Buildings of Liverpool

Detail from main entrance to Allerton Hall

University   Victoria Tower and Ashton Building

Buildings of Liverpool

Liverpool Heritage Bureau

Liverpool City Planning Department
Wilberforce House
25 The Strand
Liverpool L2 7QA

ISBN 0 9506178 0 6

Typographic Design. JT Bintley

Printed by Eaton Press Limited, Wallasey, Merseyside

Contents

Maps designed by J. Batey

Introduction

The Secretary of State for the Environment is required to compile lists of buildings of special architectural or historic interest. The administration of both local and national conservation policies is based on these lists, which are constantly under revision.

The principles of selection for these lists were originally drawn up by an expert committee of architects, antiquaries and historians, and are still followed. All buildings built before 1700 which survive in anything like their original condition qualify for 'listing' as do most buildings of 1700 to 1840. Between 1840 and 1914 only buildings of definite quality and character qualify and the selection is designed to include the principal works of the principal architects.

Selected buildings of 1914 to 1939 are also considered. In choosing buildings, particular attention is paid to:

Special value within certain types, either for architectural or planning reasons or as illustrating social and economic history (for instance, industrial buildings, railway stations, schools, hospitals, theatres, town halls, markets, exchanges, almshouses, prisons, lock-ups, mills).

Technological innovation or virtuosity (for instance cast iron, prefabrication, or the early use of concrete).

Association with well-known characters or events.

Group value, especially as examples of town planning (for instance, squares, terraces or model villages).

A survey is carried out by the Department of the Environment's Investigators of Historic Buildings, for each local authority area, and buildings are classified in grades to show their relative importance.

Grade I These are buildings of outstanding interest (less than 5 per cent of the listed buildings so far are in this grade).

Grade II These are buildings of special interest, which warrant every effort being made to preserve them. (Some particularly important buildings in Grade II are classified as Grade II*.)

In 1975 a large number of buildings were added to the statutory list for Liverpool with the approval of the Secretary of State for the Environment, bringing the number of 'listed' buildings to over 1,000. All of the buildings are Grade II with the exception of the following eight which are Grade I.

St. George's Hall
Town Hall
Bluecoat Chambers
Woolton Hall
Oriel Chambers
Speke Hall
Albert Dock
Albert Dock Traffic Office

The Grade II buildings range from the grandest civic buildings in the City Centre to small terraced cottages in the suburbs. The list also covers such artefacts as monuments, drinking fountains, gateways and pillar boxes. In terms of age the list includes such buildings as the thirteenth century Stanlawe Grange in Aigburth Hall Avenue to Barclays Bank and India Buildings in Water Street which both date from 1932.

After publication of the expanded list of buildings in 1975 the Liverpool Heritage Bureau requested the City Planning Officer to produce an illustrated book to publicise the City's heritage and so hopefully create a greater appreciation of it. *Buildings of Liverpool* is the result.

The book describes 'listed' buildings in the Dock Estate, the majority of which are not accessible to the general public without special permission from the Mersey Docks and Harbour Company, and buildings in the rest of the City. The majority of the buildings outside the Dock Estate front on to public roads and open spaces, and so may be viewed without difficulty. A small number, however, are hidden away in private grounds or behind high walls, and in these cases the permission of the owner must be obtained to view the building.

It was felt that a good way to encourage study of the City's buildings would be to divide the City up into a series of walks, each with a plan, which would collectively cover all the 'listed' buildings with the exception of those on the Dock Estate. The walks are considered sufficiently compact to be capable of completion within two hours so as not to tire the walker or overface him with too many buildings at the same time. If the reader does not wish to undertake the walks but is interested in a particular 'listed' building only, he may look it up in the alphabetical street Index at the end of the book. A short glossary of architectural terms is also included to further help the reader.

Buildings of Liverpool has been written, illustrated and graphically designed by members of the City Planning Department, and it is hoped that it will not only bring about a greater awareness of the City's considerable architectural heritage on first reading, but will also prove to be a reference book of continuing interest and enjoyment.

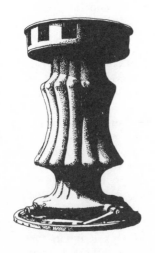

Capstan   Albert Dock

x

1 The Docks

The history of the Liverpool dock system is a story of foresight and ingenuity, and of unprecedented development on a massive scale. In 1699, Captain Granville Collins recorded that 'ships lie aground before the town of Liverpool. It is a bad riding afloat, by reason of the strong tides that run here.' No docks existed at that time and the only harbour was provided by 'the Pool', where now is Canning Place, and a creek which extended along the line of Paradise Street and Whitechapel.

With the spreading conflagration of the industrial revolution in Lancashire, Yorkshire and the Midlands, and the explosive growth of trade, particularly with the American colonies, Liverpool found itself in a position of unequalled strategic importance on the western seaboard. The ever increasing volume of shipping using the port and the relentless demand for berthing space which was to follow was matched by a continuous response by the Port authorities. It eventually took the form of seven and a half miles of docks and associated warehouses, on a scale which is still breathtaking. The use of brick, granite, timber, cast iron, steel and concrete reveals both the nature of the problems which were tackled and the development of technical solutions. The form and size of the successive works reflect the evolution of the design of shipping; from timber to iron, from sail to steam, from paddle to screw and, most significant, from small craft to the gargantuan vessels of the present day.

In 1708 Thomas Steers was appointed to advise on the building of the first dock. He recommended the abandonment of a former canal scheme and, instead, the conversion of the Pool into a wet dock controlled by floodgates. Although the idea of floodgates was not new, their use to enclose a harbour as was proposed was a bold invention which was to set the pattern for future docks the world over. The 'Old Dock' was completed in 1715 with an octagonal entrance basin and a small graving dock on the north side. Cadwick's Map of 1725 shows a pier at the entrance into the river no doubt to allow sailing ships to moor whilst waiting for a wind. By 1737, the dock was inadequate for the increasing volume of shipping and a new basin was constructed forming a large outer harbour to the Old Dock, with three graving docks opening on the west side. It was sub-

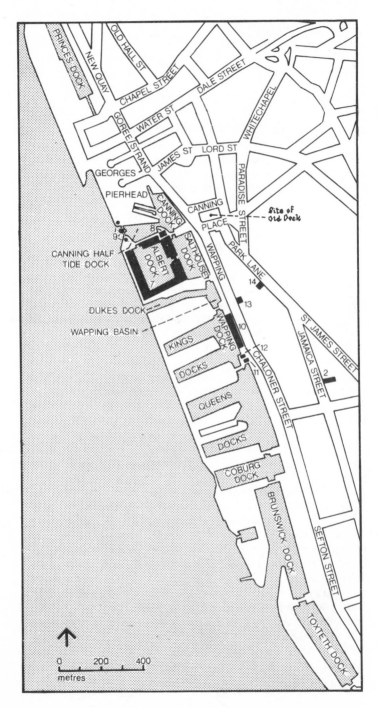

PRINCES DOCK
NEW QUAY
OLD HALL ST
CHAPEL STREET
DALE STREET
WATER ST
GOREE/STRAND
JAMES ST   LORD ST
WHITECHAPEL
PARADISE STREET
GEORGES
PIERHEAD
CANNING DOCK
CANNING
PLACE
Site of
Old Dock
CANNING HALF
TIDE DOCK
ALBERT
DOCK 7
SALTHOUSE
DOCK
WAPPING
PARK LANE
14
DUKES DOCK
WAPPING BASIN
KINGS
WAPPING
DOCK
13
10
12
ST JAMES STREET
JAMAICA STREET
DOCKS
CHALONER STREET
11
2
QUEENS
DOCKS
COBURG
DOCK
BRUNSWICK DOCK
SEFTON STREET
TOXTETH DOCK

0   200   400
metres

sequently reconstructed in 1813 and named Canning Dock. A further dock authorised by the Act of 1737 was opened in 1753 and this was known as the 'South Dock' but was renamed 'Salthouse Dock' later in the century. Between this dock and the river were several shipbuilding yards. Salthouse Dock was reconstructed in 1845.

The open harbour to the north was developed into 'Georges Dock' which extended from James Street to Chapel Street and which was opened in 1771. The dock was able to accommodate the new larger vessels requiring greater draught, and particularly Man-of-War ships. It was reconstructed and further enlarged between 1822 and 1825. Facing on to the dock, between The Strand and Goree, stood the great arcaded Goree Warehouses, built in 1793, reconstructed in 1802 after a disastrous fire, and finally destroyed in the blitz in 1941.

By 1785, the volume of shipping had increased to such an extent that two new docks were proposed to the south of Salthouse Dock. King's Dock opened in 1788, and Queen's Dock which was completed in 1796 and considerably enlarged in 1816. Both docks were originally separated from the docks to the north by the entrance section to the proposed Runcorn Canal. The Duke of Bridgewater had obtained powers under Act of Parliament in 1759 for the construction of the canal which was to have provided a link between the port and the rich salt mines of Cheshire. A terminal dock and outer channel were opened in 1773 and the old salt works, after which Salthouse Dock took its name, stood alongside. This problem of separation was not obviated until the construction of Wapping Basin in 1858, which entailed the reconstruction and narrowing of King's Dock in 1852.

Parallel to the dock road behind Queen's Dock is Jamaica Street, which runs through an area containing many fine examples of nineteenth century warehouses including the Alfred Warehouses.

In 1785 the Manchester Basin was constructed as an inlet for river craft between the Canning Graving Docks and Georges Dock and in about 1818 it was enlarged and converted into a floating dock. Another small inlet for traders from the Chester and Ellesmere Canal was constructed adjacent to George's Parade in 1795.

In 1800, the number of ships entering the port was 4,746 with a tonnage of 450,000. The docks and basins enclosed some

---

2 Alfred Warehouse
7 Albert Dock
8 Dock Traffic Office
9 Watchman's Hut

10 Wapping Dock Warehouse
11 Gatekeepers Lodge
12 Hydraulic Tower

13 Baltic Fleet Public House
14 Swedish Seamen's Church

twenty-six acres of water. A hundred years previously there was only the open river and meagre harbour facilities. The number of vessels entering the port then was 102 with a tonnage of 8,619.

The eighteenth century had been a turbulent one, with civil rebellions and foreign wars, with press-gangs in the streets of the town and privateering on the seas. Liverpool merchants grew rich on the profits of the slave trade and the rapidly expanding commerce with the West Indies and North America. Ships which sailed out of Liverpool, laden with goods from the awakening industries of the hinterland, returned with tobacco, rum and sugar, and, in the latter part of the century, with cotton. By 1800, the anti-slavery movement was in full flight and threatened the port with ruin. But the momentum which had built up in the eighteenth century was not to be stopped. In the century which followed, as mines, mills, factories and furnace chimneys transformed the Midlands and the North of England so the almost continuous work of building docks of ever-increasing dimensions progressed in Liverpool. Canals and railways were cut through to the port. Emigrants to the New World from all over the country and Europe thronged the streets and quays.

The prodigious expansion of the port was matched by the growth of the town. Between 1831 and 1891, the population within the boundaries of the town alone trebled, from 205,572 to 617,032.

In 1811 an Act of Parliament was passed for the filling in of the Old Dock and the construction of Prince's Dock to the North of George's Dock. Built by John Foster and his son, it was opened in 1821 and was the first of the docks to be enclosed by walls, an arrangement which was subsequently employed throughout the dock system. Prince's Basin was re-modelled in the 1860s and converted to a half-tide dock with three outer entrances. At the North entrance, a great brick octagonal tower was constructed to house the hydraulic equipment which powered the dock gates. The tower rose out of a spreading base with clock faces in four of the sides of the superstructure. Crowned by a deep machicolated battlement, it was surmounted by a slated conical roof with dormers and iron cresting. Together with several similar towers which punctuated the outer lines of the docks, it has now been demolished. Because of vehement opposition and continuing demand for dock space, the Old Dock was not cleared of shipping until 1826. The Custom House which was built on the site between 1828 and 1839 to the design by John Foster the younger, was undoubtedly the finest building in Liverpool destroyed by bombing in the second World War.

In 1816 work commenced on a small dock to the south of the

Queen's Dock known as Union Dock, together with its large outer basin. The two were united in 1858 with gates opening directly into the river and the new dock so formed was named Coburg Dock.

In 1824, Jesse Hartley, bridgemaster for the West Riding of Yorkshire, was appointed engineer to the docks. He was a man of enormously powerful vision who carried out his concepts with strength, solidarity and skill. Granite brick and cast iron were the materials in which he delighted to work and in which he expressed his genius, his integrity and stern independence.

The first of his works to the south, Brunswick Dock and half-tide basin, was opened in 1832. Built for the timber trade, the eastern quay was sloped to facilitate unloading. The dock and basin were built on a new massive scale, enclosing twelve and two acres of water respectively. Two large adjacent graving docks were also added. To the north work went ahead at the same time on Clarence Dock which was opened in 1830. Designed for the new steamers, the dock was laid out some distance to the north of Prince's Dock to avoid the risk of fire. It was the first to incorporate continuous covered sheds and this facility was later provided round the older docks. Waterloo was later reconstructed with inner and outer docks. Warehouses were constructed on three sides of the inner dock and were completed in 1867.

Close by on the dock road, between Barton Street and Galton Street, here called Waterloo Road, are examples of nineteenth century warehouse building.

The Victoria and Trafalgar Docks, which completed development between Clarence and Waterloo, opened in 1836. Both were built for powered vessels owing to the great increase in the use of steamers.

In 1845, the Prince Consort opened the Albert Dock, surrounded by its warehouses on a massive scale. Previously no warehouses had been provided within the Dock Estate although as early as 1803 the desirability of integrating warehousing and docks had been debated with the mercantile associations of the town. In 1810 plans for docks enclosed by warehouses had been prepared, but in the face of strong opposition from the warehouse owners in the town, the Bill for implementation was rejected by Parliament. Because of the lack of secure bonded warehousing in the town, to meet the requirements of Customs and Excise, a commission was set up in 1821 which recommended the provision of warehousing adjacent to the docks separated from areas of public access by walls or other means. At a blustery meeting at the Town Hall it was again argued that the proposals would be ruinous to the warehouse owners. The value

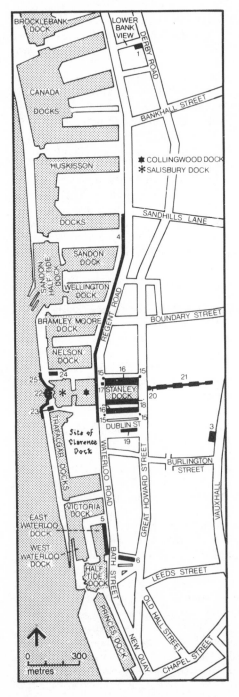

1 Lower Bank View
  Warehouse
3 Fairie Sugar Factory
4 Dock Wall
5 Waterloo Dock
  Warehouse
6 Galton Street
  Warehouse
15 Two entrances to
  Stanley Dock
16 Stanley Dock
  Warehouse
17 Stanley Dock
  Hydraulic Tower
18 Stanley Dock
  Tobacco Warehouse
19 Stanley Dock
  Bonded Tea
  Warehouse
20 Entrance to Leeds-
  Liverpool Canal
21 Two Canal Locks
22 Victoria Tower
23 Watchman's Hut
24 Dockmaster's House
25 Sea Wall

6

of the warehouses within the town at that time was estimated at £2 million. The matter was again left in abeyance until 1837 when the Municipal Council, as owners of the docks, resolved to proceed despite continued opposition and in 1839 Jesse Hartley produced designs for the Albert Dock to the river side of Salthouse. The plan was agreed in 1841 and parliamentary sanction gained.

In 1846, the year after the completion of Albert Dock, work commenced on the enlargement of Salthouse Dock and the construction of Wapping Dock, to the east of King's Dock. The new and the enlarged docks were connected by a cut behind Duke's Dock, which had been the entrance to the Duke of Bridgewater's Runcorn Canal. These works entailed the removal of much valuable property fronting on to Wapping and the construction of a new road set back from the old line. It was a long job and Wapping Dock with its fine warehouses was not occupied until 1858.

Meanwhile, 1848 saw the opening of Salisbury, Collingwood, Stanley, Nelson and Bramley-Moore Docks to the north. With the development of steam ships, the protected outer basins were no longer required and it was possible to open gates directly into the river.

The Stanley Dock is the only inland dock in Liverpool, being on the landward side of the dock road, here known as Regent's Road. It is enclosed to north and south by warehouses.

Stanley Dock, which provides access into the Leeds-Liverpool Canal is linked to the Collingwood Dock by a channel traversed by a lifting road bridge and thence to Salisbury Dock. Between the paired entrances to the river from Salisbury Dock stands one of the several great castellated towers which were built by Hartley to house the hydraulic machinery for the operation of the locks.

The following year, 1849, the Sandon Dock was completed and later modified following the Act of 1891. Huskisson Dock, opened in 1852, was subsequently extended eastwards in 1860. It reflects the rapid increase at the time in the size of vessels. The two graving docks were 950 feet in length with the provision of hydraulic lifts whereby ships of 500 feet could be raised bodily above the water.

There followed two major controversies. Firstly, an application to Parliament made in 1855 for the further expansion of the dock system and the provision of additional warehousing met with vehement opposition from a lobby of the almost bankrupt Birkenhead Dock Company. As a result, the main aims of the Liverpool Bill were defeated, and in the same session an Act was passed whereby the undertakings of the insolvent Company were transferred to the Liverpool Corporation, which agreed to purchase the property.

Secondly, in 1857, after a long and bitter contest, a Bill was introduced to the House of Commons for the transfer of the dock estate from the Corporation of Liverpool, which until this time had developed and managed the port, to an entirely new body of trustees. The ostensible promoters of the Bill were the Manchester Chamber of Commerce, the Manchester Commercial Association, and the Great Western Railway Company who had long resented Liverpool's right to levy town dues on cargoes passing through the port, a right established by King John and purchased by the Corporation in 1672. The Bill was passed by the House of Commons but amended by the House of Lords whereby £1.5 million compensation should be paid to the Corporation. As a result, the Mersey Docks and Harbour Board was established.

As the timber trade increased, for which the Queen's and Brunswick Docks had been constructed, it was decided to build new facilities to the north. Canada Dock was opened in 1859 with extensive timber yards. Later the half tide dock was extended to the north in 1872, giving access to additional docks to the east as far as Regent Road. The Canada Docks again established a new massive scale previously unseen. The increasing size of shipping, and the girth of the paddle steamers in particular, dictated that two of the entrances to Canada and Huskisson Docks were of 80 feet in width and one of 100 feet. The enormous gates were operated by hydraulic machinery housed in Hartley's magnificent double octagonal castellated tower of granite, which has now been demolished. The abandoning of paddle steamers for ocean going in favour of screw driven ships rendered these facilities unnecessary for many years to come. A further branch dock was added in 1896, together with graving docks alongside of 926 feet in length.

Opposite the Canada Docks is a street called Lower Bank View, in which can be found further examples of nineteenth century warehouses.

At the south end, the Herculaneum Dock was opened in 1864 with its extensive graving docks. It was later extended and improved in the 1880s.

By 1872 dock provision was again inadequate for the ever increasing demand. Plans were prepared in that year by G. F. Lyster, who succeeded the two Hartleys, father and son, as engineer to the Dock Board, for seven new docks beyond Liverpool's northern boundary with Bootle. The plan also proposed two new docks to the south, and Langton and Alexandra Docks were completed in 1881. Harrington followed

8

The Dock Traffic Office

in 1883 and Toxteth in 1888.

In parallel with the commercial expansion of the port, the increase in passenger traffic in the nineteenth century was prodigious. In 1847 a floating landing stage off St. George's Parade was built by L. Cubitt, engineer. Supported on iron pontoons, the stage was 500 feet long and 80 feet wide. It was rebuilt in 1873-4 and extended to 2,063 feet. In 1896, it was again extended by a further 400 feet with an additional jetty at the north end of 350 feet, giving continuous linear berthing of over half a mile. High level covered pedestrian bridges, adaptable to allow direct linkage to the liners, connected to an array of customs and baggage halls and waiting rooms.

Mechanical luggage conveyors linked from the stage and the holds of the liners to the passenger complex. In 1895, Riverside station opened which allowed passenger trains to stand along the quayside under cover and contiguous with the covered Princes Parade where carriages, cabs, and later, taxis could queue.

In 1893, the world famous overhead railway, which ran parallel to the dock road for seven and a half miles from Seaforth in the north to Dingle in the south, was opened. At the close of the century George's Dock was drained and filled and the Pier Head area was formed.

The Waterloo Warehouse

The Lower Bank View Warehouse is dated 1885 and is on seven storeys, principally of red brick. The windows have segmented arches with small panes set in iron glazing bars. There are six recessed loading bays with round arches in blue brick and iron doors.

The Alfred Warehouses form a large square block between Jordan Street and Bird Street. Built in 1867 and extended in 1879, the building is of brick articulated by the use of blue brick. The warehouse accommodation is on five storeys and a basement and hoists are provided on the side elevations. All the windows are small with segmental heads and the building has a cornice and parapet with a central gable and 'eye'.

The Fairrie Sugar Factory is some distance from the docks in Vauxhall Road. The warehouse block is dated 1847 and is of red brick. It has a very high ground floor with five floors above and a tower projecting above the roof line to the north-east. There are eight windows with segmental heads on each floor with small pane glazing. The later buildings to the south are not listed.

The Dock Wall from opposite Sandhills Lane to Collingwood Dock with the entrances was the work of Jesse Hartley. The wall itself is of large irregular shaped blocks of granite and is about 18 feet in height. It incorporates large carved plaques with wording such as 'Sandon Graving Dock 1848' and 'Collingwood Dock 1848'. The wall is punctuated by massive gate posts and turrets at the entrances. The main entrance to Sandon Dock has two large square stone piers with cornices and iron lampholders and in the centre is the gatekeeper's lodge with its cornice and parapet, ornamented at the corners. The nameplate on the front is in a pedimented panel and the lodge has a central chimney. The vast wooden doors to the entrance were designed to slide back into the thickness of the wall. The entrance to docks 47, 49 and 50, opposite Boundary Street, has three round, tapering turrets with heavy tops and deep slits at the side to receive the gates. The former entrance further south is similar but the centre turret is oval in plan. The entrance to North Collingwood, North Salisbury and Nelson Docks again has three towers, but the centre one is taller and larger. The entrance to Nelson, South Wellington and Bramley-Moore Docks, opposite Fulton Street, is similar, as is the now blocked entrance near Bramley-Moore pumping station.

The Waterloo Dock Warehouse was built in 1867 by George Fosbery Lyster as a grain store and it incorporated machinery for raising, storing, turning, ventilating and discharging the grain. The ground floor is an open arcade supported by rusticated granite piers and arches with five vaulted floors above. The structure above the ground floor is of brick and the

The Albert Dock

openings in each storey are double windows with semi-circular heads on four floors. The cills of the windows are formed by continuous rough stone string-courses. The buildings are surmounted by a bold cornice carried on stone brackets and a parapet above. The windows of the top floor are single, the cornice forming a continuous lintel. Hoisting machinery is housed in turrets which rise above the general line of the structure.

Galton Street Warehouses. These brick warehouses, dating from about 1870, form a group on the north side of Galton Street. At the corner of Waterloo Road stands a seven-storey warehouse with round-arch doorways, windows with vertical iron bars and stone lintels and recessed loading bays. The warehouse between Greenock Street and Glasgow Street is of five high storeys and that to the east of Glasgow Street is of six storeys. **The cobbled roadways** forming Galton and Greenock Streets are also worthy of note.

The Albert Dock is a Grade I listed building. Built 1841-5 by Jesse Hartley and Philip Hardwick, the five-storey warehouses enclose the almost square dock on all four sides, creating a courtyard of mighty proportions which are doubled by the reflections in the sheltered water. The design is enormously powerful by virtue of its scale, its uncompromising simplicity and the repetition of elements which are both an obvious response to functional needs and to the strong overall design discipline. The quays are of granite; the warehouses are of brick and cast iron. The four upper floors are carried on a colonnade of massive cast iron Doric columns supporting iron lintels. At intervals the columns are more widely spaced and here support segmental brick arches which cut into the accommodation on the floor above. The upper floors are lit by regularly spaced windows with small panes set in iron frames. The floors are formed by shallow brick vaults restrained by iron tie bars and supported on cast iron columns and beams.

The Dock Traffic Office, also a grade I listing, 1846-7, by Philip Hardwick, with the top storey added by Jesse Hartley in 1848 forms one external corner of the Albert Dock courtyard. It is built in the form of a classical temple, but again the materials used are predominantly brick and iron. The main Tuscan portico with frieze, entablature and pediment which faces Canning Place is all of iron. The building has two floors below the cornice and parapet with a third floor above and windows at the level of the entablature. A central chimney rises above the level of the roof.

Watchmen's Huts, Canning Half-Tide Dock. These three octagonal granite cabins which guard the gates into the river were built by Jesse Hartley in 1844 as part of the Albert Dock project. They are of very low proportions with shallow pyramidical roofs in three tiers and overhanging cornice eaves. The doors are on the landward side with windows on each of the other faces.

The Wapping Dock Warehouse, 1856, by Jesse Hartley, is similar in construction and materials to the Albert Dock warehouses with an open colonnade of iron columns to the dockside with five large segmental arches spaced at intervals. Above are four floors in brick with segmental headed windows and small panes set in iron glazing bars.

The Gatekeeper's Lodge at Wapping Dock, 1856, by Jesse Hartley, takes the form of a fortress turret. Oval in plan with tapering walls and surmounted by a high spired roof, it is built of random granite. It has an arched doorway and cruciform slot windows.

The Hydraulic Tower at Wapping Dock, 1856, probably by Jesse Hartley, is one of the several towers which stood along the outer lines of the docks and which housed machinery for the operation of the lock gates into the river. The tower is octagonal in form of brick with stone quoins above a random granite plinth. Above the crenellated cornice it is crowned by a battlemented parapet.

The Baltic Fleet Public House is an example of the many hostelries which lined the dock road. Opposite the dock entrance at the north end of Wapping Dock, it stands on a triangular site and takes the form of a Victorian palazzo on two floors. The round-arched windows on the ground floor are divided by Tuscan pilasters supporting a cornice. On the first floor the windows are pedimented and in moulded architraves with Tuscan pilasters between the windows carrying top cornice with decorated brackets.

The Swedish Seamen's Church, or Gustaf Adolfs Kyrka in Park Lane, is a lively asymmetrical building designed by W. D. Caroe, erected in 1882-3. The compact design is dominated by a central octagonal tower with a pyramid roof. Although the hard brick facades are of indeterminate style, there are traces of Norse timber church detail in the gabled dormers, curved finials to gables and the thin lead covered spire.

The Two Entrances to Stanley Dock, Great Howard Street and the Regent Road Entrance, are each formed by three round granite towers with sliding gates set into the thickness of the wall. Probably built by Jesse Hartley in 1848, they are similar to the Regent Road entrances.

The Stanley Dock Warehouses, 1848, by Jesse Hartley, are of the same construction and materials as the Albert Dock and Wapping Dock warehouses, although the ground level cast iron columns do not have entasis; they are widest at their bases but follow a slightly concave line up to the Doric capitals. Originally

The Baltic Fleet Public House

The Swedish Seamen's Church

15

the two five-storey blocks to the north and south faced each other across the dock but the southern wing was separated from the quayside by the interposing of the later tobacco warehouse. The eastern end of the north wing has been demolished and replaced by a later building. The original warehouses were equipped with hydraulic loading and lifting machinery.

Stanley Dock Hydraulic Tower, probably 1848, by Jesse Hartley, is built of smooth stone in irregular blocks. It is a tall octagonal tower with castellations at the top and a round chimney. The windows are narrow slots.

The Stanley Dock Tobacco Warehouse extends along the whole of the south front of the dock and is dated 1900. Built of red and blue brick with eleven storeys above a high rusticated stone base, it is said to be the largest in the world. The building is panelled with pilasters and crowned by small parapets and pediments.

Stanley Bonded Tea Warehouse. This large and solid rectangular brick warehouse fills the block between Dublin Street and Dickson Street, and presents a regular front to Great Howard Street. It dates from the 1880s. The two long sides are punctuated by deeply recessed loading bays with arched tops and iron doors, and each of the six storeys has rows of typical small arched windows. The Great Howard Street facade is decorated by a carved and painted shield of arms and a motto, no longer readable.

The Entrance to the Leeds-Liverpool Canal from Stanley Dock is crossed by a stone bridge with concave sides built of large and small irregular granite blocks.

The Four Canal Locks, rising 160 feet, are formed with stone side walls and wood and iron gates date from the 1840s.

The Victoria Tower, Salisbury Dock, by Jesse Hartley, is dated 1848. It is constructed of granite of irregular shaped blocks and takes the form of an octagon with a high tapered circular base which is pierced by round-arched openings. Above the base is a string moulding and narrow slits at the first floor below a continuous balcony carried on stone brackets. Higher again are eight circular clock faces and long open slits and round eyes at the top. The tower is crowned by a projecting castellated parapet carried on corbels.

The Watchman's Hut, Salisbury Dock, on the sea wall to the south of the Victoria Tower is a small oblong building of two storeys, constructed of smooth and small irregular stone blocks. It carries a corbelled battlemented parapet and the doorway and windows are in a Tudor style.

The Dockmaster's House, Salisbury Dock, is on the sea wall to the north of the Victoria Tower, and is by Jesse Hartley. It is built of brick and is on three floors with wooden moulded eaves and wood mullions. The south side has a small brick porch with a stone cornice and round arched window.

The Sea Wall from the Dockmaster's House to the Watchman's Hut, including the **Basin Entrance** and the **cobbled paving** to the quays, Salisbury Dock. This section of the sea wall is by Jesse Hartley and is dated August 1848. This Cyclopean granite walling forms great sweeping curves and is constructed of huge smooth blocks of stone of irregular shapes carefully and precisely fitted together. The cobbled paving extends about 12 feet from the top of the wall and is constructed of very large flat white stones.

The Victoria Tower   Hydraulic Tower, Wapping Dock

Watchman's Hut, Salisbury Dock

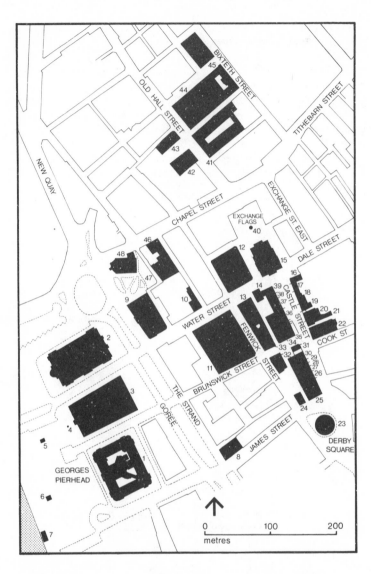

1 Mersey Docks and
  Harbour Board
2 Royal Liver
  Building
3 Cunard Offices
4 The War Memorial
5 Monument of
  Edward VII
6 Monument to Sir
  Alfred Lewis Jones

7 'Heroes of the
  Marine Engine
  Room' Memorial
8 White Star Building
9 Tower Building
10 Oriel Chambers
11 India Building
12 Barclays Bank
   Building
13 National

   Westminster Bank
14 Branch of the
   National
   Westminster Bank
15 Town Hall
16 Midland Bank
17 3-5 Castle Street
18 Queen Insurance
   Building
19 17-21 Castle Street

2 Pier Head and Castle Street

The growth of the docks on which Liverpool's wealth and trade were based was accompanied by the development of commercial premises in the old part of the City. Until the 1820s traders carried out their work from their houses and shops, which were packed together with warehouses in the narrow thoroughfares around the Castle Street, Water Street, Chapel Street and Old Hall Street area. Gradually, with their expanding wealth and greater social aspirations, the leading merchants moved their households out to more spacious premises in Duke Street and beyond, leaving the old core to take on a more intensley commercial character. Rents and land values soared, and redevelopment was carried out with increasing zeal. Before the mid-nineteenth century, office buildings were not a specific building type of any significance, but the growing power of Victorian commerce gave companies the desire and means to express their prestige and importance by erecting splendid and dignified premises for their business operations. Liverpool's zenith was reached at the turn of the century with the construction of the Pier Head group of office buildings, in spirit profoundly expressive of the Imperial optimism of Edwardian enterprise.

It is these three buildings constructed on the land gained by filling in the George's Dock that give Liverpool her famous skyline, reminiscent of the great North American Cities with which her principal trade was then carried out. The first to be built was the **Offices of the Mersey Docks and Harbour Board** completed in 1907 to the designs of Arnold Thornley. This impressive symmetrical block takes the form of a Renaissance palace with cupolas at its corners and in the centre a large classical church dome on a high drum. Internally an octagonal hall reaches up to the dome with arched galleries running around it at four levels. **The Royal Liver Building,** erected in 1908-10, has no counterpart in England and is one of the world's first multi-storey buildings with a reinforced concrete structure. It was designed by Aubrey Thomas in a remarkably free and original style. The sculptural clock towers are surmounted by domes on which the famous mythical Liver Birds are perched. The last of this trio of waterfront buildings is the **Cunard Offices** designed by Willink and Thicknesse with Arthur Davis (of Mewes and Davis) as consultant, and constructed during the Great War. It is built in the style of an Italian palazzo but with Greek revival details, and it is very nicely proportioned. Less of a *tour de force* than either the Mersey Docks and Harbour Board or the Liver Building, it can nevertheless stand a closer and more critical architectural examination.

The Pier Head also contains a number of monuments of note. **The War Memorial,** in front of the Cunard Building takes the form of a granite pedestal crowned by a copper figure of Victory. **The Monument of Edward VII** by Sir W. Goscombe John was intended by the sculptor to stand on the steps of St. George's Hall. Fortunately, after a vociferous public campaign organised by Sir Charles Reilly, this was prevented and the equestrian statue was dispatched to its present site. **The Monument to Sir Alfred Lewis Jones** by Sir George Frampton, unveiled in 1913, consists of a square stone pedestal with a bronze figure at the top representing Liverpool and its shipping. **The Memorial to the 'Heroes of the marine engine room'** also by Goscombe John was paid for by international subscription and erected in 1916. It shows lifesize standing figures of engineers and firemen in high relief, and was originally intended to commemorate those lost in the *Titanic* disaster of 1912.

On the corner of The Strand and James Street, opposite the Mersey Docks and Harbour Board building, stands the **White Star Building** erected in 1898 and the first of the new generation of giant office blocks built in the City. It was designed by Norman Shaw with J. Francis Doyle, and, like New Scotland Yard, is striped with bands of brick and white portland stone. Its height is emphasised by angle turrets and tall chimneys which make a striking effect when viewed on approach from the south along the dock road. After serious war damage the main gable to The Strand was rebuilt to a simpler design.

Tower Building on the corner of Water Street was designed by Aubrey Thomas predating his other work, the Royal Liver Building, by two years. It is similarly inventive, and, built in 1908, was one of the earliest steel framed buildings in the country. It

Mersey Docks and Harbour Company Offices

The Royal Liver Building

Cunard Offices

lacks any architectural refinements however, the designer being more concerned with functional requirements such as the large windows which admit good light and the use of self-cleaning white glazed tile as an exterior cladding. Tower Building is so called because it stands on the site of the Tower of Liverpool, a fortified house on the river's edge belonging to the Stanley family, Earls of Derby. This building was used by the Stanleys as an embarkation base for the Isle of Man and their property in Ireland, but towards the end of the eighteenth century it fell into disrepair and became a gaol for criminals and debtors.

In the eighteenth century Water Street was a fashionable place of residence for the wealthy class of Liverpool merchants: it is now one of the finest of the commercial streets. **Oriel Chambers** (grade I) designed by the practically unknown Liverpool architect, Peter Ellis, and built in 1864 is one of the most significant buildings of its date in Europe. The Water Street and Covent Garden elevations have tall stone mullions with nail head decoration separating graceful cast iron windows which provide excellent lighting to the offices behind. At the rear, stripped of all decoration, the long projecting bands of windows are remarkably prophetic of the twentieth century. The building's functional design aroused a great deal of controversy in its day — it was described as 'a great abortion' and 'an agglomeration of protruding plate glass bubbles.' Today we appreciate its honesty, its elegant detailing and its reflective qualities, and we can admire its revolutionary impact.

Opposite Oriel Chambers is **India Buildings** designed by Herbert J. Rowse, the most influential Liverpool architect of the inter-war years, as the result of an architectural competition. It was built between 1924 and 1932 at the cost of £1.25 million for Holt's Blue Funnel Line, and is one of the largest office blocks in the City. Such a huge provision of offices being considered highly speculative at the time, the building was so designed that it could be converted into a warehouse. In its simplified neo-classical style it is typical of American office designs of that time, and Rowse was certainly influenced by his extensive travels in North America. The most notable feature is the barrel vaulted arcade that runs through the centre of the block lined by small shop fronts. **The Barclays Bank Building,** originally the headquarters of Martins Bank and completed in 1932, was also a competition success for Rowse. This building is similarly monumental in scale and is American-French classical in origin. It has a steel-framed construction, and the design of servicing which incorporated completely ducted pipes and wires and low temperature ceiling heating was very advanced. The bronze entrance doors in low relief are of note, and having passed through them the Jazz Age

Window Detail

Oriel Chambers

Parisian interior with its Egyptian motifs is particularly splendid.

The National Westminster Bank on the corner of Fenwick Street, built in 1850 is distinguished by giant fluted Doric columns rising through first and second floors. This monumental treatment is given stability by heavy rustication to the ground floor and a plinth of polished red granite. Note the bronze doors with sculptured tigers' heads, and the fine classical interior with ornamented plasterwork and columns.

Adjoining this and also now a branch of the **National Westminster Bank** is an attractive early Renaissance style building. This is typical of the mid-nineteenth century Liverpool bank buildings with its closely spaced classical windows and heavy cornice.

It was said by Sir James Picton that 'the history of Castle Street is the history of Liverpool' and this fine street still remains the identifiable centre of the City. The streets of the town were laid out at the beginning of the thirteenth century, the seven original ones being Dale Street and Water Street, Tithebarn Street and Chapel Street and, running across Old Hall Street, High Street and Castle Street ending at the castle which was built in 1235. After the civil war the castle fell into disuse and was finally demolished in 1721 to make way for St. George's Church, now Derby Square. This area formed the market place which gradually encroached so far along Castle Street that it reached the Town Hall, in front of which the merchants at that time congregated. By the mid-eighteenth century Castle Street had become a street of shops, and the most fashionable place in town, but when the market was moved, it was abandoned to commerce and was widened to its present generous proportions in 1786.

The existing **Town Hall** (grade I) is the City's third and was designed by John Wood of Bath and built in 1749-54. It was intended that the ground floor should act as an exchange for the merchants to transact their business, whilst municipal functions would be carried out on the floors above. The building was seriously damaged by fire in 1795 and James Wyatt was commissioned to reconstruct it, which he did adding first the impressive dome on its high drum and later, with John Foster, the two storey Corinthian portico. Wood's work, elegant and finely etched, can best be seen from Exchange Flags, whilst Wyatt's additions give weight and grandeur to the main facade. The interiors were not completed until 1820, but together they form an exceptionally fine example of late Georgian decoration, and one of the best suites of civic rooms in the country. The building has survived numerous attempts at damage. In 1775 seamen protesting against the reduction in their wages attacked it with a cannon, for their employers were sheltering inside, and in 1881

Iron grille at entrance

Elephant Sculpture

Minerva

Town Hall

25

there was an abortive attempt by the Fenians to blow it up. War damage, following a raid in June 1941, was more serious, but since then it has been well restored.

On the corner of Dale Street and Castle Street is the late nineteenth century **Midland Bank** by Edward Salomons, distinguished architect of the Manchester Reform Club. Built as an art gallery for Thomas Agnew & Co., it is of red brick and has a deep frieze at the top with swags and wreaths. **Nos. 3-5 Castle Street** were built in 1889 to the design of Grayson and Ould for the British and Foreign Marine Insurance Company whose inscription can be seen on a colourful mosaic frieze over the first floor. Distinctive features are the balustraded balconies and dormer windows with their unusual gables and curved pediments. **Nos. 7-15** are part of the **Queen Insurance Buildings** whose principal front is on Dale Street. On the ground floor of the facade to Castle Street is the access to Queen Avenue, an arcade with walls of glazed brick and oriels with pargetted aprons, accessible through a wide shallow arch decorated with iron spandrels. The side arches are filled in with modern shops and, on the floors above, the brick and dressed stone facade is of great decorative variety and richness. **Nos. 17-21 Castle Street** are a typical Victorian commercial building of polished granite and stone. The facade is divided on each floor by pilasters and columns of different orders with friezes and cornices forming bands between floors. **No. 25,** which extends over the entrance to Sweeting Street, is of similar composition, but with even greater surface decoration. The top floor rises over the three centre bays only and is surmounted by a curved pediment with acroteria. **The Huddersfield Building Society,** formerly the Norwich Union building is a little earlier in date than these other buildings, and, although smaller in size, has greater architectural distinction. Its portico of four giant fluted attached Corinthian columns and pediment rests on a heavy stone cornice and parapet with ground floor granite pilasters. It is a valuable neighbour to the famous **Bank of England** built in 1845-8 which is considered to be C. R. Cockerell's best work. Cockerell's design for the main facade is a free adaptation of Greek motifs on a grand scale giving the building an importance greater than its height, which is in fact little more than the adjoining buildings. This facade forms a striking closure to Brunswick Street which is virtually on its main axis. The interior has unfortunately been altered.

In Derby Square, the former St. George's Church was used by John Foster as the centre of an imaginative plan to create a circus as a cross axis between the newly widened Lord Street and Castle Street which extended south to his monumental Customs House. The Customs House, Lord Street/St. George's Crescent and

The White Star Building   The Barclay's Bank Building

Tower Building

S. Long

South Castle Street were unfortunately destroyed by enemy action, the church already having been demolished in 1897, and post-war replacements have been a poor substitute for this grand conception; however (perhaps by divine intervention) the **Victoria Monument** survived. This was designed by E. M. Simpson, Professor of Architecture at Liverpool University, with the sculptures by Charles Allen, Vice Principal of the School of Art, and was completed in 1905. The four bronze groups around the memorial represent Agriculture, Commerce, Education and Industry, and there is a plaque recording the site of the Liverpool Castle. **Castle Moat House** on the north side of Derby Square stands on the site of the moat of the Castle. It was built in 1841 for the North and South Wales Bank and designed by Edward Corbett. The fine three bay, pedimented front has been brought forward and the giant composite pilasters substituted for original columns.

Returning along Castle Street, the west side presents a completely intact Victorian commercial street frontage. The end building, **Bank Buildings** occupied by the Midland Bank, displays the most exuberant of Victorian features with its elaborate entrance bay, balustraded iron balconies and carved reclining figures. This was designed by Lucy and Littler and built in 1868. The Scottish Provident Building, **Nos. 52-54,** is part of the late eighteenth century classical rebuilding of Castle Street which followed the widening in 1786. As can be seen from the remnants of the pediment on either side of **Nos. 48-50, No. 46** is a further original portion, and in detail more complete. Nos. 52-54 have been much altered, with bay windows added, the central pilaster removed and the front refaced. Nos. 48-50, the building inserted between the earlier facades, is by Picton and was built in 1864. It is interesting that so scholarly an architect did not feel any necessity to relate his building to what would then have formed a regular street front. **No. 44** is a later and eccentric nineteenth century replacement faced in ashlar and green vitreous tiles. The curious curved pediment contains a profusion of gilt foliate carving and bands of coloured tiles. **Nos. 40-42,** now occupied by the Burnley Building Society, are thought to be the work of Grayson and Ould. They are of four storeys, with three gables forming a picturesque roofline, and can be seen to their best advantage from Cook Street where they serve to close the view at the westerly end. **The Co-operative Bank** on the corner of Brunswick Street, originally the Adelphi Bank, is the most inventive of this group. It was designed by W. D. Caroe, a highly original architect, and built in 1892. Contrasting bands of granite and sandstone and lively Victorian detail culminating in the corner turret with its unusual green copper onion dome give the

Co-operative Bank

Halifax House

34-36 Castle Street

Mersey Chambers

building its distinctive appearance. Of particular quality are the bronze doors designed by the sculptor Stirling Lee showing historical pairs of inseparable friends. This incongruous subject was perhaps intended as a symbol for encouraging good relations with the bank manager.

At the top of Brunswick Street are two distinguished bank buildings. **Barclays Bank** was built as a private bank for Arthur Heywood and Sons in 1800. It has a plain five bay front with rusticated ground floor and blind arcading. Opposite is **Halifax House** built for the Liverpool Union Bank in a quiet palazzo style. The coat of arms on the Fenwick Street facade is inscribed with a date of 1835, though this is probably too early. The central round arched entrance is flanked by large windows each of which is divided by Tuscan pilasters with a frieze of triglyphs and metopes and a modillioned cornice.

The final block of Castle Street contains several Victorian buildings in the Loire style such as **Nos. 34-36** which are again by Grayson and Ould. The corner into Brunswick Street is skilfully turned by the use of a round turret surmounted by a small dome. This is echoed on the Brunswick Street facade, the part between these turrets forming a steep gable elaborately decorated with a balustraded balcony, arcading, a carved frieze of ships and liver birds, and crowned by a niche. **The National Westminster Bank Overseas Branch,** another variation on the French Renaissance style, has an interesting variety of window types — second floor windows are ogee headed and cusped, third floor are narrow and round headed, and fourth floor are round arched. Tall clustered stone chimneys rise from the steep roof. The next building, a further **National Westminster Bank,** was designed by Norman Shaw and built in 1899-1902 for the former Parr's Bank. Like the White Star Building it is striped, but otherwise it is not as striking. The massive round headed and rusticated entrance leads to a fine circular interior with central lantern and radiating coffered and carved panels with painted swags of fruit. In front of this building is a Sanctuary Stone embedded in the road surface. This is the only surviving mark of the boundary of the old Liverpool Fair held on July 25th and November 11th. In this area for ten days before and after each fair debtors were able to walk free from arrest providing they were on lawful business. **Nos. 10-18** have a series of shops on the ground floor; the chemist's shop retains its original front. Above there is an irregular rhythm of windows, those on the second floor having panelled pilasters and pediments. **Nos. 6-8,** the United Kingdom Provident Institution, are distinguished by an order of giant Ionic columns to the third and fourth floors with a broken curved pediment. Finally, **Nos. 2-4,** another National Westminster Bank, are again in the Loire style and are richly decorated.

After the widening of Castle Street and the surrounding improvements at the end of the eighteenth century it was felt that the commercial community required better accommodation for transacting business. As a result, a new exchange was built on a large area that was cleared to the north of the Town Hall. Due to expanding trade, this building soon became inadequate and was replaced in 1862 by a larger exchange, designed by T. H. Wyatt in a French Renaissance style, this in turn being demolished to make way for the present building. Exchange Flags, created at the time of the first exchange, formed an open air exchange floor, and when in 1851 Queen Victoria looked down from the balcony of the Town Hall at the merchants assembled below, she is reported to have remarked that she had never before seen so large a number of well dressed gentlemen collected together in one place. In the centre of the Flags is the **Nelson Monument,** Liverpool's first public sculpture, erected in 1813. It was designed by M. Cotes Wyatt, with much of the modelling by Richard Westmacott, and shows four chained prisoners seated around a circular drum with relief panels and festoons. The drum was designed as a ventilator shaft for the bonded warehouse of which Exchange Flags formed the roof. These warehouses have now become a car park, but the monument still performs its necessary respiratory function.

Old Hall Street is named after the Old Hall, a thirteenth century mansion situated close to Union Street. Initially the seat of the Moore family, this house passed into the possession of the Earls of Derby in 1712 and was demolished for road widening in 1820. Old Hall Street had been a private road to the Hall, but after its becoming public, the northern end was developed up to the end of the eighteenth century, as the aristocratic part of the town. Here were leafy Ladies' Walk, Love Lane, and the promenade of Maidens' Green, all soon to be rudely destroyed to create an area of intense industrial and commercial activity and crossed by canals and railway tracks. Much rebuilding has again occurred here in recent years, but there remains a group of good Victorian commercial buildings, the finest of which is **The Albany Building** situated a short way along Old Hall Street on the right. The Albany was built in 1856 for Richard Naylor, a wealthy banker of Hooton Hall, and designed by J. K. Colling, a scholarly London architect. It is one of the best and earliest of the large Victorian office buildings in the city, successfully combining company offices with warehouse accommodation, a specific requirement of the cotton trade at that time. Before the cotton exchange was built adjacent, it formed the meeting place of cotton brokers who rented the offices. In style it is a very free Renaissance design with highly individual decorative treatment based on natural forms. This decoration can best be seen on window heads, tympana, frieze, and particularly in the fine entrance gates. The spacious courtyard is crossed by two elegant cast iron bridges, each approached by a delicate spiral staircase, and more ironwork can be seen in the ingenious top lit corridors which run the full length of the building.

Opposite The Albany is **Harley Chambers,** a classical neo-Greek style offiice building of 1860. The centre bay has a series of Venetian windows, that on the first floor has Ionic columns and a pediment. **City Buildings,** on the corner of Fazakerley Street, is a 1906 remodelling by Frederick Fraser of a mid-nineteenth century sugar warehouse. It is a spectacular job, the whole front being given a sheer cast iron and glass skin which sweeps around the corner in a manner used 25 years later by Sir Owen Williams in the celebrated Daily Express Buildings in London and a number of other principal cities.

The Cotton Exchange is another building that has been remodelled; however this recent refacing is an irretrievable loss, for the Old Hall Street frontage was the supreme architectural expression of the great power of the cotton trade and an extravagantly self-confident Edwardian Baroque design. Built in 1905-6 and designed by Matear and Simon, all that remains is the side and rear elevations. The one to Edmund Street is iron framed, with iron spandrel panels having delicate classical detail and large areas of plate glass rising through several storeys. The stone figures in front of the building on Old Hall Street represent Science, Industry and Commerce and were once part of the towers of the original frontage. **Orleans House** in Bixteth Street, also by Matear and Simon, is iron framed and clad in a similar manner to the Cotton Exchange. Liverpool has a strong and pioneering tradition of cast iron in buildings both as a structural and cladding material.

It is now necessary to cross Old Hall Street and follow the narrow Fazakerley Street and Rumford Place through to Chapel Street. The large modern development Richmond House stands on the site of Richmond Buildings, which was a dignified palazzo style commercial block and probably the finest work of Picton. Fragments of this building can be seen in the first floor entrance hall. On the opposite side of Chapel Street is another fine building by Picton, **Hargreaves Building,** erected in 1861. This is a five bay Venetian palazzo with round arched windows and, in roundels above, busts of historical figures connected with South America. Adjacent to the Covent Garden facade of Hargreaves Building can be seen the rear of **Mersey Chambers** with aggressively projecting glass and iron oriel windows. This was built between 1860 and 1870 for T. and J. Harrison the

Shipbuilders, and has a very different face on to Old Churchyard. Here note the carved Liver Bird over the central bay. The churchyard was laid out as a public garden in 1891 in memory of James Harrison, a partner in this firm.

At the south-west corner of the churchyard formerly stood the Merchants' Coffee House with a fine view of the river. In this meeting place were carried out the principal auction sales of property and ships. Similar gatherings were held at The Exchange Coffee House in Water Street, where, according to a notice in the *Liverpool Advertiser* in 1766, there was to be a sale of eleven negro slaves.

The Church of Our Lady and St. Nicholas is the parish church of Liverpool and was known as the Sailors' Church, St. Nicholas being the patron saint of sailors, and the tower being a landmark visible from the river. The tower is in fact the oldest part, for although the rest of the church was built in the fourteenth century as a chapel of ease, it was destroyed during the last war. The tower was designed by Thomas Harrison of Chester and built in 1811-5, replacing a previous tower with a spire which collapsed in 1810 killing 25 people including 17 girls from the Moorfields Charity School. Harrison's tower is a good example of early Gothic revival with flying buttresses supporting a graceful open lantern which is surmounted by a ship weather vane.

The Church of Our Lady and St. Nicholas   S. Long

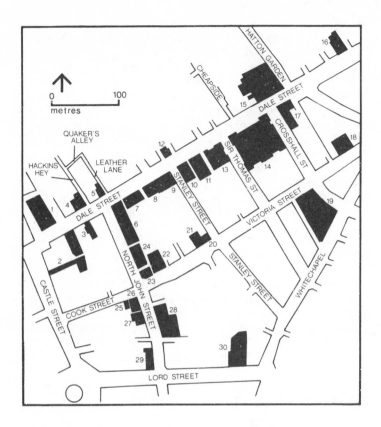

1 Liverpool, London
   and Globe Insurance
   Building
2 Queen Insurance
   Building
3 Stage Insurance
   Building
4 Union Marine
   Building
5 Rigby's Building
6 Royal Insurance
   Building
7 The Temple
8 Prudential
   Assurance Building
9 Buckley's Building
10 Muskers Buildings
11 Imperial Chambers
12 National
   Westminster Bank
13 Municipal Annexe
14 Municipal Buildings

15 City Magistrates
   Courts
16 135-139 Dale Street
17 Westminster
   Chambers
18 Jerome/Carlisle
   Buildings
19 Midland Railway
   Goods Office
20 The Bank of Ireland
21 Union House
22 Fowler's Building
23 Regina House
24 Solicitors Law
   Stationery Society
   Building
25 16 Cook Street
26 18-22 North John
   Street
27 24-26 Harrington
   Chambers
28 Central Buildings

29 Marldon Chambers
   and
   Clarence Building
30 81-89 Lord Street

3 Dale Street and Victoria Street

The second city centre walk starts in High Street, at the junction of Castle Street and Dale Street. High Street previously ran through to Old Hall Street and was the main street of the town. Dale Street was then the principal route into the town from Manchester and London, and was a very busy and populous thoroughfare. At the east end of the street was a bridge over the brook which ran along the line of Byrom Street and Whitechapel into the Pool. The street was first widened in 1786 and buildings were erected on the north side corresponding with the stucco terraces of Castle Street. Since it was the main entry to and from the town, inns and taverns were numerous, but gradually during the nineteenth century these were replaced by a series of large and impressive commercial premises. One of the first of these was the **Liverpool and London and Globe Insurance Building** erected in 1855-7 and designed by C. R. Cockerell, architect of the nearby Bank of England. It is a fine classical building of seven bays with attached columns on the second floor and an imposing, very original doorway set in a French niche of banded rustication. Also original is the diagonal treatment of the staircases on the High Street facade. The mansard roof and dormer windows are later additions which mar the original proportions.

On the other side of Dale Street is the **Queen Insurance Building** designed by Samuel Rowland for the Royal Bank and built in 1839. It has a grand facade with giant upper Doric and Ionic columns and a big top balustrade supporting the coat of arms of the Royal Bank. Segmental arches surmounted by ornamental iron screens lead to Sweeting Street and Queen Avenue, at the end of which is an elegant and finely proportioned building by the same architect. Inside is a large hall with a marvellous rich classical plaster ceiling. Next in Dale Street is the **State Insurance Building,** half of the front of which has been demolished. This is another original building by Aubrey Thomas, architect of the Royal Liver Building, and was built in 1906. The design shows a very free treatment of Gothic forms which in their flowing lines are almost Art Nouveau. Behind this facade the offices are placed around a galleried court with a glass tunnel vault. **The Union Marine Buildings** opposite is a typically robust design by Sir James Picton. The ground floor has large round-arched windows with keystones and marble panels

Prudential Assurance Building

between, and at the top is a very heavy projecting cornice with rope moulding on round arched machicolations. Across Hackins Hey is **Rigby's Buildings** a Victorian stuccoed building with rich decoration. Although the facade carries the date of 1726, the present building is probably not earlier than 1850. The second floor is the most elaborate with small balconies and pediments, and at the top is a balustraded parapet with urns and actoreria and the inscription 'Rigby's Buildings'.

The small alleyways behind Rigby's Buildings including Hackins Hey, Quaker Alley and Leather Lane are worth examining, for although they contain no listed buildings they give an indication of the character of Liverpool before the main streets were widened.

Opposite this area, on the corner of Dale Street and North John Street, is another of the early twentieth century giant office blocks **The Royal Insurance Building** erected in 1897-1903. The architect, J. Francis Doyle, was chosen from a limited design competition with seven entrants, the assessor Norman Shaw being retained as advisory architect. Doyle, who had worked with Shaw on the White Star Building, was so heavily influenced by Shaw's style that he was able to refashion it, the gable being taken straight from the earlier building. It is however, an extremely impressive building; the granite and Portland stone exterior conceals a steel frame of advanced design giving a column-free general office occupying most of the ground floor. The sculptured frieze a typical Arts and Crafts motif by C. J. Allen, takes as its theme insurance in its various forms, and runs around three sides of the building. The campanile with an octagonal cupola, gilded dome and sundial forms a prominent feature in the City skyline. The adjacent building in Dale Street is **The Temple,** designed by J. A. Picton and Son for Sir William Brown and erected in 1864-5. It is in an Italianate style with a central turret forming a large rusticated round arch on the ground floor leading to an open arcade.

Facing the end of Moorfields is the **Prudential Assurance Building** by Alfred Waterhouse and built in 1885-6 (the tower was added in 1906) in his typical harsh red terracotta and brick late Gothic style. The decoration is much simplified, relying mainly on scale and rhythm for effect, but the corner treatment with its oriel window and twin gable shows Waterhouse's compositional skill. The adjoining **Buckley's Buildings** is included in the listing for its group value. It is also of brick, but with stone dressings and turns the corner into Stanley Street. Then **Muskers Buildings,** formerly the Junior Reform Club, is more conventionally Gothic, with large pointed arched windows with cusped tracery. The neighbouring **Imperial Chambers** is

Queen Avenue

Municipal Buildings and Annexe

38

also Victorian Gothic. The central office entrance with composite columns leads to a glass roofed hall crossed by iron bridges.

Opposite the end of Stanley Street is the **National Westminster Bank** a stuccoed three storey Victorian Building with a banded rusticated ground floor supporting pilasters and giant fluted columns with elaborate Corinthian capitals. Further east is the **Municipal Annexe** built in 1883 as the exclusive Conservative Club and designed by F. and G. Holme. It is in a bold French Renaissance style with an iron balcony on the first floor and symmetrical wings topped by high truncated roofs with pedimented windows. **Municipal Buildings** was built in 1860-6 to the designs of the Corporation Surveyor, John Weightman, and completed by his successor, E. R. Robson. This large building is in a mixture of Italian and French Renaissance styles with symmetrical French pavilion roofs, in the centre of which is a tower with a curious freely shaped spire or steep pyramid roof. This has a wrought-iron balcony half way down which was described by C. H. Reilly as 'like a skirt popped over the head (if that is ever done) and not allowed to settle into its proper place.' The giant Corinthian columns and pilasters have different designs to all the capitals, which is a Gothic rather than Renaissance conception, and the building is further adorned by its sixteen fine sculptured figures.

The City Magistrates Courts on the north side of Dale Street were built in 1857-9 and also designed by Weightman. This is a dignified three storey ashlar building with a central pediment and carriage entrance below. Around the corner in Hatton Garden, the Fire Station is by Thomas Shelmerdine, Corporation Surveyor after E. R. Robson. Built in 1898 it is an interesting composition combining Jacobean and Art Nouveau motifs. Then the City Transport Offices, also by Shelmerdine, built in 1905-7 and another good facade, this time with Edwardian Imperial features including architectural sculpture. Behind these buildings, but accessible from Cheapside, is the Main Bridewell designed by John Weightman and built in 1860-4. It is a typically severe neo-classical prison building, the main front being separated by a courtyard from the massive rusticated gate piers at the entrance.

The last buildings of note in Dale Street are **Nos. 135-139,** a terrace of late eighteenth century brick houses. No. 139 was built for John Houghton, a distiller, whose works were nearby. On the Trueman Street elevation is a Venetian window with some Adam style decoration and a fine tripartite doorway.

On the south side of Dale Street, between Crosshall Street and Preston Street, stands **Westminster Chambers** built in 1880 in the Gothic style. The Crosshall Street facade has two pointed

The Royal Insurance
Building

135-139 Dale Street

Midland Railway Goods Office

arched doorways with carved mouldings and granite columns. The adjacent Juvenile Court was formerly a Wesleyan Chapel built in 1878-80 and designed by Picton junior. It is an original building in an early thirteenth century style built of small rusticated stones. Round the corner in Victoria Street, between Crosshall Street and Kingsway, are the matching **Jerome Buildings** and **Carlisle Buildings** dated 1883. These have a distinctive roofline with their projecting dormers with three light windows and pagoda like roofs.

Victoria Street is a new street formed in 1867-8 to improve the flow of traffic and produce a new and impressive location for commercial development. The western section of the street followed the line of the existing Temple Court, which accounts for the gentle curved frontage of the Fruit and Produce Exchange Buildings. Probably the most impressive building in Victoria Street is, in fact, not commercial but principally a warehouse, the **Midland Railway Goods Offices** erected about 1850. A bold and functional design it was built by the Midland Railway for the receipt and dispatch of their goods, the great doorways being sufficiently high to admit the largest load. The main front has a slightly concave face with the windows set in giant round arches with keystones and imposts. The Victoria Street facade has carved spandrels with shields of arms and carved names of Midland Railway Stations.

The General Post Office of 1894-9 was designed by Sir Henry Tanner but had its first floor removed after war damage which accounts for its unfinished appearance. **The Bank of Ireland,** formerly the Westminster Bank, on the corner of Stanley Street, was built circa 1870. It has an interesting functional facade to Stanley Street with cast iron mullioned windows and tall lift shafts. Adjacent to the Bank of Ireland is **Union House** built in 1882, a five storey block with polished granite columns to the ground and first floors. The most interesting feature of the building is the cast iron staircases with a wall of stained glass depicting the harvesting and packing of merchandise in foreign lands. It is possible to see this glass at night from the side passage, Progress Place, where it fits within a robust cast iron and glass facade. **Fowler's Buildings** is an office block built in 1864 to the design of J. A. Picton. It is of stone with eight granite Tuscan columns, round arched windows and a heavy top cornice on brackets. Adjoining this, on the corner of North John Street, is **Regina House** which includes the Beaconsfield Public House, and then around the corner in North John Street the **Solicitors Law Stationery Society Building** of 1854. This is a narrow four storey building stuccoed on the upper floors and enriched with balconies, carved lintels, and on the top floor, three round eyes,

Fowler's Building

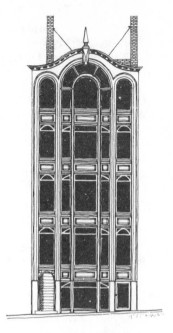

16 Cook Street

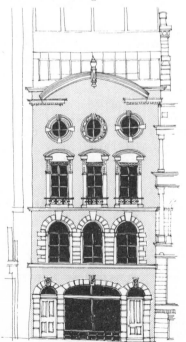

Solicitors Law Stationery
Society Building

42

the centre one decorated as a laurel wreath. An ingenious roof extension has recently been added.

At the bottom of Cook Street is the second and only other recorded building by Peter Ellis, architect of Oriel Chambers. It is **No. 16,** built two years later than Oriel Chambers in 1866, and is just as original. The front has three giant bays in a Venetian window head filled in with plate glass, but in the courtyard to the rear is the most remarkable feature. Here a surprisingly 'modern' glazed cast iron spiral staircase cantilevered from each floor is squeezed into the corner against a wall of glass with slender iron mullions. In its stripped aesthetic it is far in advance of its time, and Ellis would seem to have paid the penalty by receiving no further architectural commissions. After this date he is recorded only as working as a civil engineer.

The adjacent corner building, **Nos. 18-22 North John Street,** is a mid-nineteenth century office building with modern shops on the ground floor and upper walls stuccoed. **Nos. 24-26 (Harring-ton Chambers)** is similar, but later in date and has giant panelled pilasters and pedimented dormers. **Central Buildings** opposite is a huge and imposing symmetrical block. The heavily moulded upper floors are seated on a colonnade of red granite Doric columns filled in with plate glass, giving light to the shops behind.

Marldon Chambers and Clarence Building, situated on the corner of North John Street and Lord Street, are an example of the Victorian classical style, being later than the original classical facades of Lord Street by John Foster in the 1820s. The giant fluted composite pilasters and deep frieze and cornice above the second floor windows give the facade a grand scale, and the end three bays are emphasised by a pediment and four half columns instead of pilasters.

The only other building of special note in Lord Street is **Nos. 81-89.** This is a late nineteenth century block which achieves a striking effect by the use of alternate horizontal bands of white and yellow stone. Three segmental arches frame three upper floors, the middle one recessed to form a reversed bay. Above this are three steep gables containing a series of lancet windows and punctuated by octagonal turrets.

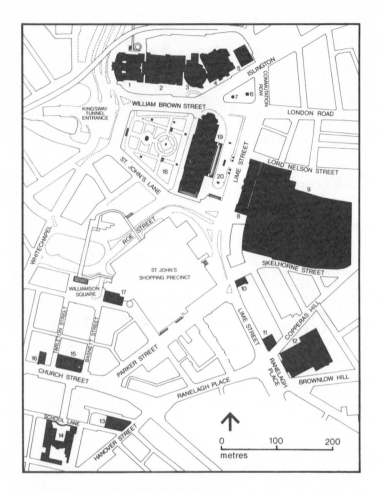

1 College of
   Technology and
   Museum Extension
2 William Brown
   Library and Museum
3 Picton Reading
   Room and Hornby
   Library
4 Walker Art Gallery
5 Sessions House
6 Wellington Column
7 Steble Fountain
8 Former
   North Western Hotel
9 Lime Street
   Station Sheds
10 Crown Hotel

11 The Vines
12 Adelphi Hotel
13 Crane Building
14 Bluecoat Chambers
15 Compton House
16 25 & 25A
   Church Street
17 Playhouse Theatre
18 St. John's Garden
   Monuments
19 St. George's Hall
20 St. George's Plateau
   Lime Street

4 William Brown Street, Lime Street, Church Street Area.

The walk starts in William Brown Street, formerly called Shaw's Brow after a Mayor who owned some properties on the site. In 1860 it was renamed William Brown Street after the wealthy merchant who paid for the William Brown Library and Museum.

College of Technology and Museum Extension, William Brown Street. Opened in 1902 and designed by E. W. Mountford, this three storey stone building in the Edwardian imperial style exhibits a wealth of sculpture by F. W. Pomeroy. On the pediment of the first bay below the museum can be seen a symbolic figure of Liverpool holding a globe and sceptre, supported by figures typical of the City's commerce and industries. On the pediment nearest the Mersey Tunnel, Minerva is located typifying the wisdom of the City and presiding over the education of the community.

William Brown Library and Museum, William Brown Street. This building, designed in stone by Thomas Allom, was opened in 1860. It was subsequently modified by John Weightman, the Corporation Architect. Damaged in the Second World War, it was reconstructed with an unfortunate addition on the skyline by the City Architect, Dr. R. Bradbury. It has a portico of six Corinthian columns with a pediment modelled on that at the south side of St. George's Hall. The building was constructed to house the 13th Earl of Derby's Natural History Collection which he bequeathed to the town in 1851. The proposal to build created a controversy and the wealthy merchant, William Brown, came forward and offered to defray the cost. His offer was accepted and the building eventually opened amid much celebration.

Picton Reading Room and Hornby Library, William Brown Street. Sir James Picton, the then Chairman of the Libraries and Museums Committee, laid the foundation stone for the Reading Room in 1875 and the building was opened in 1879. It was designed by Cornelius Sherlock and modelled on the British Museum Reading Room. The Hornby Library, designed by Thomas Shelmerdine, was added in 1906. The Reading Room performs a valuable civic design function by acting as a pivot to William Brown Street and Islington, which are at an angle to each other. It consists of a stone drum raised on a podium with a peripheral colonnade of Corinthian columns. The exterior surface of the drum contains small niches with statues, an enriched frieze and a domed rotunda roof. The Hornby Library at the back has an Edwardian imperial interior. The Reading Room, on completion, was nicknamed 'Picton's Gasometer'. It was the first public building in Liverpool to have electric lighting, which was introduced to it by Picton.

Walker Art Gallery, Islington. Consisting of a single storey Grecian stone facade with a portico of freestanding Corinthian columns, this building was opened in 1877 to a design by H. H. Vale. It was enlarged in 1822 by Cornelius Sherlock and Sir Arnold Thornley designed the rear extension which was completed in 1931. Statues of Raphael and Michaelangelo, designed by Warrington Wood, are positioned at each side of the entrance. The friezes on the building portray four local events — the Duke of Edinburgh laying the foundation stone of the Gallery, King William III embarking at Hoylake for Ireland in 1690, King John granting the first charter to the burgesses of Liverpool and Queen Victoria in Liverpool in 1851. The figure above the portico is not Britannia but Liverpool personified as a majestic matron wearing a civic crown wreathed in laurels. She holds a ship's propeller in her left hand and a trident in her right.

A public subscription was launched to erect the first building but it met with considerable opposition. After he was elected Mayor in 1873 Alderman Andrew Barclay Walker, a brewer, announced that he would pay the entire cost. The opening day was observed as a public holiday in Liverpool and the ceremony attracted great crowds of festive well-wishers.

Sessions House, Islington. Opened in 1884, this stone building in a free classical style was designed by F. & G. Holme. It consists of a five bay front with a portico of four paired Corinthian columns and a high enriched parapet. The coat of arms of the Lancashire County Council is located in the pediment. The interior includes a charming Italian Renaissance staircase hall with a series of little saucer domes.

Wellington Column, William Brown Street. Sited where the Folly Fair was once held, the column was inaugurated in 1863. It was designed by George Anderson Lawton of Glasgow and is an exact replica of the Melville monument in Edinburgh. It is a fluted Doric column, has an overall height of 132 ft. and is built of Darleydale stone. The four sides of the plinth contain reliefs and the south panel depicts the grand charge at Waterloo. It is said that the statue of the Duke is cast in metal salvaged from guns captured at Waterloo. In the north-eastern corner of the triangular enclosure to the west of the column may be found the Board of Trade Standard Measurement Table marked out in iron pegs. This will become a museum piece when metrication is completed.

William Brown Library and Museum

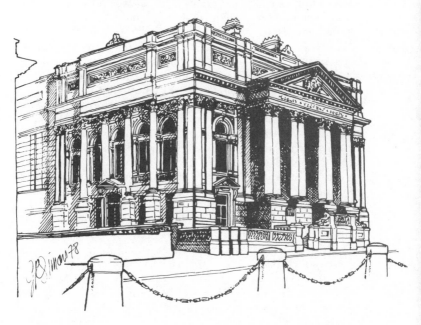

Sessions House

Steble Fountain, William Brown Street. Designed by W. Cunliffe, this fountain was erected in 1879. It consists of a circular stone basin with a bronze centrepiece of figures representing the four seasons. It was the gift of Colonel R. F. Steble, the Mayor of Liverpool in 1874/75.

To the east of the Steble Fountain and Wellington Column lies Commutation Row, which owes its name to an incident in the days of 'Window Tax'. The residents in the Row, apparently compelled to pay for their windows, decided to make the few they had as large as possible, which led to a dispute with the Inland Revenue. The situation was resolved by a 'Commutation' being agreed upon, hence the name. Lime Street until 1790 was known as Lime Kiln Lane after a Mr. William Harvey's kilns, which stood on the site of the present railway station. In 1804 doctors at the Infirmary which was located where St. George's Hall now stands, objected to the fumes from the kilns and after litigation the kilns were relocated elsewhere.

Former North Western Hotel, Lime Street. Opened as a 330 room hotel in 1871, the building was designed by Alfred Waterhouse, who also designed the Prudential building in Dale Street. The seven storey facade is faced with Caen and Stourton stone, towards which the Corporation made a contribution as it considered the site one of the most important in the town. The building is massive, monumental and symmetrical in the French Renaissance style.

Lime Street Station Sheds, Lime Street. The first station built on this site was designed by John Fowler and was completed in 1836. It included a two storey masonry screen to Lime Street. A second station was built in 1851 which consisted of a train shed, an adjoining office building and Fowler's screen. The train shed was designed by Richard Turner and William Fairburn and the adjoining office block by William Tite. Part of Tite's building can still be seen fronting on to the service yard off Lord Nelson Street. The third station was started in 1867 and included the present northern train shed which, at the time, was the largest in the world with a span of 200 ft. The present parallel southern train shed was completed in 1879 and is of dry construction with each bay taking only three days to construct. The sheds are too low to be impressive but do follow a graceful curve which is particularly visible when viewed from adjoining high buildings.

Crown Hotel, 43 Lime Street. The architect is unknown but the building was completed in 1905 and has one of the richest 'Art Nouveau' exteriors in Liverpool. It consists of a brick super-structure with moulded plaster friezes and gilded letters on a polished granite base with shallow box windows to the first and second floors. The cut glass windows and beaten copper panels to

Steble Fountain

Former North Western Hotel and Lime Street Station

49

the ground floor pick up the evening light. The rich plaster ceilings of the interior are visible through the cut glass windows.

The Vines, 81-87 Lime Street. This exuberant Edwardian Baroque building, designed by Walter Thomas, was completed in 1907. Thomas also designed the Philharmonic Hotel in Hope Street. The building, constructed of stone, is capped by a steep slate roof, florid gables and an ill-proportioned tower. The ground floor has four convex glazed windows of cut and etched glass. The building was constructed for Mr. Walker, the brewer, and the interior of mahogany, beaten copper and rich plaster was designed to take his favourite paintings which still remain.

Ranelagh Place and Ranelagh Street take their name from a Pavilion and Tea Garden which were located between 1722 and 1790 on the site of the Adelphi Hotel. The Garden, in which entertainments were provided, was a popular rendezvous for the well-to-do.

Adelphi Hotel, Ranelagh Place. The architect, Frank Atkinson, also designed ships' interiors and Selfridges in Oxford Street, London. The hotel was completed in 1912 and has a cladding of white ashlar on a steel frame. It was originally intended to enclose a courtyard but the back was never built. It was unusual when it was built in that the windows were brought forward to the surface of the building making the walls appear very thin. The first floor has round arched windows with face masks on the keystones. The elegant interior has Greek details in the marble panelling and plaster columns.

Hanover Street was probably named in honour of the Duke of Cumberland, George III's brother. The Duke had honoured the town by a Royal inspection in appreciation of Liverpool's support for his brother when the Scots rebelled in 1745.

Crane Building, 85 Hanover Street. The architect and exact date of completion are not known but the building is late Victorian and in the Greek style. The three upper storeys are of brick, the remainder being stone. The ground and first floors have Greek ornament and round-headed windows to the first floor. The three brick upper storeys have carved capitals to flat pilasters with a rich top cornice above. The theatre interior has a panelled ceiling and walls with fluted Ionic pilasters.

Bluecoat Chambers, School Lane. Grade I. Originally built as a charity school in 1717, this use ceased in 1906. The architect is not known. The inscription below the pediment reads — 'Dedicated to the promotion of Christian Charity and the training of poor boys in the principles of the Anglican Church. Founded this year of Salvation 1717'. In 1913 it was bought by W. H. Lever, the first Lord Leverhulme, with proceeds from a libel action he won, as he intended to promote it as a centre for the arts.

Crown Hotel

Adelphi Hotel

A scheme was drawn up in 1914 but shelved due to the war and his enthusiasm waned. In 1927 enthusiasts launched an appeal and bought it from Lord Leverhulme's executors and formed the Bluecoat Society of the Arts, which now owns the building.

The building was damaged in the Second World War and a plaque in Latin over the entrance reads 'Struck down from the sky by the firebrands of the enemy and partly destroyed on 4th May 1941 restored with dutiful affection in the year 1951'. The building is 'H' shaped in plan with a cross link at the southern end which encloses a courtyard. The entrance court on the other side of the middle link is open on the northern side. The centre link building originally contained the chapel and hall and is of two storeys with five bays to the front, surmounted by a pediment, slate hipped roof and a small cupola. The building is in a stately and crisp Queen Anne style showing a Wren influence with three-quarter Ionic columns, dark brickwork, painted stone quoins and dressings. All windows have cherubs on the keystones. The 'listing' includes the forecourt railings, the gates and gatepiers.

The City's principal shopping street, Church Street, lies to the north of Bluecoat Chambers and was laid out at the end of the seventeenth century. It takes its name from the Parish Church of St. Peter which was built parallel to it in 1704. The church, demolished in 1922, was located where Woolworth's store now stands and its former position is commemorated by a brass Maltese Cross in one of the paving stones in front of Woolworth's.

Compton House, 33-45 Church Street (Marks & Spencer). This building was erected in 1867 by Jeffrey & Company as a department store. The architect is not known. In 1877 the firm went bankrupt and the building was subdivided partly into an hotel. The centre of the Church Street facade is emphasised by a large round arch and broken pediment to the first floor. The end bays have symmetrical square towers with Venetian windows on the second floor rising to an additional storey above the eaves containing Ionic columns.

25 & 25A Church Street. The date and architect are not known but the building is Victorian. It consists of four storeys of painted stucco over brick. The first floor comprises three glazed round arches topped by keystones and divided by panelled pilasters. The second floor windows have ornamental balustraded balconies. The building is also interesting in that Frank Winfield Woolworth opened his first shop in Britain here in 1909.

Williamson Square is connected to Church Street by Basnett and Tarleton Streets, both named after old Liverpool families who resided in the area at the time the streets and Williamson Square were laid out. Williamson Square was built by the Williamson family in the early eighteenth century adjacent to the

Bluecoat Chambers

Playhouse Theatre

watercourse that originally ran down Whitechapel. Formerly known as Frog Lane, the street was changed to Whitechapel in the 1770s. Williamson Square in the early and mid-eighteenth century was a select place of residence and its founder published the Liverpool Advertiser. Gradually it took a turn for the worse and by the end of the eighteenth century was the hub of the town's vice and crime. In the late nineteenth century it was popular on Saturday afternoons for the public displays that took place there and records tell of a giant that smashed stones on his chest, a dwarf who licked hot irons, a snake charmer and a spotted lady.

Playhouse Theatre, Williamson Square. Built in 1865 as the Star Music Hall by an unknown architect, the building was reconstructed as a repertory theatre by Professor Adshead in 1912-13. The building has a three storey seven bay plaster front with a broken pediment and Corinthian pilasters between the windows on each floor. The elegant and graceful neo-Greek auditorium has cast iron columns. The extension, consisting of circular glass and plaster drums was completed in 1967 and was designed by Hall, O'Donohue and Wilson. It is one of the best new buildings in the City.

Roe Street takes its name from Mr. William Roe, a merchant who lived in a house overlooking Queen Square. Mr. Roe had a fine garden with a fountain fed by a conduit from the Old Fall Well which sprang from a site now occupied by the Royal Court Theatre. This well was one of the principal water sources for the town until the end of the eighteenth century.

St. John's Garden and It's Monuments.

St. John's Garden takes its name from St. John's Church which stood here from 1783 until 1887. Many French prisoners of war who were detained in Liverpool during the Napoleonic Wars were buried in this churchyard. The former church site and churchyard were laid out as terraced gardens by Thomas Shelmerdine, the City Surveyor, and opened to the public in 1904. The garden contains a number of monuments commemorating people associated with reforming some of the most pressing social problems of the nineteenth century.

Gladstone Monument. Erected in 1904 and designed by Sir Thomas Brock. Gladstone, the Liberal statesman and Prime Minister, was born in Rodney Street in 1809 and died in 1898. The tall pedestal between seated female figures of 'Truth' and 'Justice' carries a relief entitled 'Brotherhood'. Gladstone stands holding a roll of parchment and books.

Rathbone Monument. Designed by George Frampton and erected in 1889, the monument commemorates William Rathbone, 1819-1902, a member of the distinguished Liverpool family of social reformers. Rathbone was an M.P. for nearly 30 years and was one of the founders of Liverpool University and pioneered Liverpool District Nursing.

Forwood Monument. Erected in 1903 and designed by George Frampton. Forwood, who died in 1898, was elected Tory M.P. for Ormskirk in 1885 and eventually became Secretary to the Admiralty.

Balfour Monument. Balfour died in 1886 and the monument designed by A. Bruce Joy was erected in 1889. Balfour was a philanthropist of Scottish origin and championed temperance and neglected children.

Lester Monument. Designed by George Frampton and erected in 1907, the monument commemorates Canon Major Lester, a worker for neglected children, who died in 1903.

Nugent Monument. Erected in 1906 and designed by F. W. Pomeroy. Monsignor Nugent, 1822-1905, worked on behalf of neglected children and founded ragged schools and orphanages. The monument is composed of a standing bronze figure in a blessing attitude with a ragged boy.

Regimental Monument. It commemorates the South African War and is of white stone with a central bronze wreath, helmet, flag and sword and a standing soldier at each side. The central pedestal contains a figure of Britannia. The monument was designed by Sir William Goscombe John and erected in 1905.

St. George's Hall and Plateau, Lime Street. Grade I. In the early nineteenth century Liverpool held a four-day musical festival every three years in St. Peter's Church. In 1836 the City felt that a new hall was required to house this important event. A fund was raised and in June 1838 a foundation stone was laid as a tribute to mark the coronation of Queen Victoria. As no design had then been prepared a competition was held for the new Concert Hall on the site of the present Wellington Column and the winner was a 23 year old architect named Harvey Lonsdale Elmes. A second competition was held by the City for new Assize Courts and was also won by Elmes. The Corporation then decided to combine the two buildings and Elmes produced a design. Work started in 1842 on the site of the Old Infirmary but during the course of construction in 1847 Elmes became ill and was advised to take a rest in Jamaica where he died shortly after arrival, 'a martyr to architecture' according to his father. Professor C. R. Cockerell was appointed to take over and the Hall was inaugurated on the 18th September 1854.

The building of Darleydale stone combines the massiveness of a Roman bath with the delicacy of a Greek temple. The complete building is 490 ft. long and contains two courtrooms, a central Great Hall and a small elliptical Concert Hall together with ancillary rooms. The south front is a Greek temple with a

St. George's Hall

Cast Iron Dolphin
Lamp Standard

A balcony carried
by maidens

56

tympanum and frieze, the sculpture of which has had to be removed as it was in a dangerous state. The sculpture, representing 'Britannia with Commerce and the Arts', is by Cockerell with help from the Victorian sculptor, Alfred Stevens. A Latin inscription below the south front pediment reads 'Free citizens have here dedicated a place for Arts, Laws and Councils'. The east front facing Lime Street consists of thirteen bays of giant Corinthian columns and a colonnade 200 ft. long. Relief panels at the base of the east front by Stirling Lee, Conrad Dressler and Charles J. Allen were introduced in 1894. The north front is an ellipse and the west front overlooking St. John's Garden containing a large number of windows is of considerably less power than the east front.

The Great Hall of the building contains red granite columns carrying a mighty tunnel vault inspired by Blouet's reconstruction of the Baths of Caracalla which was published in 1828. The partially sunken floor, when uncovered, is surfaced with Minton's tiles of a strong brown and blue colour which owe something to Alfred Stevens. The organ, located between the Northern Court and the Great Hall, was placed there by Cockerell which, however, blocks the axial view deemed important by Elmes.

The small Concert Hall, dubbed the 'Golden Concert Hall' by Professor Reilly, the first Professor of Architecture at the University, is by Cockerell and is considered by many the best room in the building. It consists of wood panelled walls, papier mache friezes and a balcony carried by maidens; the material of which they are made is still unrecognised. The room with its mirrors and chandeliers is magical and was the scene of many of Charles Dickens' 'Readings'.

St. George's Hall is of considerable engineering interest. The Consultant Engineer, Sir Robert Rawlinson, was instrumental in introducing hollow blocks for the vault over the Great Hall which lightened the load from a possible one thousand tons to six hundred tons, and Dr. Boswell Reid, the heating engineer, produced a most advanced heating and air conditioning system. Air was introduced under the long portico on the east side and passed over jets of water which cleaned it before it was heated and distributed to the main rooms of the building by way of steam operated fans and huge ducts. Four giant shafts, each with three ducts, were strategically incorporated in the plan. Two ducts withdrew smoke from boilers and individual fireplaces below and the third extracted vitiated air. The building has received praise from many people — Queen Victoria said that it was 'worthy of Ancient Athens'. Richard Norman Shaw, the architect of Scotland Yard, called it 'one of the great edifices of the world'. Sir Nicholas Pevsner in his book *Buildings of England, South Lancashire* published in 1969, states that it is the 'Freest neo-Grecian building in England and one of the finest in the world'.

Over the years architectural historians have been puzzled how such a young architect could have produced such an accomplished and original building. It has been likened to the work of Schinkel, the German architect who built a number of important buildings in Berlin, including the Altes Museum, in the early nineteenth century.

In a B.B.C. broadcast in January 1977, entitled *A Temple for the Merchant Princes*, Stephen Bayley, lecturer in Art History at the Open University, stated that although Elmes visited Munich after he produced the final design for St. George's Hall, he never visited Berlin and could not, therefore, have seen Schinkel's work with his own eyes. Bayley admits that Elmes may have seen Schinkel's work illustrated in books but believes Elmes obtained his inspiration for St. George's Hall nearer home.

Elmes was born in Hampshire, near Chichester, and his father, although not an architect, was interested in architecture. He greatly admired Grange Park in Hampshire, designed by William Wilkins. The house had a clumsy but unusual longitudinal plan and it is known that the younger Elmes was also interested in it and made measured drawings of it. Bayley suggests that the inspiration for St. George's Hall may have been Grange Park rather than Germany.

St. George's Plateau, Lime Street.

Cast Iron Dolphin Lamp Standards — by Alfred Stevens, date unknown.

War Memorial. Designed by Professor Lionel Budden of Liverpool University. The memorial was unveiled on the 11th November 1930. The two bronze reliefs are by H. Tyson Smith. One shows marching soldiers, the other mourners. The memorial is unfortunately sited in that it blocks the view of the Hall colonnade when viewed axially from Lime Street.

Queen Victoria Monument. This equestrian statue on a plinth was designed by Thomas Thorneycroft and erected in 1870.

Prince Albert Monument. Also by Thomas Thorneycroft and erected in 1866.

Recumbent Lions. Two pairs in stone designed by Nicholl and erected in 1855.

5 Bold Street and Duke Street Area

The part of the City Centre through which this walk leads was laid out mainly in the eighteenth century and some of the streets were shown on a map of 1725. The latter part of the century was a very wealthy period in the history of Liverpool, accounted for in part by the lucrative and infamous slave trade which flourished again in the mid 1780s following the American War of Independence and until its abolition. Gentlemen's clubs, newsrooms, libraries, concert and meeting halls and many other institutions throughout the area are evidence of the wealth and 'enlightenment' of the times. Some remain; others have gone without trace.

The walk starts at Waterloo Place which is at the Church Street junction with Hanover and Ranelagh Streets and from here Bold Street forms a long straight ascent to St. Luke's Church, its slender tower dramatically terminating the view. Bold Street was laid out in 1780 having originally been a 'rope walk' used in connection with the craft of ropemaking for the sailing ships of the time. It became a fashionable residential street and many of the dwellinghouses on the south-west side (the right side looking up to St. Luke's) were occupied by merchants who had their counting houses at the back, fronting Wood Street. Between 1785 and 1796, the whole of this side was completed and about half of the opposite frontage. The original residential use rapidly gave way to shopping and for over a hundred and fifty years Bold Street was one of the most fashionable and exclusive shopping streets outside London, and frequently compared to Bond Street. The lower part of the street was pedestrianised in 1972-3.

On the left facing on to Waterloo Place and Bold Street is the **Lyceum,** the last remaining building in Liverpool by Thomas Harrison of Chester. It was built 1800-2 jointly for the Lyceum gentlemen's club and to rehouse the Liverpool Library which was the first circulating library in Europe, being founded in 1757. The accommodation was originally on one floor with a basement and mezzanine, the library and the club having separate entrances from the recessed Ionic portico facing Bold Street. The old library is circular, roofed with a decorated saucer dome with a central roof light. A first floor circular gallery supported by reeded Doric columns gives access to the librarians room, situated above the club's smoking room to the right of the portico. The main original club room was the newsroom facing on to Waterloo Place, with a

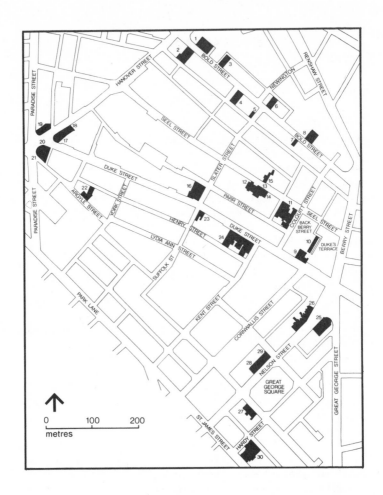

1 Lyceum
2 12-16 Bold Street
3 Palatine Club
  7 Bold Street
4 Marlborough House
  52 Bold Street
5 4 Slater Street
6 43-47 Bold Street
7 92 Bold Street
8 75-79 Bold Street
9 169-175 Duke Street
10 1-9 Dukes Terrace
11 Royal Institution
12 St. Peter's Church
13 76 Seel Street
14 78 Seel Street
15 55 Seel Street

St. Peter's
  Presbytery
16 105 Duke Street
17 1 and 3
  Duke Street
18 24-30 Hanover
  Street
19 Church House
20 12 Hanover Street
21 Warehouse 1863
22 21, 21A and 23
  Argyle Street
23 Monroe Public
  House
24 116-126 Duke Street
25 Congregational
  Church

26 10-26 Nelson Street
27 10, 18 to 21 Great
  George Square
28 28 to 34 Great
  George Square
29 8 and 8A
  Grenville Street
  South
30 Church of
  St. Vincent de Paul
  and Presbytery

shallow barrel vaulted roof. A weather vane on the roof of the building controlled an indicator which still exists in the news room showing the direction of the wind for the benefit of the sailing shipowners and captains using the club. Sadly, the many unsympathetic additions at roof level have destroyed the simple form of the building. The library closed before the war and the building now has an air of blackened dilapidation.

Almost opposite are **Nos. 12-16 Bold Street,** an early Victorian cast iron framed shop with two storeys of glass between slender iron columns and stuccoed front above. The whole front is in its original form apart from minor modifications and retains its crenelated canopy to the ground floor shop fronts and above its Ionic capitals and ornamented balustrading.

Moving up the street on the left hand side is the former **Palatine Club (No. 7 Bold Street)** by Charles Octavius Parnell, 1854. Built of Bath stone it takes the form of a Florentine palace on four storeys. Above a rusticated base there is a centralised group of three windows on each floor with Doric and Corinthian columns and pediments on the first and second floors respectively.

On the corner of Concert Street further up the street stands **Marlborough House (No. 52 Bold Street).** On this site stood one of the first buildings in Bold Street constructed 1785-6 by Charles Eyes as a concert hall capable of seating 1400 together with an orchestra of 150. The hall was carried over the footwalk on Wood Street by means of an arcade. The original concert hall was famed for its excellent acoustics but in 1836 it was altered to create shops with a hall above. Following a fire it was again rebuilt in 1853 by A. H. Holme and the present building, which is no longer used as a concert hall is of stucco of the late classical period. The reliefs on the facades depict musical instruments and musical scores and the inscription 'Halle des Modes' is a later addition.

The next street off Bold Street to the right is Slater Street and the second building on the right, **No. 4 Slater Street,** is an interesting example of a conversion into a shop of two typical late Georgian houses. The shop fronts are worth looking at, formed by six arches richly decorated in stucco.

Opposite Slater Street are **Nos. 43-47 Bold Street,** a stone building of five bays built in about 1864 by William Culshaw and Sumner for the Liverpool Savings Bank. At street level there are now three modern shop fronts but the three upper floors survive with a central curved pediment formerly above the main door to the bank. Above are four curved iron balconies and a large cornice at the roof level. Higher up the street on the right is **No. 92 Bold Street,** a Victorian building with a stone facade in the classical tradition. The two upper floors both carry carved friezes and cornices supported on columns and pilasters.

Lyceum

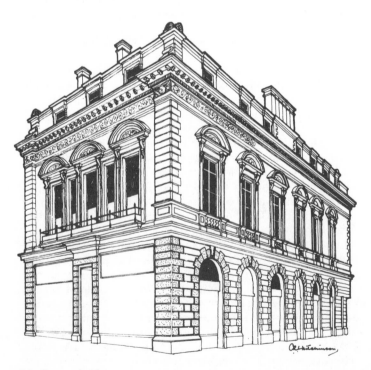

Marlborough House

Diagonally opposite are **Nos. 75-79 Bold Street,** again of Victorian classical style. The facade is of stucco and three storeys high. At the ground floor level columns remain between three shop fronts, carrying a frieze and cornice and, above, giant order pilasters and half columns measuring two storeys in height support a central pediment and two smaller side pediments.

Continue on to the top of Bold Street and turn right into Berry Street. St. Luke's Church, now a ruin, is described on page 78. Berry Street too was an eighteenth century 'rope walk'. On the right hand side between Wood Street and Seel Street can be seen the remnants of the facade of a once imposing terrace built in about 1798 by John Walmsley and altered about 1812 when it was converted to shops and a coach factory. What remains is not 'listed', nor are the other brick Georgian houses on this side of the street which were converted to shops at about the same time.

Duke Street was laid out by 1725 in the form of a long avenue, although it was possibly not named until later. For a century it was a fashionable residence of the wealthiest merchants and is associated with most of the families who were instrumental in the prodigious growth of Liverpool to become one of the world's greatest ports. There are frequent reminders of this period throughout the length of the street.

Nos. 169-175 Duke Street are examples of early nineteenth century houses. Nos. 171 and 173 have retained pedimented entrances with fanlights. An alleyway leads to 'back-to-back' terraces of artisans dwellings, **Nos. 1-9 Dukes Terrace,** which are the last surviving examples in the City.

Turn right into Colquitt Street where, on the left hand side, stands the **Royal Institution** (now the University Extra Mural Department). It was built originally as a house for Thomas Parr, an important Liverpool Banker, in about 1799. In the local tradition it had its offices and warehouses at the back abutting Parr Street. The Royal Institution, for the cultivation of literature, science and the arts, was established by William Roscoe and the house was converted for this purpose by Edmund Aitken who added the central Greek Doric porch. The Institution opened in 1817 and was incorporated by royal charter in 1822. The main front is five bays of two-and-a-half storeys in brick with restrained stone dressings. The two symmetrical side wings are a floor lower and linked to the main block. Many of the paintings and sculptures of the Royal Institution can be seen in the Walker Art Gallery.

Further down Seel Street on the left is the oldest Roman Catholic church in Liverpool, **St. Peter's.** It is dated 1788 and the sanctuary was added in 1845. The church is faced in stucco with two tiers of windows and a two storey pedimented porch.

75-79 Bold Street

Royal Institution

Inside there is a gallery on three sides supported on columns. The sanctuary with its two storey pilasters, gilded capitals and arched roof contrasts richly with the simplicity of the rest of the interior.

Adjoining the church, **No. 76 Seel Street,** is an early nineteenth century three storey brick house with a panelled door and round traceried fanlight. **No. 78 Seel Street** dates from about the same time and may have been a school. It is two storeys high, pedimented, and has a stone string course.

Opposite, **No. 55 Seel Street (St. Peter's Presbytery),** is an early nineteenth century Georgian house of brick with stone dressings.

Continue down Seel Street and turn left into Slater Street. On the right hand side you will come to **105 Duke Street,** the former Union News Room opened on the 1st January 1801, on the day England was united with Ireland. Built by John Foster Senior it is of ashlar on two storeys, with a central Ionic pediment on the Slater Street facade. Failure to reach agreement on the plans for the Lyceum Club in Bold Street led to a group of dissidents establishing the Union Newsroom. Between 1852 and 1862 the building was bought by the Corporation who established there the first public library and museum in Liverpool. It is now used as offices.

At the river end of Duke Street there is an interesting group of Victorian offices, each one utilising the curved segment of a corner site. **Nos. 1 and 3 Duke Street** is a five storey stuccoed office/warehouse with ground floor shop windows and, above, giant three storey high Tuscan pilasters. The adjoining warehouses, **Nos. 24-30 Hanover Street,** are simpler in treatment with a long round-headed goods entrance and pulley.

On the opposite corner stands **Church House** dating from the 1870s. This richly ornamented building is constructed of terracotta bricks with bands of coloured brick and has Romanesque style round-headed windows.

Opposite is **No. 12 Hanover Street** (Brimley's Ltd.) a splendid red brick Victorian office block. The angled pilasters terminate above the balustraded roof as tall moulded chimneys. An attractive feature of the building is the iron balcony at first floor level. Attached to this building in Argyle Street is an 1863 warehouse.

Also in **Argyle Street, Nos. 21, 21a and 23,** are two early nineteenth century brick warehouses. No. 21 is a former dwellinghouse and warehouse with adjoining loading bay.

Returning to Duke Street, diagonally opposite to the former Union Newsroom, is the **Monroe Public House.** Built originally as a private house in the late eighteenth century it is of three storeys in brick with stone trimmings.

105 Duke Street

1 - 3 Duke Street

66

Nos. 116-126 Duke Street form a late eighteenth century brick terrace with stone dressings and decoration. No. 118 is also notable for being the birthplace in 1793 of Felicia Browne who achieved fame, both as a child and later as Mrs. Hemans, a poetess.

At the top of Duke Street turn right into Nelson Street. On the left on the corner of Great George Street is the former **Congregational Church** built in 1840-1 by Joseph Franklin, the younger Foster's successor as Corporation Surveyor. It is a distinguished late classical stone building with a semi-circular porch of giant order monolithic Corinthian columns screening the stone drum which is continued above the entablature to a domed roof. The drum is lit below the dome by circular windows set into a continuous guilloch frieze. The giant order is continued in the facades to the main body of the church with Corinthian pilasters above a rusticated plinth. The arched windows between express the line of the oval gallery which formed part of the interior. The presbytery on the far side of the church and linked to it forms part of the composition and continues the architectural treatment of the church itself.

Nelson Street and the area through which it runs was first developed in the first quarter of the nineteenth century and the street names recall the history of the times; battles such as the Nile, Camperdown, Cape St. Vincent and heroes such as Cornwallis, Hardy and Duncan as well as Nelson are all commemorated as too are the statesmem Pitt and Grenville. The naming of Great George Square epitomised national loyalty.

Nelson Street is part of Liverpool's Chinese quarter and many of the Georgian buildings remain.

For example, **Nos. 10-26 Nelson Street,** on the right hand side, is a terrace in the late Georgian tradition with original entrances, fanlights and semi-circular iron balconies.

The Nook Public House opposite is not 'listed' but provides a fine blend of the East and the West.

Nelson Street runs into Great George Square, once one of the finest of Liverpool's Georgian squares. Little survived the war time blitz but its scale and former elegance can be gleaned from the original buildings which have remained, **Nos. 10, 18 to 21 and 28 to 34 Great George Square and 8 and 8a Grenville Street South.** All are architecturally similar being of three storeys and many of the original details are intact.

Cross the Square and continue along Hardy Street at the end of which on the left you will find the **Church of St. Vincent de Paul** and its **presbytery.** The church was built by E. W. Pugin in 1865-7 in Gothic geometric style and is of stone. Note the iron lantern belfry and spire which springs out of the apex of the gable on the St. James Street front. The presbytery behind the church is of brick and stone in Gothic style and is possibly contemporary with the church.

76-78 Seel Street

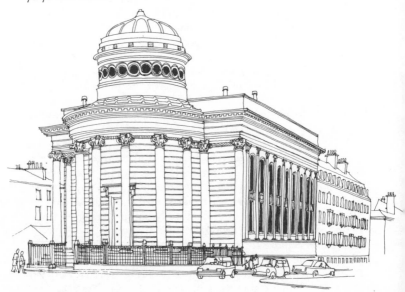

Former Congregational Church, Great George Street

6 *Mount Pleasant and the University Precinct*

Mount Pleasant, as the name implies, was first developed in the latter half of the eighteenth century with elegant Georgian houses in spacious grounds overlooking the bustling town below. The atmosphere of these early pleasure gardens is reflected by the playful **monument** behind the Central Hall, with its eight Doric columns and pagoda dome, even though this is of much later date. This commemorates the Renshaw Street Chapel built in 1811 on the site now occupied by Central Hall.

At this point it is worthwhile making a detour along Benson Street where **Nos. 57B and 59-67 Renshaw Street and Nos. 4-10 Benson Street** are a reminder of the well-mannered street architecture which at one time comprised so much of the City Centre. The Renshaw Street frontage and curving stuccoed corner are early Victorian classical buildings, but still very much in the Georgian tradition. Three storeys high with an attic storey above the cornice, they have small shop fronts below, upper windows in moulded architraves, some with pediments and continuous string courses. Nos. 8 and 10 Benson Street are an unusual design in ashlar sandstone: two pedimented doorways flank three arched windows on the ground floor, whilst above the first floor windows is a blank panel and large carved pediment, surmounted again by a singular parapet. It is said to have been built by the architect or builder of St. George's Hall for his own occupation, but has affinities in its use of stone and Greek Revival detailing with Percy Street (see page 92).

Behind the north side of Leece Street, and below Roscoe Street, is Oldham Street, where **Nos. 15-17** is the **Caledonian Free School,** dated 1812 on a stone plaque. This is a simple Georgian brick building of two storeys, with a pediment over the three centre windows. **No. 19** adjoining is built in the same style, and was probably the school master's house.

Returning to Mount Pleasant, **No. 50** on the south side is the first of the surviving Georgian houses. The classical gate piers, paved forecourt and flight of steps are an imposing approach to the front door, which is surmounted by an unusual broken pediment supported on splayed brackets.

Nos. 52-54 Mount Pleasant, long known as Hunts Hotel, are two and three storey brick houses of the same period, distinguished by a wide columned portico and the later bay windows

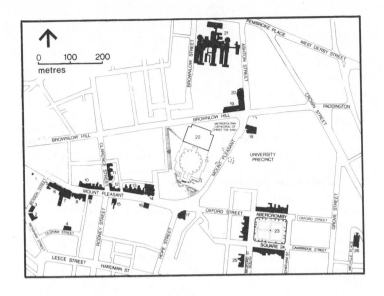

1 Monument
2 57B and 59-67 Renshaw Street
3 4-10 Benson Street
4 15, 17 and 19 Oldham Street
5 50 Mount Pleasant
6 52-54 Mount Pleasant
7 Y.M.C.A. Building
8 62-66 Mount Pleasant
9 68 Mount Pleasant
10 73-95 and 95A Mount Pleasant
11 21A, 21-29 and 33 Clarence Street
12 97-107 Mount Pleasant
13 109-125 Mount Pleasant
14 Wellington Rooms
15 76 and 78 Mount Pleasant
16 96 Mount Pleasant
17 Medical Institution
18 Students' Union
19 Victoria Building
20 Ashton Building
21 Royal Infirmary
22 Metropolitan Cathedral Crypt
23 Abercromby Square
24 Pillar Box Chatham Street
25 78-82 Bedford Street South
26 School for the Deaf

70

which add a pleasant informal air to the regular Georgian facades.

The Y.M.C.A. Building is a complete contrast to its classical neighbours, an exuberant Gothic extravaganza of dark brick and stone, designed in 1875 by the Liverpool architect, H. H. Vale. The great pinnacled tower with its castellated turret and pointed dormers is exactly placed on the curve and slope of Mount Pleasant to dominate the entire length of the street. **Nos. 62-66** continue the Georgian brick street facade, and then on the corner of Roscoe Street is **No. 68,** an elegant symmetrical design with a wide brick arch line traced over the centre of the facade below the pediment.

On the north side of the street **Nos. 73-95 and 95a** is a row of simple three storey terraced houses built around 1800, slightly later than the first houses opposite. More of these are seen around the corner in Clarence Street (**Nos. 21a, 21-29 and 33**) but the next row on the north side of Mount Pleasant, **Nos. 97-107** (particularly Nos. 101-107) appears to be of an older style: note the different window details. A terrace is shown in this location on Charles Eyles' map of 1785.

Nos. 109-125, now mostly converted to hotel uses, is a terrace of larger scale town houses, dating, according to a rainwater head on No. 113, from 1816.

The Wellington Rooms (now the Irish Centre) was designed by Edmund Aikin and built as a subscription assembly room for the Wellington Club in 1815-6. An elegant stone front with a central projecting semi-circular entrance of Corinthian columns which was originally an open colonnade. The blank stone walls at each side are relieved simply by one finely carved panel.

Returning to the south side of Mount Pleasant, **Nos. 76 and 78** are more three storey Georgian terraced houses, now in office use. The remainder of the block, as far as Hope Street, is occupied by the Notre Dame Convent, whose Victorian Gothic buildings of 1857 and later are 'unlisted', but are wrapped around **No. 96** Mount Pleasant, a late Georgian house of five bays.

The Medical Institution of 1836, by C. Rampling, occupies the further curving corner of Hope Street, a fine stone frontage with six large Ionic columns.

At the far end of Mount Pleasant is the University **Students' Union,** 1910-13, by Sir Charles Reilly. A brick and white stone building of three storeys and classical style now occupying a corner site where its three rather different principal elevations can be seen in conjunction, whereas originally the surrounding buildings and the railway cutting separated them.

Facing is the **Victoria Building** of 1887-92 by Alfred Waterhouse, built to house University College before it became

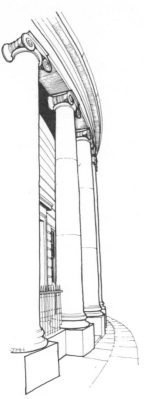

The Medical Institution

Corner of Benson Street
and Renshaw Street

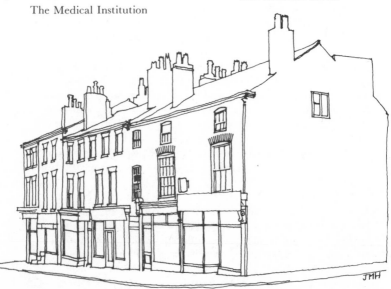

97-107 Mount Pleasant

the University of Liverpool. A romantic Gothic-style building in red brick and terracotta, its corner turret and tall clock tower are elegant features on the skyline, although the view up Brownlow Hill is now marred by the insensitive mass of the modern Mechanical Engineering block. (cf. Prudential Building, Dale Street, p. 37).

Round the corner on Ashton Street is the **Ashton Building,** formerly the Faculty of Arts 1913, by Briggs, Wolstenholme and Thornely (although the design is probably by Frank Simon, architect of the demolished Cotton Exchange). In contrast to the Victoria Building, this is stone and classical, with giant pilasters and pediments to street and courtyard facades.

Further down Ashton Street, and with its main covered entrance on Pembroke Place, is the **Royal Infirmary,** 1887-90, contemporary with the Victoria Building, and also designed by Waterhouse. Gables and gabled dormers, turrets and round arches, and all in common brick and red brick. The interiors are extensively tiled, and in the small chapel the colours are green, grey and blue on the round columns and arches.

Returning to Mount Pleasant, the Metropolitan Cathedral of Christ the King (1960 by Sir Frederick Gibberd) stands on a vast plateau, below which is the **Crypt** of Sir Edwin Lutyens' cathedral of 1932, and the only part to have been built. The scale of these mysterious brick vaults stretching away beneath the earth perhaps indicates the enormous size of Lutyens' conception, which would have had a higher and larger dome than St. Peter's, Rome, or St. Paul's, London.

A little further south in the University precinct is **Abercromby Square,** named after Sir Ralph Abercromby, the general killed at Alexandria in 1801. Although John Foster, Senior, had planned this area in 1800, the square and surrounding streets were not laid out until 1816, and it was a further twenty years before the majority of the houses were built. These are three storey brick terraces with continuous cast-iron balconies at first floor, each side of the square a single composition with a central stone Doric porch. The east side of the square contained the fine Ionic portico of Foster's St. Catherine of 1831, but this was destroyed in 1966 to make way for the University's new Senate House.

Also listed are the **iron railings, gates and piers,** replaced in 1952, which surround the garden in the manner of the London squares, and the central **garden house** with its iron trellis and domed roof.

On the corner of Chatham Street is a **Post Office Pillar Box,** possibly c. 1866, hexagonal in plan with a cornice, a top with curving petal forms, and an acorn finial.

Monument behind
Central Hall

Pillar Box,
Chatham Street

View down Mount Pleasant

Abercromby Square

74

Nos. 78-82 Bedford Street South are three attached Regency villas, two storey stucco houses with wide overhanging eaves and surviving ironwork.

Nos. 14-30 Oxford Street, leading into Abercromby Square from Mount Pleasant, and a good three storey brick Georgian terrace with traceried fanlights and inset Doric doorcases, is not 'listed'.

Further east beyond Abercromby Square is the former **School for the Deaf** in Melville Place, off Oxford Street, built in 1840. Now standing isolated, surrounded by cleared sites, its imposing entrance steps and Ionic porch once dominated a small urban square.

Mount Pleasant

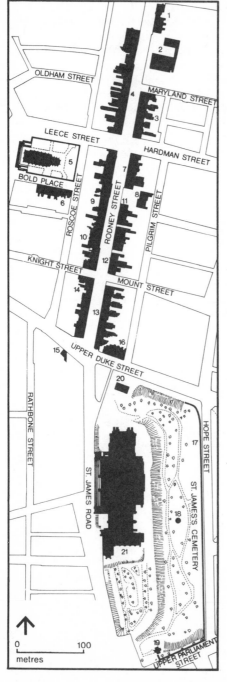

1 1, 3 and 5
  Rodney Street
2 St. Andrew's Church
  of Scotland
3 2 Maryland Street
  and 7-23 Rodney
  Street
4 4-16, 16A and 18-32
  Rodney Street
5 St. Luke's Church
6 6-15 Bold Place
7 25 and 27-31
  Rodney Street
8 33 and 33A
  Rodney Street
9 34 Rodney Street
10 36A, 38, 40, 50,
   52 and 62
   Rodney Street
11 35 Rodney Street
12 47 and 49
   Rodney Street
13 51-75 Rodney Street
14 74-78 Rodney Street
15 24 Upper Duke
   Street
16 Mornington Terrace
   Upper Duke Street
17 St. James Cemetery
18 Huskisson Memorial
19 Lodge to Cemetery
20 Mortuary Chapel
21 Anglican Cathedral

7 Rodney Street and Anglican Cathedral

Rodney Street was first projected shortly after Lord Rodney's 1782 naval victory over the Comte de Grasse, and was one of the earliest and largest of the new residential areas springing up on the outskirts of the City at that time. After a slow start, building was rapid in the last years of the eighteenth century as the wealthy merchants moved away from the increasing urban pressures on their houses in Hanover Street and Duke Street. By 1807 it appears that most of the street had been developed, and its line was extended northwards along Clarence Street, Russell Street and Seymour Street towards St. Anne Street (see page 99).

Nos. 1, 3 and 5 Rodney Street are three attached late Georgian houses which set the pattern for the street: red brick, three storeys high with stone string course and cornice, two sash windows on the ground floor and three on the upper floors, iron balconies to the first floor windows, and ornament concentrated on the doorway. Within this pattern it is interesting to see the rich variations of proportion and detail which are revealed.

St. Andrew's Church of Scotland was built in 1823-4 to the design of John Foster, Junior. The body of the church is a simple two storey design with arched windows and stuccoed walls, but the stone facade is an imposing composition of massive Ionic entrance columns flanked by corner towers, each crowned with smaller Corinthian columns and domes.

In the churchyard to the north is the smaller **Sunday School** of 1872, its round-arched windows and classical details echoing the style of the church.

The Georgian terrace pattern is resumed with **No. 2 Maryland Street,** its fluted Tuscan columns and traceried fanlight facing the churchyard, and then a continuous row of houses from **Nos. 7-23 Rodney Street.** No. 7 has a round-headed doorway with a fanlight over inset fluted Doric columns, whilst Nos. 9 and 11, 13 and 15, 17 and 19 have coupled doorways with Doric columns surmounted by pediments. No. 9 was the birthplace of Arthur Clough, poet (born 1819) and Anne Clough (born 1820), first principal of Newnham College, Cambridge. No. 23 forms the corner with Hardman Street, a slightly later Victorian building, but of the same proportions, with elaborate curved pediments on brackets (some missing) over the ground floor openings. Built as an assembly room, the fine hall on the first floor still retains much of its original decoration.

On the west side of the street opposite St. Andrews, the three storey brick terrace pattern recurs in **Nos. 4-16 and 16A and 18-32,** but here with iron railings around basement areas. Some houses retain original glazing bars, and some have iron balconies on the first floor. Nos. 16 and 16A have modern shop fronts on the ground floor, and No. 32 on the corner of Leece Street has an early twentieth century stone bank facade.

Just below Rodney Street on Leece Street, is **St. Luke's Church.** Designed as early as 1802 by John Foster, Senior, it was built by his son, John Foster, Junior, with some alterations, from 1811-31. The style is perpendicular Gothic, with large traceried windows, now seen to advantage silhouetted against the empty bombed-out nave, stepped buttresses and a multitude of decorated pinnacles. The west tower, approached by imposing flights of steps on three sides, is most dramatically seen in the view up Bold Street.

The formal gardens round the church are enclosed in heavy **cast iron railings** with cusped ornaments, and **stone octagonal gate piers.**

To the south of the church is Bold Place, **Nos. 6-15,** a row of narrow fronted three storey brick houses, early nineteenth century, particularly notable for paired doorways, the adjoining round fanlights under a common segmental brick arch. Nos. 9, 11 and 12 have semi-circular iron balconies to the first floor.

Returning to Rodney Street, the corner house on the east side, **No. 25,** is of later nineteenth century date, but then **Nos. 27-31** return to the Georgian style, No. 29 with a heavy stone Doric portico projecting, No. 31 with a later Ionic portico added.

Nos. 33 and 33A Rodney Street are set back behind a garden whose trees and foliage, like St. Andrew's churchyard, provide a pleasant break in the continuous line of buildings. No. 33 is three storey brick Georgian again, with a modern doorway, but No. 33A is a much later (early twentieth century) addition.

Across the street, **No. 34,** the corner house, has a pedimented gable on to Leece Street and fine iron lampholders on the railings at each side of the entrance.

Continuing along the western side of the street, **No. 36A** has a large projecting Ionic portico, and **Nos. 38 and 40** have pedimented doorways with ornamented Ionic capitals and frieze. The three storey terrace form continues, but with a variety of entrance forms and iron balcony designs and a wall-mounted iron lamp bracket between **Nos. 50 and 52,** until we reach **No. 62.** Originally standing detached, it is a large five-bay house (i.e. five windows wide) with the centre three bays projecting slightly and crowned by a pediment. Built in 1796, it was the birthplace in

St. Andrew's Church of Scotland

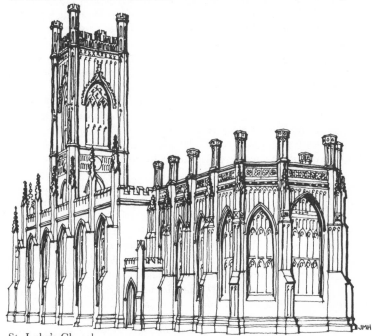

St. Luke's Church

79

1808 of William Ewart Gladstone.

Returning to the east side of the street, **No. 35,** is also a large five bay house, with a pediment over its whole width and an ornate doorway and first floor centre window.

It is reputedly the first house to be built on Rodney Street, and was occupied by Pudsey Dawson, Mayor of Liverpool in 1799.

Further on, two basically identical houses, **Nos. 47 and 49,** demonstrate again the variety of Georgian detail, in the way that rusticated quoins, brackets below the cills, and rich ornamentation on the Tuscan entrance, have been applied to No. 47 and not to No. 49.

Beyond Mount Street, **Nos. 51-75 Rodney Street** were built as one architectural composition, with a five bay pediment over No. 63 in the centre and a continuous iron balcony.

On the west side again, the row of houses, **Nos. 74-78,** contains some particularly fine doorways, with delicate fanlights and columns set inside a brick arch.

Beyond the southern end of Rodney Street, and a slightly smaller version of these houses, is **No. 24 Upper Duke Street,** one of the few surviving Georgian remnants of a large area now cleared for new housing.

Mornington Terrace, Nos. 29-37 Upper Duke Street, slightly later in date than Rodney Street, is also brick, three storeys and basement, with the centre house breaking forward and surmounted by a pediment. The entrances have pilastered doorcases and fanlights set inside semi-circular arches.

Facing Mornington Terrace, and overshadowed by the Anglican Cathedral, is the great chasm of **St. James' Cemetery.** Originally a quarry from which the stone for many public buildings of the eighteenth century had been cut, the cemetery was created in 1825-9 by John Foster, exploiting to the full the picturesque features of the site. The east side below Hope Street presents a Piranesian spectacle of wide intersecting ramps running up battered and rusticated walls, monuments and arched vaults.

In the centre of the cemetery lies the **Huskisson Memorial,** 1836, also by John Foster, a domed rotunda of Corinthian columns. John Gibson's statue of Huskisson, the Liberal politician and M.P. for Liverpool who had been killed at the opening ceremony of the Liverpool to Manchester railway in 1830, has now been removed from the memorial to the Walker Art Gallery.

At the main entrance to the Cemetery, the imposing rusticated archway at the south-west corner, is the **Lodge,** again by Foster, a small stone house with simple classical detailing. At the northwest corner lies the **Mortuary Chapel** of 1829 designed by the same architect, dramatically sited on a cliff overlooking the

35 Rodney Street   62 Rodney Street

80 Rodney Street   Huskisson Memorial

81

original tunnelled entrance to the old quarry. Built in the form of a miniature Greek temple, with Doric porticos at either end, the fine interior now contains a number of neo-classical monuments from the cemetery, including some by John Gibson.

Towering above the cemetery, and visible from many distant parts of Liverpool and the Wirral, is the **Anglican Cathedral.** It is built on St. James' Mount, or Walk, originally named Mount Sion when this promenade and park was laid out by the Corporation as relief work in the severe winter of 1767.

In 1901 an architectural competition was held for the design of a new cathedral, and the young Giles Gilbert Scott was chosen, to be assisted at first by G. F. Bodley. Work started in 1904 and the Lady Chapel was completed 1906-10, although by this time Scott had radically revised his scheme, adopting the one massive central tower (1924-42) instead of two smaller towers. The cathedral is sometimes cited as the last anomalous example of the outdated Gothic revival, but is nevertheless a unique and personal creation, a fusion of Gothic and Art Nouveau, and a truly monumental building.

Anglican Cathedral

Having left the Anglican Cathedral, we continue up the hill away from the City centre, and return to the quieter virtues of the Georgian street.

In 1800 the Corporation Surveyor, John Foster, Senior, prepared a grid iron street plan for the development of a large area once of peat bog known as Mosslake Fields, to the east of the Georgian houses then springing up along Mount Pleasant and Rodney Street. Building was slow, however; it was twenty years before the northern area was developed around Abercromby Square, and not until after 1835 did the plans for Canning Street and Falkner Square become reality.

Turning into Hope Street from Upper Duke Street, **Nos. 33-47 Hope Street** is a three-storey brick terrace of c. 1830, some with fluted Doric columns to the doorways inside semi-circular arched openings, and some with a plainer pedimented doorway, rather early eighteenth century in style.

Opposite is the **College of Art,** the Hope Street frontage of 1910 by Willink and Thicknesse with Doric porch flanked by two-storey curved bows, the earlier Mount Street corner 1882 by Thomas Cook.

Adjoining in Mount Street is the **Liverpool Institute,** originally the Mechanics' Institute, 1835-7, by A. H. Holme. Built in ashlar sandstone, like the Art College, it has an imposing portico of giant Ionic columns looming over the small houses opposite.

Nos. 3 and 5 Mount Street retain something of the scale of the Rodney Street houses round the corner, but **Nos. 9-25** are much smaller, with only one sash window on each floor.

No. 35 Mount Street is larger again, and its elaborate doorway contained in a brick arch is worth closer examination and comparison with similar designs in Rodney Street.

Nos. 60-66 Hope Street, between Mount Street and Rice Street, is another row of varied Georgian facades, mostly three-storey, but No. 62 two-storey, with a large two-storeyed bow.

Nos. 2-22 and 11-17 Hope Place are two more terraces of three-storey Georgian style brick houses, set behind gardens.

Further along Hope Street is the Police Headquarters, with a long, symmetrical stone front to Hardman Street. Two-storeyed, the facade is articulated by classical detailing and projecting

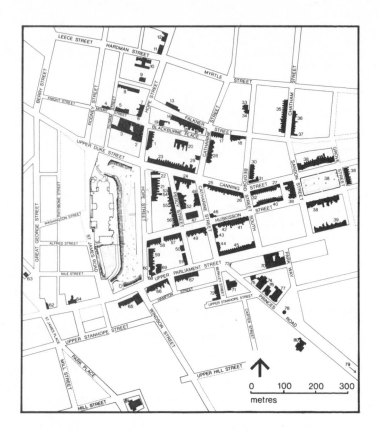

84

pavilions, and a large centre bay with unusual curved corners. Set behind the facade over a crossing of rear wings of the building, and not easily visible from the street, is a stone and stucco dome with a raised lantern.

The building was originally the **School for the Blind,** designed by A. H. Holme in 1850. The 1931 extension to the School on the corner of Hardman Street and Hope Street occupies the site of the Chapel, originally designed by John Foster, Junior, in 1818, in London Road, and removed from there as Lime Street Station expanded.

On the opposite corner of Hardman Street is the **Philharmonic Hotel,** a magnificent Art Nouveau confection of stepped gables, turrets, balconies and oriels designed in 1898-1900 by Walter Thomas. The rich gin palace interior, even extending to the gentlemen's toilets, reveals the collaboration of many artists and craftsmen from the University's then School of Architecture and Applied Art, notably Blomfield Bare's work on the copper panels and the iron and copper entrance gates.

Beyond the 'Phil' are **Nos. 28 and 30 Hope Street,** two-storey Georgian brick houses; No. 28 particularly attractive with its projecting 3-bay centre below a pediment and elaborately

---

43 47-57 Catharine Street
44 59-67 Catharine Street
45 79-109 Upper Parliament Street and 180 Bedford Street South
46 3 Huskisson Street
47 Church of St. Bride
48 44-52 Catharine Street
49 30-42 Huskisson Street and 54 Catharine Street and 19 Percy Street
50 34-38 Percy Street
51 40-50 Percy Street
52 13-17 Percy Street
53 2 and 4 Percy Street
54 6 Percy Street
55 8-18 Percy Street
56 20-32 Percy Street and 1 Huskisson Street
57 14-28 Huskisson Street

58 2-12 Huskisson Street and 51 Hope Street
59 53-65 Hope Street
60 67-71 Hope Street
61 St. Patrick's Roman Catholic Chapel
62 1 Upper Parliament Street
63 3 and 4 Great George Place
64 15A and 17 Upper Parliament Street
65 24-34 and 36 Upper Parliament Street and Toxteth Public Library
66 40-50 Upper Parliament Street
67 58-74 Upper Parliament Street
68 33 Upper Parliament Street
69 Third Church of Christ Scientist
70 102 Upper Parliament Street

71 Greek Orthodox Church
72 2-12 Berkley Street, 68 Hampton Street and 123 Upper Stanhope Street
73 Florence Nightingale Monument
74 Church of St. Margaret
75 St. Margaret's Vicarage
76 5 Princes Road
77 Jewish Synagogue
78 Huskisson Statue
79 Drinking Fountain
80 Welsh Presbyterian Church

85

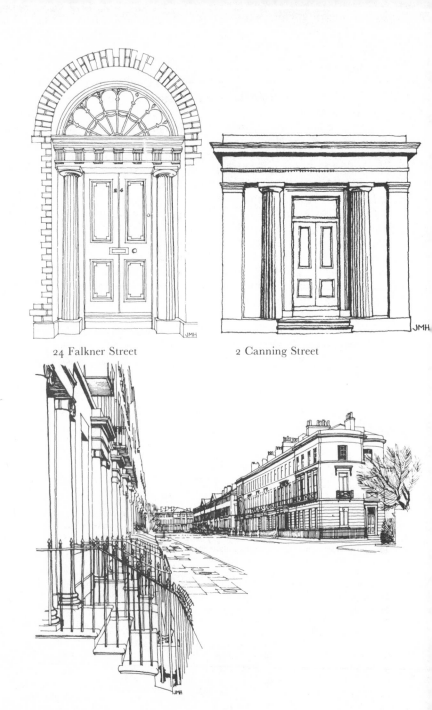

24 Falkner Street

2 Canning Street

1-43, 18-50, 2-16 Canning Street

86

decorated central doorway (now unfortunately converted to a window).

Returning along Hope Street towards the Anglican Cathedral, we pass Falkner Street on the left, originally Crabtree Lane but renamed after the merchant family who had leased a large tract of the Mosslake Fields land from the Corporation for development. **Nos. 19-33 Falkner Street** are relatively small three-storey houses over a basement, with simple pilastered entrances and two windows to each floor.

Nos. 6-14 opposite are similar, but then the scale increases and **Nos. 16-30** are much grander houses with three sash windows, some surviving iron balconies and fine semi-circular fanlights and inset Doric columns to the doorways. The terrace continues with **Nos. 32-38,** dropping down to two-storeys in height.

Beyond Catharine Street are two similar terraces, **Nos. 42-50** and the adjoining **1 Catharine Street,** and **Nos. 54-66 Falkner Street,** all brick, three-storeys over a basement, with fluted Doric entrance columns and semi-circular fanlights, iron railings, and either two or three sash windows to each floor. No. 66 has a round-arched stair window over the doorway.

Returning to Hope Street, the Liverpool Institute High School for Girls is a large Italianate building dating from 1874, but the core of the school is **Blackburne House,** built in 1785-90 as a detached mansion in the countryside by John Blackburne, who was mayor of Liverpool in 1788. The surviving portion of this Georgian house has a curved bow at the rear and an elegant portico of four Ionic columns over a double entrance stairway on to Blackburne Place.

Blackburne Terrace, a single composition of six three-storey brick houses, dates from 1826, and is set back in a private carriageway behind trees. The four centre houses have projecting stone Doric porches, whilst the outer two entrances have plain pilasters with foliated capitals.

We have now returned to the corner of Hope Street above St. James Cemetery, and facing the cathedral are **Nos. 2-10 Gambier Terrace,** built in 1832-7, probably to the design of John Foster, Junior. It is a monumental composition, with two-storey Ionic columns to the projecting north wing, a long ground floor arcade of Doric columns, and then simpler pilasters to the south wing. The latter was no doubt intended to form the centre section of a much longer terrace, but building stopped during the slump of 1837, the demand for large city houses declined as the affluent took the railway to new suburbs, and the design was never completed. The return end of the block, **No. 2 Canning Street,** has an enclosed Greek Doric porch.

Nos. 1-43 Canning Street is a brick Georgian style terrace begun in 1835 and illustrating in its slight variations and breaks in cornice line, the common development pattern of a number of builders each erecting a few houses to a standard design set by the Corporation surveyor. The houses are large, three storeys over a basement and three bays wide, with iron railings, a variety of iron balconies, and Ionic columns framing panelled doors and rectangular fanlights. **Nos. 4-16 Canning Street** is a similar design, but here the entire facade is in stone, rusticated on the ground floor, the Ionic porches project, and the first floor windows over each porch have architraves, cornice and console brackets.

The long terrace, **Nos. 18-50 Canning Street, and Nos. 156-8 Bedford Street South,** is also similar, but returns to brick. The Ionic porches project again, and there are two forward breaks in the row, with large pediments over paired houses.

Nos. 52-76 Canning Street carries the same brick terrace theme on towards Falkner Square, here with dentilled cornices to the Ionic porticos.

Nos. 3-23 and Nos. 38 and 40 Catharine Street are slightly smaller in scale, although each house is still three bays wide, and the entrances have plainer Tuscan pilasters.

Nos. 151-163 Bedford Street South are almost identical to these Catharine Street houses. Adjoining is the curved end of **Nos. 57-61 Canning Street.** On the opposite corner of Canning Street is **No. 165 Bedford Street South,** forming the end of its terrace and symmetrically designed with a projecting Ionic portico and an ornamented window over.

Nos. 120 and 122 Bedford Street South, almost swallowed by later hospital buildings, are two stuccoed mid-nineteenth century houses set back behind small gardens. With their Ionic porticos, iron balconies and moulded architraves around the windows, they make an interesting contrast with the slightly earlier brick houses next door, **Nos. 124 and 126 Bedford Street South.**

In Chatham Street, another of the cross streets joining Falkner Square to Abercromby Square, **Nos. 142-172** is a continuous terrace of three-storey brick houses over a basement, with semi-circular entrance fanlights and inset Doric columns.

On the other side of the cobbled street, **Nos. 161-171** are wide-fronted two-storey houses with a central doorway, again with semi-circular brick heads, decorative fanlights and inset Doric columns. Two tall iron lampholders survive on the front railings. No. 171 is dated 1816, which makes this row rather earlier than much of the surrounding development. **No. 173 Chatham Street** is similar to its neighbours, but three-storeys high.

Falkner Square is a part of the spacious plan for the new

57 Canning Street

8 Percy Street

3-17 Percy Street

residential quarter conceived by Foster as early as 1800, but the garden, with its **iron gatepiers and railings,** was not planted until 1835, and even that was before any building was begun by the Falkner family. The square has a pleasant informal character lent by the painted stucco, bay windows, the rows of plane trees in the wide pavements, and the relatively low, two-storey buildings (all of which are 'listed') although Picton, the Liverpool historian, thought that this 'imparts to the general aspect a somewhat undignified effect'. Each side of the square is, or originally was, of symmetrical design, although this has been obscured by later attic additions and varied colour schemes. The east side on to Grove Street, **Nos. 17 to 24,** is the most formal, with three storeys, a continuous iron balcony across the first floor, and the centre emphasised by a large top pediment.

Falkner Terrace, Nos. 151-179 Upper Parliament Street, was another venture by the same developer. Started in 1831, it pre-dates the square, and stood for so long surrounded by empty sites that it was known as 'Falkner's Folly'. It is a long stuccoed terrace of three storeys and a basement, with Tuscan pilastered doorways, the ground floor walls horizontally grouted to simulate masonry, and pilasters between the first floor windows of the projecting end and centre houses.

From Falkner Square we will now return along Huskisson Street towards the Anglican Cathedral.

Nos. 25-51 Huskisson Street is a three-storey brick terrace of the 1830s, symmetrically designed with projecting ends, each house with an Ionic portico and most with iron balconies.

Nos. 58-70 Huskisson Street are later houses, c.1860, introducing the bay windows which were to be such a favourite feature of Victorian domestic design, but which are quite acceptable here when built in the same materials, brick and stone, as the surrounding Georgian houses.

Nos. 44-56 Huskisson Street return to the standard plain facades of the 1830s, here with Ionic porticos. This terrace continues around the corner into **Nos. 47-57 Catharine Street,** where the porticos have fluted Ionic columns. Beyond Egerton Street with its tiny two-storey cottages, **Nos. 59-67 Catharine Street,** is a very similar terrace, but some of the porticos have fluted Greek Doric columns. Continuing around the next corner, the design is repeated endlessly down the long imposing row of **Nos. 79-109 Upper Parliament Street and 180 Bedford Street South. No. 3** Huskisson Street faces No. 44, on the corner of Catharine Street. Another three-storey brick house of the 1830s, it now supports (or is it supported by?) a dense growth of ivy, but is distinguished architecturally by an iron lampstandard on a stone pier beside the entrance, which is a later stone porch

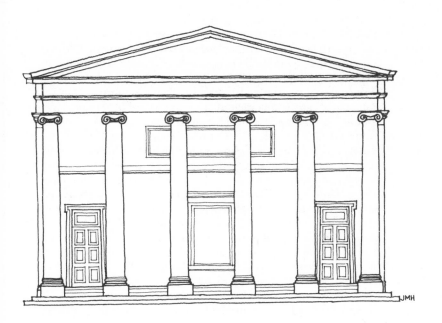

Church of St. Bride

67, 69, 71 Hope Street

with round-arched window and a segmental-headed doorway.

Across the road is the **Church of St. Bride,** designed in 1830 by Samuel Rowland in the form of a classical temple. The sides and chancel are simply detailed in stucco, with six high windows capped by cornices on console brackets, but the entrance front to Percy Street has a monumental portico of six unfluted Ionic stone columns and a pediment. The large gatepiers to the railings around the churchyard are constructed of cast iron sections.

Beyond the churchyard, **Nos. 44-52 Catharine Street** is a row of large three-storey stuccoed houses. The projecting porticos have fluted Ionic columns and a decoration of honeysuckle on the frieze. **Nos. 30-42 Huskisson Street (and 54 Catharine Street and 19 Percy Street)** is another stuccoed terrace, designed as one symmetrical composition overlooking the churchyard, with continuous iron balconies on the first floor, and a greater elaboration of classical detail on the centre and end houses, particularly the gable on to Catharine Street.

In Percy Street, **Nos. 34-38** are in brick again, three storeys over a basement, with fluted Ionic columns to the doorcases and traceried fanlights in an enriched round arch. **Nos. 40-50 Percy Street** are similar, but with simpler Tuscan pilastered entrances. Turning towards Canning Street, the remaining two terraces are quite unique in Liverpool, and in the words of C. H. Reilly, the first Professor of Architecture at the University, 'strongly to be recommended'. They are faced entirely in ashlar sandstone, Greek revival in detail, and have been ascribed, on somewhat flimsy evidence, to John Foster, Junior.

The shorter terrace, **Nos. 3-17 Percy Street,** is a strong composition, small in scale yet palatial, with projecting centre block and wings, and a free-standing colonnade of Greek Doric columns in front of the recessed parts. Across the street, **Nos. 2 and 4,** dated 1835, are Gothic in style, with tall gables, pinnacles, and carved heads to the side street. **No. 6** is classical again, with a rusticated ground floor, and Doric pilasters to the first floor. **Nos. 8-18** have two-storey high Corinthian pilasters below, and coupled pilasters, pediments and Greek acroteria on the third floor. The projecting entrance porches have heavy square pillars.

Nos. 20-32 Percy Street and 1 Huskisson Street is a plainer terrace with similar Greek details and an incised decoration around the doors.

Percy Street still retains its original **Gas Lamps** (now converted to electricity) in iron, with slender fluted stems, cross arms and lantern tops.

Nos. 14-28 Huskisson Street is all stuccoed, but not of one design: Nos. 26 and 28 are larger buildings with iron balconies and moulded architraves to the first floor windows, the centre one of each with a pediment.

Nos. 2-12 Huskisson Street, known as Cathedral Mansions, is a severe stuccoed terrace with horizontal grouting to the ground floor and a continuous first floor balcony. The doorways have rectangular fanlights, moulded architraves and cornices on curved brackets. **No. 51 Hope Street** forms the return end to the terrace, overlooking St. James' Cemetery and the Cathedral.

Nos. 53-65 Hope Street are three-storey and basement terraced houses, c.1830, mainly in brick, although some are stuccoed.

Nos. 67-71 Hope Street is a stucco Regency villa style group, the centre (which once had a fine cast iron verandah) recessed between gabled wings with broad flat eaves rather like the University's houses in Bedford Street South.

Upper Parliament Street, which we have now reached, took its name from the 1775 Act of Parliament which the landowner, the Earl of Sefton, obtained in order to grant building leases and erect a new town of Harrington in the Mill Street area. Until 1807 the road, climbing the steep hill from the river, ended at St. James' Cemetery, at that time still a quarry, but it was then extended eastwards to form the boundary between the new housing on the Mosslake Fields and Toxteth Park to the south.

St. James' Church, which strangely is not 'listed', was the first public building erected in Lord Sefton's development, built in 1774-5 by Cuthbert Bisbrowne. A very simple brick building with a square tower and round-arched side windows, the interior is of interest for the early structural use of cast iron columns supporting the gallery.

A little further south on Park Place is **St. Patrick's Roman Catholic Chapel,** 1821-7 by John Slater, another rather severe brick building, with projecting central pediment to the street flanked by two stone porticos of four Greek Doric columns. The statue of the saint originally adorned the St. Patrick Insurance Company in Dublin.

Returning to Upper Parliament Street, **No. 1** is a fine example of a Georgian town house, equal to anything in Rodney Street. Three storeys, built in brick with stone dressings, it has a central pediment over a slight forward break in the facade, architraves and cornices to the central windows on first and second floors, and a Doric entrance with delicately carved stonework and semi-circular fanlight.

Nos. 3 and 4 Great George Place, built for the North and South Wales Bank and now occupied by the Midland Bank (and still retaining some Victorian woodwork in the banking hall), is a complete contrast: stone Victorian Gothic with high gables and chimneys, and busy pointed arches and foliated capitals.

3 and 4 Great George Place

94

Ascending Upper Parliament Street, **Nos. 15A and 17** are early nineteenth century brick houses anticipating a much later Victorian pattern of two-storey semi-detached villas with bay windows. No. 17 is derelict but still retains its sash windows, fanlight and pedimented doorway.

Across the road, **Nos. 24-34 Upper Parliament Street,** is a three-storey late Georgian terrace set back behind small gardens. **No. 36** adjoining is a large double-fronted house of the same height, stuccoed, with an imposing entrance at one time approached by a double circular stone stairway with decorative iron railings. It is now a day nursery.

On the corner of Windsor Street is **Toxteth Public Library,** built in 1902 by Thomas Shelmerdine, who was Corporation Surveyor from 1871-1914. The design is typical of his work throughout the City in its exuberant Edwardian Baroque. The library presents a symmetrical facade to Windsor Street, the round-arched entrance with bulbous Ionic columns and projecting hood flanked by large Venetian windows in gabled wings, and above is a steep dormered roof and small cupola.

The Georgian street frontage continues with **Nos. 40-50 and 58-74 Upper Parliament Street,** broken only by the gap where Nos. 52-56 used to be. A variety of houses within the same discipline, both two and three storeys, and some built on a much larger scale than the usual terrace. No. 40, for instance, is a detached double-fronted house with a projecting Ionic portico, and was once the town house of the Earl of Derby.

No. 64 has three iron balconies and giant panelled pilasters on the upper two floors. Nos. 70, 72 and 74 are two storeys, with a considerable weight of stone detailing to the brickwork. The centre house of the three has a top pediment and moulded window architraves with cornices.

Opposite No. 40, **No. 33 Upper Parliament Street** forms the return end to Hope Street, a two-storey brick Georgian house set high over a basement, with steps up to the brick-arched doorway and traceried fanlight.

The Third Church of Christ Scientist was designed in 1914 by W. H. Ansell as a Temple of Humanity. Built of brick with a patterning of tiles, the flying buttresses over the aisles give a strong vertical emphasis, but the austerity is softened by the curving gable lines and the inviting entrance garden.

No. 102 Upper Parliament Street, now a racquet club, is a large Regency house in brick and stone, two storeys and basement, with a second floor behind a mansard roof. The Venetian central doorway has a carved coved cornice; the windows are alternately triple and single sashes in stone architraves with cornices and Greek anthemion motifs.

Princes Road was laid out as early as 1846 as a monumental boulevard approach to Princes Park, but most of the development did not take place until the 1870s and later. The two-thirds of a mile length of the avenue was, until recently, particularly remarkable for its inordinate number of ecclesiastical edifices.

The Greek Orthodox Church is a large Byzantine style building of 1865-70, by Henry Sumners. Red brick with stone dressings, it has a round-arched entrance on Berkeley Street and arched windows with roundel-patterned glazing bars. Most distinctive, though, are the domes raised on drums, three over the entrance and one in the centre of the eastern arm.

Nos. 2-12 Berkeley Street, No. 68 Hampton Street and No. 123 Upper Stanhope Street is a stuccoed Georgian terrace facing the church. It is of three storeys, now seriously decayed or marred by later alterations, but still retains some iron balconies and traceried fanlights over Doric doorcases.

The Florence Nightingale Monument is set into the boundary wall of the William Rathbone Staff College (the entrance decoration of which is also worth looking at) on the corner of Upper Parliament Street and Princes Road. It was designed by Willink and Thicknesse and executed in granite by C. J. Allen, who also worked on the Philharmonic Hotel. The central relief carving of the 'Lady with the Lamp' succouring two wounded soldiers is set in a temple facade frame and flanked by wall seats.

The Church of St. Margaret, 1868-9, by G. E. Street, was paid for by the stockbroker, Robert Horsfall, whose family built several churches in Liverpool. Externally it is a severe, simple building in common brick and red stone dressings, with a small wooden belfry over the steep slate roof. The interior is richer, particularly the extensive stencilled decorations on walls and roofs, which have recently been repainted.

Adjoining the church is **St. Margaret's Vicarage,** probably also designed by Street, and also brick Gothic, with pointed relieving arches in blue brick over the windows.

No. 5 Princes Road, 'Streatham Towers', is a Victorian Gothic mansion built in brick and stone, sporting a round staircase tower with a tall conical roof.

The Jewish Synagogue, 1874, by W. and G. Audsley, is built in brick, stone and red brick, with a large rose window in the castellated gable flanked by octagonal turrets. A massive front, combining both Moorish and Gothic features. The interior is rich in marble and gold, with a tunnel-vaulted nave.

At the beginning of the boulevard is the **Huskisson Statue,** 1847, by John Gibson, which was made for the Customs House in Canning Place. The figure of the politician is dressed in a toga, holding a scroll, and mounted on a granite base. Further down the boulevard is a **Drinking Fountain,** with a square stone base containing four round basins and niches, and surmounted by an iron lampstandard.

The Welsh Presbyterian Church on the corner of Upper Hill Street, was built in 1865-7 by W. and G. Audsley. The style is early English Gothic, in a rubble stone with white stone dressings. The graceful pinnacled spire rising from the buttressed corner tower is a most impressive feature in the avenue.

3 Princes Road, St. Margaret's Vicarage, Church of St. Margaret, 5 Princes Road, Jewish Synagogue

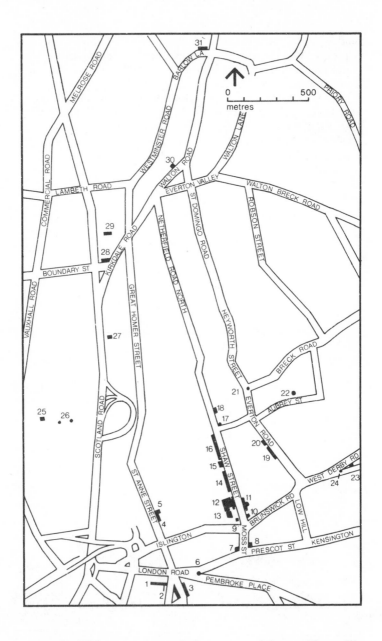

1 9-33 Lord Nelson Street
2 12 St. Vincent Street
3 6-50 and 11-53 Seymour Street
4 24 and 26 St. Anne Street and 1 Springfield Street
5 Owen Owen Warehouse
6 Statue of George III
7 Prince of Wales Public House
8 1 Prescot Street
9 3 Islington Square

9 From the City Centre to Everton

Immediately to the north of Lime Street Station, and climbing the hill westwards away from St. George's Plateau, is a street of small Georgian houses, **Nos. 9-33 Lord Nelson Street,** one of the few surviving remnants of this period in the city centre. Together with **No. 12 St. Vincent Street,** the return end of terrace with a pedimented gable, they are narrow three-storey brick houses with Doric pedimented door cases.

No. 17, in the centre of the terrace, is a three storey stucco building, six bays wide with two arched entrances on the ground floor (and a new carriage entrance in the middle), erected c. 1840 as the Owenite Hall of Science. Lord Nelson Street (or Great Nelson Street as it was then called) appears on the map of 1807, but **Nos. 6-60 and 11-53 Seymour Street** were built a few years later, although the street itself had been laid out as a northward continuation of Rodney Street and Clarence Street through Norton Street to St. Anne Street (see p100) before the end of the eighteenth century. Similar to Lord Nelson Street, the brick houses are narrow, three storeys high, with some iron balconies surviving and a variety of fanlights and inset Doric doorcases. Rainwater heads are dated 1810 and 1828.

St. Anne Street was laid out prior to 1785, even before Rodney Street, as part of an extensive new suburban quarter. It soon became one of the most fashionable streets of the city, and by 1803, according to Picton, the Liverpool historian, presented 'a goodly array of mansions on both sides, inhabited by the *creme de la creme* of the Liverpool society of the day'. Nothing now remains of this early period, but in **Nos. 24 and 26 St. Anne Street and No. 1 Springfield Street,** later Georgian brick houses of three storeys with panelled doors and semi-circular fanlights, one can catch a glimpse of the elegant residences which so soon were overtaken by the developing city. Nos. 5-11 Springfield Street are of the same date, with pedimented doorways, but are not 'listed'.

Adjoining No. 26 St. Anne Street is the **Owen Owen Warehouse,** built c.1859 for the Export Carriage and Wheel Works, with an elegant cast iron facade of slender Corinthian columns and entablatures framing large areas of glass. The potential of iron as cladding as well as structure begins to be realised here: Peter Ellis' Oriel Chambers (page 22) and No. 16 Cook Street (page 43) explore the same theme.

Returning to London Road, in Monument Place, at the junction with Pembroke Place, is the **Statue of George III,** a bronze equestrian figure in Roman dress. It was modelled by Sir R. Westmacott and intended for Great George Square (see page 67) where a pedestal was laid in 1809, but the statue was finally erected in its present location in 1822.

Further on, the **Prince of Wales** public house turns the corner into Moss Street with a curving three storey facade of rich Victorian Gothic detail. All in stone, it has arched entrances and windows with granite columns, classical busts in roundels, and a centre tower with a steep roof.

No. 1 Prescot Street, on the opposite corner, was designed in 1905 by J. Francis Doyle as a Martins Bank, now a Barclays. Edwardian Baroque and white Portland stone, with rich modelling and a profusion of classical ornament. The splayed corner above the entrance has an octagonal tower surmounted by a domed open pavilion.

Islington Square marks the junction between Islington, climbing up the hill away from the city centre, and Shaw Street which Thomas Shaw, the Everton landowner opened up from Moss Street through to Netherfield Road in 1829, when he began to develop the family estate. **No. 3 Islington Square** dates from this period, a substantial three-storey brick house with large top pediment and a Greek Doric porch. The adjoining house, which is not 'listed', was a stuccoed Regency musical academy. **Nos. 6-12 Shaw Street** form the eastern side of the square: a three-storey brick terrace of the late Georgian type which has survived extensively in the Rodney Street and Canning Street area, here with Ionic doorways.

The Liverpool Collegiate School is an imposing red sandstone building in Tudor Gothic style, 1840-3, won in a competition design by Harvey Lonsdale Elmes. The centre has a huge arched entrance projecting the full height of the building,

Seymour Street

Bowden Fountain,
West Derby Road
left-hand balustrade restored

Islington Square

flanked by two-storey perpendicular windows and pinnacled buttresses. The end bays again project, with two-storey oriel windows. At the rear is an octagonal lecture hall.

A little lower down the hill, and facing Salisbury Street, is the **Roman Catholic Church of St. Francis Xavier,** designed 1845-9 by J. J. Scoles, with the Lady Chapel added in 1888 by E. Kirby. The church is stone, in an early English Gothic style with geometrical tracery. The entrance is set below a corner tower and spire, and leads to an aisled interior with slender polished limestone columns. Adjoining are the **College High School** buildings, largely by Henry Clutton, 1856, and later. The main facade on to Salisbury Street, built in red brick and terracotta, with a heavy emphasis on the repetition of buttresses and round arched windows, and dormers set behind an openwork balustrade, may be by Scoles in 1877.

Nos. 37a-71 Shaw Street is a long imposing terrace of late-Georgian brick houses dating from c.1830. Three-storeys high over a basement, and each three windows wide, they have Ionic doorways and first floor ornamental iron balconies.

Nos. 73-79 and Nos. 93-119 Shaw Street are similar, although some of these houses are partly demolished or derelict. All, again with Ionic doorways except No. 75, which has a heavy rusticated square surround surmounted by a shield.

On the Green above Shaw Street at the upper end of Everton Brow, is the **Lock-up** of 1787, a small round sandstone building with a conical roof.

Facing south down Shaw Street from a commanding site between Everton Terrace and Netherfield Road South, is the **'Ann Fowler' Salvation Army Memorial Home for Women,** built in 1867 as a Welsh Independent Chapel. The south entrance front has a row of round-headed arches, flanked by square four-storey towers. The approach has a stone retaining wall to the street, with stone gatepiers and iron gates, railings and lamp brackets.

Another remnant of the gentry's residence in Everton sits on top of the ridge above Shaw Street: **Nos. 47-67 and 71 Everton Road,** a terrace of three-storey brick houses dating from 1824, when they were laid out by the owner of the land, one James Plumpton. Although many are neglected and several have been roughcast, with altered doorways, Nos. 47-55 and Nos. 63-67 each have a central panelled door up steps, with Doric columns and traceried fanlight in a round brick arch. No. 71 is a detached three-bay house with a central projecting Doric porch of two columns.

On the corner of Everton Road and Breck Road is a **Victorian Post Office pillar box** of c.1863: cylindrical with an octagonal

Salvation Army Memorial Home for Women   Netherfield Road

top and a crown.

The Everton Water Works in Aubrey Street, by Thomas Duncan, the Corporation's first water engineer, was begun in 1854 with the underground reservoir, which has high battered stone walls and a parapet formerly crowned by two corner turrets. In 1857 the high level tank was added, a tremendous circular structure supported by concentric rings of plain and rusticated stone arches. The iron tank, 90 feet above the pavement, holds 2,700 gallons.

The Locarno on West Derby Road was formerly the Olympia Theatre designed in 1903 by Frank Matcham. A large corner building, rather bald, of brick and stone giant pilasters, parapet, centre fan window, balconies, round eyes and pedimented windows. The original rich interior of the theatre largely remains, with two galleries, boxes and ceilings dripping with plaster ornamentation.

Nearby, at the corner of Boaler Street is the **Bowden Drinking Fountain** of 1913, a rich Edwardian Baroque memorial of red polished marble.

The following listed buildings, although widely separated, are also to be found in the Everton and Kirkdale areas.

The Roman Catholic Church of Our Lady of Reconciliation in Eldon Street, near to Vauxhall Road, was built in 1859-60 by E. W. Pugin. Stone, in decorated Gothic style, with a large west rose window and bell turret, an eastern apse, and inside arched arcades on round stone columns.

Nearby, the enclosed playground in front of the half-timbered flats in Eldon Grove, dating from 1911, has **two cast iron street lamps,** one at each end. These are set high on a large square plinth, originally with a drinking fountain on two sides, and have a fluted column above with two ornamented arms holding the lamp and crowned by a liver bird.

Also well below the Everton ridge is the **Roman Catholic Church of St. Anthony** on Scotland Road, 1833, by John Broadbent, a pupil of Thomas Rickman, who also built the tower of St. Mary's Church at Walton Village. It has a severe and simple stone exterior with buttresses and lancet windows, and a plain interior relieved by three grouped arches to chancel and chapels.

Further north along Scotland Road are two more Georgian survivals surrounded by recent municipal housing developments. **Nos. 223-247 Boundary Street** date from c. 1830, a three-storey terrace of brick houses each two windows wide, with round-arched doorways. Great Mersey Street has now largely been demolished, but **Nos. 107-117,** three-storeys built high over a basement, with steps to the entrances, are in good condition. The street was formed as early as 1817 and, in the words of Picton, 'long continued a distant rural suburb, built on one side, the houses having a pleasant outlook over fields and gardens towards the town'.

The Church of St. Mary, Walton Road, is a brick building of 1835 with a decorated Gothic front in stone added in 1841-3 by A. H. Holme. The interior, now stripped of furniture, has galleries on three sides and an open timber roof.

Nos. 59-73 Barlow Lane, Kirkdale, is an early Victorian terrace of small brick houses with stone band and cornice, sash windows and a traceried fanlight over the door. A few other buildings of this period remain in the area, particularly on Westminster Road, indicating what must have been a suburban retreat along the lanes out of the City, but soon swallowed by the dense bye-law housing of the later nineteenth century.

St. Anthony's, Scotland Road

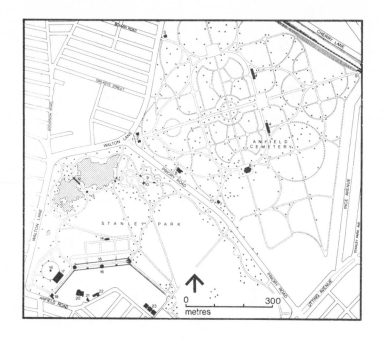

1 Gatepiers, Clock
  Tower and Wall
2 Sandstone Lodges
3 Lodge and Entrance
  Walton Lane
4 Catacombs
5 Cherry Lane
  Entrance
6 South Chapel
7 Priory Road
  Lodge and Entrance
8 'Lansdowne House'
9 Two ornate iron
  bridges
10 Wooden Pavilion
11 Third iron bridge
12 Sandstone bridge
13 Stone shelter
14 Iron Pavilion
15 Terrace
16 Red Sandstone
  Screen Wall
17 Glass Conservatory
18 Small Bandstand
19 Anfield Road Lodge
20 Early nineteenth
  Century House
21 5 Anfield Road
  'Roseneath Cottage'

22 9 and 11
  Anfield Road
23 35-45 Anfield Road

10 Anfield Cemetery / Stanley Park Area

The Victorian pre-occupation with death is illustrated by this splendid Gothic cemetery laid out in 1862 by Lucy and Littler as a complete necropolis, although their work here is more restrained than in other parts of the City.

The main entrance to Anfield Cemetery is very fine comprising **gatepiers, ornate iron gates, a tall clock tower and a rubble wall** all in pink sandstone. The clock tower is decorated with a very finely carved, although now much decayed, coat of arms of Liverpool and Gothic tracery, with, as a macabre touch, a skull carved at the base of the coat of arms.

The entrance is flanked by **sandstone lodges** with stone mullioned and transomed windows and tall gabled roofs in bands of blue and green slate. The left hand lodge has heavy iron strapwork on its front door in a pattern that is repeated at the Catacombs in the Cemetery.

The Lodge and Entrance on Walton Lane are not as ornate as the main entrance but nevertheless the iron gates are very fine and the lodge is in sandstone with a square porch and pointed entrance.

The Catacombs are on either side of the central pathway through the cemetery. They are identical sandstone buildings with Gothic decoration and gargoyles projecting from the eaves. There is a central arch through each building and a door with iron strapwork at each end. There are many fine contemporary tombs in this area.

At the end of the central pathway is **Cherry Lane Entrance.** This entrance is a fine example of Victorian ingenuity for it is separated from the roadway by a railway embankment. A large coach entrance and two smaller pedestrian entrances have been cut through the embankment and are supported by sandstone columns. Both inside and outside of the cemetery grounds a large coat of arms of Liverpool has been carved, and 'look out turrets' have been built in the style of a Gothic fortress. Sadly Gothic fortresses do not keep out vandals even though the splendid iron gates are sealed.

The tall sandstone spire of the **South Chapel** makes this building easy to identify. Protruding from the spire are gargoyles, and the steep roof has bands of green and blue slates. In comparison to the main entrance gates and nearby tombs this building is pleasantly restrained.

The Priory Road Lodge and Entrance is similar to the other entrances but the lodge has a squat octagonal stair turret with a castellated top, and a triangular oriel window on the west side.

'Lansdowne House', at one time the registrar's office, is the final building in this group and is larger than the other lodges. It has stone mullioned and transomed windows with labels over the windows in the upper storeys. There are tall octagonal chimney stacks and the steep roofs have green and blue slate bands.

On the opposite side of the road to the cemetery stands Stanley Park, laid out in 1867-70 by Edward Kemp with the Bandstand, Pavilion, iron bridges, terracing and curtain wall possibly by E. R. Robson the Architect of the Municipal Offices in Dale Street. Turning left at the entrance the path crosses **two ornate iron bridges** between which there stands a **wooden pavilion,** on a stone base, with Gothic traceried windows. The boating lake is reached by passing under a **third iron bridge; a fourth iron bridge** can be seen at the eastern end of the lake. The lake is crossed by a fine six arched **sandstone bridge,** facing which is a six sided **stone shelter** with pointed arches, timber and slate roof and a glazed lantern with an iron crest.

Directly opposite the bridge and across the park is a bowling green and terraced gardens. Facing the terrace is a small **iron pavilion** comprising a solid six sided core with iron panels decorated with floral reliefs. Surrounding the central core is an iron verandah having a glazed and tiled roof.

The terrace opposite to the pavilion is a long low sandstone wall with buttresses. The weight of this wall acts as a foil to the ornamental gardens above it. Directly behind the gardens is a long **red sandstone screen wall** with pointed arches, arcading, buttresses and **two small attached pavilions.** There are **three large, sandstone pavilions** evenly spaced along the wall facing the bowling green, the central one being attached to the wall. The large pavilions are open with pointed arches and timber and slate roofs.

The glass conservatory is later than the other buildings in the park, dated 1899 by Mackenzie and Moncur who were responsible for the ornate Palm House in Sefton Park, it is very light with Gothic decoration in cast iron. Standing in front of the conservatory is a **small bandstand.** This pretty little structure has an octagonal slate roof supported by slender iron columns with delicate tracery.

The final building in this group is the **Lodge** on Anfield Road which is also in the Gothic style with steep gables. A nice feature is the relieving arch over one of the ground floor windows.

Leaving the park and turning into Anfield Road, we find

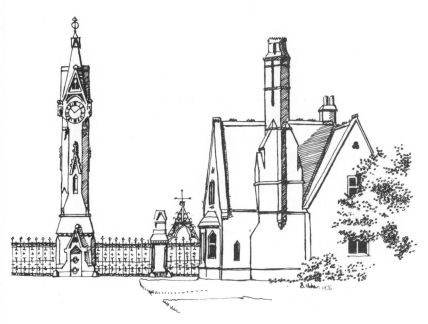

Main Gate, Liverpool Cemetery

Liverpool Cemetery Gate

sandwiched between two later extensions an **early nineteenth century house** now used as a school. This is a stuccoed building and unlike the Gothic buildings in the area is in a bland classical style. It has a square porch with pilasters, windows in moulded cases and a moulded eaves cornice.

No. 5 Anfield Road, 'Roseneath Cottage', a sandstone lodge, adjoins the school. It is a small Gothic house with a square battlemented porch set into an angle between two walls.

Nos. 9 and 11 Anfield Road are semi-detached Victorian Gothic villas with No. 11 spoiled by having a red brick extension fronting on to the roadway. Originally both houses were in scored stucco with Gothic traceried windows and square labels. The chimneys have blind pointed lancet 'windows'.

More in keeping with the Gothic atmosphere of the park and cemetery are the three stuccoed semi-detached Victorian villas, **Nos. 35-45 Anfield Road.** These houses were originally identical but are now in varying states of repair. The doors are set in shared porches each having a fanlight. The single storey bays are battlemented. Windows in the upper storeys have labels and the steeply gabled roofs have moulded barge boards; each house has tall octagonal chimney stacks.

Liverpool Cemetery Lodge

11 St. Domingo Grove Area

Although St. Domingo Grove is physically separated from Anfield Road, they have much in common for they are both areas of mid-Victorian speculative building, with, in the case of St. Domingo Grove, three or four house types. All the houses are built in red sandstone and stuccoed; when new they would have been very desirable residences, and although they are now in varying states of repair, it is still possible to see the attention to detail and craftsmanship that typifies the architecture of this period.

Nos. 55-67 are three-storey semi-detached houses with single-storey bay windows. No. 67 has original moulded door and window cases which are missing from the other houses in the group.

Nos. 49 and 51 differ from their immediate neighbours in that they have three windows along the front and not two. The door to No. 51 is set in a nicely detailed case and the ground floor windows to No. 49 have shallow projecting hoods.

A house type common in St. Domingo Grove is used for **Nos. 41-47, 25-35, 17 and 19, 40 and 42, 32 and 34, 20 and 22, and 16 and 18.** It is semi-detached with three-storeys and pointed gables at the front. The ground floor windows are rectangular with a single mullion; the upper windows have pointed arches. Set back from the front of the houses are large two-storey 'lean-to's' with ogee curved cornices and Tudor arched doorways. Some of the houses have quoins and No. 40 is in particularly good condition with a label over the ground floor window, carved barge boards and a nicely panelled door.

Nos. 28-30, 24-26, and 21-23 are three pairs of semi-detached houses with two-storeys and a central projecting front portion. These houses are simpler than other properties in the Grove with plain moulded door and window cases and a convex frieze over the ground floor windows in the projecting part of the houses.

Nos. 12 and 14 St. Domingo Grove is a finely detailed semi-detached house with a moulded eaves cornice supported on decorated brackets, quoins, moulded window cornice and ground floor windows with cornices and brackets.

Nos. 9-11 and 13-15 are two semi-detached houses with pointed gables and decorated barge boards, quoins and labels over windows. The entrances are at the side with, in the case of

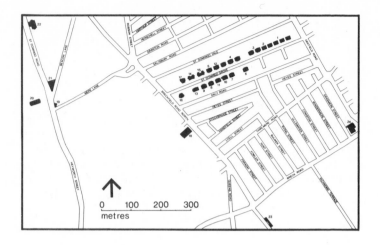

1 55-67 St. Domingo Grove
2 49-51 St. Domingo Grove
3 41-47 St. Domingo Grove
4 25-35 St. Domingo Grove
5 17 and 19 St. Domingo Grove
6 40 and 42 St. Domingo Grove
7 32 and 42 St. Domingo Grove
8 20 and 22 St. Domingo Grove
9 16 and 18 St. Domingo Grove
10 28-30 St. Domingo Grove
11 24-26 St. Domingo Grove
12 21-23 St. Domingo Grove
13 12 and 14 St. Domingo Grove
14 9 and 11 St. Domingo Grove
15 13 and 15 St. Domingo Grove
16 4 and 6 St. Domingo Grove
17 5 and 7 St. Domingo Grove
18 Church of St. Saviour
19 The Mere Public House
20 St. George's Church
21 Everton Library
22 Church of Our Lady Immaculate
23 Cardinal Godfrey High School
24 Richmond Baptist Church

No. 13, decorated barge boards.

The last properties in this group are **Nos. 4 and 6, and 5 and 7;** these semi-detached houses have pointed, moulded gables, quoins and a side entrance on a large outrigger.

Left high and dry amongst desolation in nearby Breckfield Road North is the **Church of St. Saviour,** 1868-9, by Gordon M. Hills. Built of stone, now very black, in the late thirteenth century style, it is impressive in the height of its nave.

It is a short walk from the decayed gentility of St. Domingo Grove to Heyworth Street, and three excellent buildings. The first of these is the **Mere Public House.** This is a truly splendid early twentieth century half-timbered pub with three gables on its main facade and a fourth gable on its canted corner; this is topped by an open turret with a cupola. The upper half-timbered floor is supported by decorated columns and on either side of the centre gable are carved standing figures in Elizabethan costume. The white panels are pargetted and the upper lights of the windows have stained glass panels. The ground floor has mullioned and transomed windows and all surfaces are richly decorated.

Opposite the public house stands **St. George's Church,** built in 1812-4 by Thomas Rickman, who is celebrated for his *avant garde* use of prefabricated cast iron sections in buildings. Externally St. George's Church is a very pleasing example of the early Gothic revival in the perpendicular style. It is castellated and has a square clock tower with perforated castellations all in sandstone. The sandstone, however, is merely a facing material supported by a skeleton of cast iron vaults, columns and ribs, made by the Liverpool iron founder, Thomas Cragg, who also worked with Rickman at St. Michael's Hamlet. St. George's is a meticulous translation of Rickman's Gothic principles into cast iron and is triumphantly light and airy.

On the triangular junction of St. Domingo Road and Beacon Lane stands **Everton Library** dated 1896 by Thomas Shelmerdine, the Corporation Surveyor. As with Shelmerdine's other public libraries, this is a freely designed and exciting building in red brick and stone. The entrance has stone columns, wrought iron gates and very ornate panels bearing the inscription 'Everton Library. Erected AD 1896'. There is a second entrance at the 'point' of the triangular site with similar ornamentation. This entrance is extended upwards to form a squat octagonal tower which is topped by a concave-sided turret.

A little way along St. Domingo Road stands the **Church of Our Lady Immaculate,** the final building is this group. This Church, built in 1856 by E. W. Pugin, was originally intended as the Lady Chapel of a proposed Roman Catholic Cathedral. It is

Mere Public House

St. George's Church

built of stone and has three gables with green slate roofs; the St. Domingo Road frontage consists of a high red sandstone rubble wall and has a steeply gabled entrance with a pointed arched doorway. Although the intended Cathedral was not built the surrounding jumble of municipal flats gives this church a mediaeval atmosphere of being part of a community.

In Breckfield Road South is the **Cardinal Godfrey High School,** an early nineteenth century scored stucco building. In the centre it has a Greek Doric portico of two columns, dentilled friezes and cornice.

The Richmond Baptist Church in Breck Road was designed by Sir James Picton and built in 1864-5. It is an imposing but unfriendly building, with much dogtooth ornament. The interior has galleries on four sides supported on fluted iron columns with composite capitals.

Everton Library

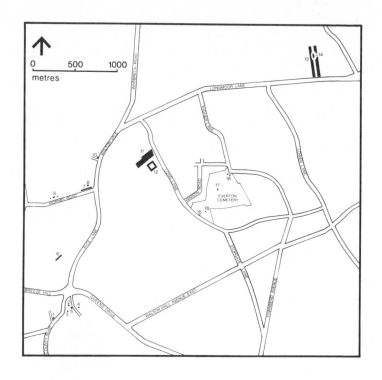

1 Glebe Hotel
  195 County Road
2 Church of St. Mary
3 Old School House
4 Old Rectory
5 Victorian Mortuary
6 Walton Hospital
  Rice Lane
7 2-54 Hornby Road
8 1 and 2
  Hornby Place
9 Walton Gaol
  Gate House and
  Italianate Villas
10 Barclays Bank
  Rice Lane
11 Hartley's Jam
  Factory
12 Hartley's Village
13 Cottage Homes
  Longmoor Lane
14 Dining Hall
15 Sandstone Lodge
16 Lodges on
  Higher Lane

17 North Chapel
18 South Chapel

Glebe Hotel, 195 County Road. Situated on a busy main road
the Glebe Hotel is one of those strange Victorian buildings
which might be happier in a Gothic cemetery. It occupies a
corner site and is constructed of roughly cut yellow sandstone
blocks with ashlar bands and quoins. The main entrance is
flanked by Norman pillars supporting a round arch.

The most interesting features of the building are the details of
the three main gables which have rose windows, and the
treatment of the chamfered corner which has a two-storey turret
and a fish scale spire. It is the painstaking attention to Gothic
detail particularly in the ornamental carved bands around the
turret and the carved friezes between the storeys, which add to
the character of this building.

County Road/Walton Village. The Church of St. Mary,
together with the Old School House and the Old Rectory, form
a very pleasant village group in a densely populated area of the
City. Surrounding the church and old school house is a
Victorian **red sandstone ashlar wall** containing **three
entrances** and a **marble drinking fountain** dated 1861.
Each entrance is flanked by two tall stone gatepiers with carved
Gothic details; one gateway has a large octagonal iron lamp
supported by an iron traceried arch.

The Old School, dating from the seventeenth century, stands
just inside the southern gateway to the churchyard and is now
used for community purposes. It is built of red and cream
sandstone rubble with ashlar quoins and mullioned windows.
There is a continuous stringcourse over the ground floor
windows, the upper floor windows having labels. The building
has twin gables, one of which is weathered sandstone ashlar as is
the rear of the building, perhaps indicating different dates of
construction.

Set into the eastern side of the churchyard wall is a small
Victorian **mortuary** constructed of roughly cut large rusticated
blocks of sandstone and having a very roughly formed triangular
pediment.

Adjoining is a **hearse house** which is gabled and has a
pointed arch; this portion is castellated and is constructed of
ashlar blocks. A strange and somewhat disturbing building.

Standing in the churchyard is a **seventeenth century**

sundial, the shadow casting finger or gnomon has been removed.

The Church of St. Mary was originally the parish church of Liverpool. It has been extensively restored and the sandstone ashlar cleaned revealing it as a very fine building. The west tower dates from 1828-32 by John Broadbent; the north side dates from 1840 and the large south aisle chapel was built in 1911. All the work is of a very high standard and even the modern additions do not detract from the appearance of the building.

The final building in this group is the **Old Rectory,** Walton Village. This building dates from the early nineteenth century and is built of red sandstone ashlar blocks, with three castellated narrow gables on the south side. The rectangular windows have sandstone labels and Gothic tracery. The most notable feature of the building is the large *porte-cochere* at the main entrance; this is castellated and has three Tudor arches topped with round moulded finials.

Walton Hospital, Rice Lane, was built in 1868 as a workhouse; although there is nothing of the Dickensian grimness associated with workhouses about this building, which in the nineteenth century was set in open countryside. It is a three-storey brick building with stone dressings; an interesting feature of the slate roof is the square louvre ventilating turrets which have pagoda tops to them. The most notable feature of the building is the fine clock tower which surmounts the central entrance block. The clock face is set inside a Gothic arch and the tower is topped by a high fish scale tiled roof with an iron parapet.

Walton Gaol, Hornby Road, together with the adjacent prison officers' houses, **Nos. 2-54 Hornby Road,** are a fine example of the Victorian attitude to the penal system when apparently everybody involved with prison had to suffer — even the staff, for the prison officers' dwellings are only a little less bleak than the prison itself. They comprise two long terraces of brick houses punctuated by three-storeyed towers. Where the terraces break the two facing gable ends form **Nos. 1 and 2 Hornby Place.**

Rather more cheerful are the **two Italianate villas** which flank the original gatehouse. These two buildings are of brick with stone dressings. The windows are rectangular with those on either side of the doorways round arched. Both houses have large two-storey bays with six windows.

The Gate House to the prison is now defaced by a modern addition and has lost its fine Norman arch. Enough remains, however, to give some indication of what the original structure

Church of St. Mary

Old School House

was like. Dating from 1855, by John Weightman, the use of the Norman style and red brick gives an impression of uncompromising solidity emphasised by the deeply recessed round arched windows. A macabre sense of humour was responsible for the almost featureless masks that gaze balefully down.

It is to be regretted that Barclays Bank mark their ownership of Martins Bank properties by insisting on fixing an illuminated plastic sign to the face of each building. It is such a sign that spoils the appearance of the **Barclays Bank** situated at the junction of Rice Lane and Eskdale Road. This building, dated 1898 by Willink and Thicknesse, is built of red pressed bricks with stone dressings and a green tiled roof. The ground floor windows are round arched supported by Doric pillasters. Each corner on the front elevation has a round turret topped by shallow domes and the gables are elaborately treated in the Dutch style. It is pleasing to note that the designers of the building included egg and dart moulding under the cornice which has been carefully carved by the Victorian builders, and a frieze of swags just under the windows.

Hartley's Jam Factory is a good example of the Victorian taste for eccentricity in architecture for this 1866 monument to confectionery is an immense red brick medieval castle. The main entrance to the building has an iron portcullis flanked by round castellated turrets and a crenellated parapet. A tall brick clock tower situated in the centre of the factory complex can also be seen from the front of the building. The octagonal brick chimney belongs to the **Engine House** situated inside the factory and to the left of the entrance.

The Dining Hall to the factory, dated 1895, is now owned by Messrs. Marcus H. Barlow & Co. Ltd. This attractive building with Dutch gables was built as part of the workers' amenities which also include the **49 dwelling-houses** which form a square and are known as Hartley's Village. These are modest houses in comparison to workers' cottages associated with other nineteenth century industrial estates and many of them have been altered by the addition of modern porches, walls and gates; nevertheless, they are an important contribution to our knowledge of the social conditions that prevailed in the late nineteenth century.

The Cottage Homes, Longmoor Lane, all of which are listed, are by Charles Lancaster, dating from 1887-9, and were built as homes for deprived children. The Cottage Homes are virtually identical red brick buildings with care taken over the details of design in the form of labels, terracotta ornaments in the gables and red tile cresting on the roofs. Whilst using the same basic design for his houses the architect has added interest to the

Hartley's Village

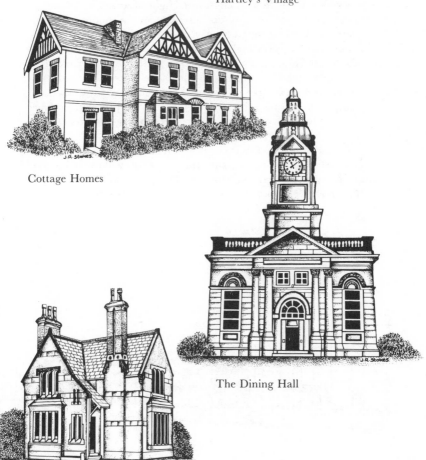

Cottage Homes

The Dining Hall

Kirkdale Cemetery Lodge

group by half timbering some houses and adding bay windows to others.

Of the single storey buildings, **Willow House** is the most notable. It has a glazed porch at the front supported by Doric pillars, and the double central gables have red ornamental tiles.

The most impressive building of the group is the Dutch classical style former **Dining Hall** which is set in the middle of the central avenue and forms a focal point for the estate. The main entrance is a large round arched doorway flanked by ashlar pillasters which support a triangular pediment. On either side of the entrance is one tall round arched window. The roof is balustraded and is topped by a square brick and ashlar tower having a clock face on each side and a three tier curved roof.

Everton Cemetery, Long Lane/Higher Lane. The Victorian approach to death was enthusiastic and although Everton Cemetery is not as magnificent a necropolis as Anfield Cemetery it does have a certain elan. **The Long Lane Entrance** has a yellow sandstone lodge with a steep slate roof; it is similar in style, although not so ornate as the Glebe Hotel, County Road. There are **two lodges** on Higher Lane similar to the Long Lane Lodge but having tall stone chimneys. All three lodges have windows with ogee tracery. **The entrance gates** are of cast iron.

Inside the cemetery there is a **North Chapel** and a **South Chapel** which are similar and built of yellow rusticated sandstone with red sandstone ashlar quoins and steeples and both have ogee mouldings around their entrances.

Hornby Road

Wavertree is at first sight an unpromising area for a walk taking in 'listed' buildings. A busy main road and brash shop fronts are not normally associated with the restrained style of the Georgian age or the vivacity of the Victorians; however, a walk around this area proves to be more than rewarding for both the student of architecture and the casual observer.

The main thoroughfare through the area is Picton Road/ High Street, and the walk commences at **238 Picton Road,** a small brick cottage set back from the road and sandwiched between a corner public house and **Minster Soft Drinks Ltd., 240 Picton Road,** a three-storey brick building dating from the nineteenth century.

The Wavertree District Library, 244 Picton Road, is a large red brick building by Thomas Shelmerdine dating from 1902-3. Ashlar quoins give 'weight' to this fine building and stone columns have been used to form a Venetian entrance. The porch is balustraded and further character is added by the use of a Dutch gable rather than a more conservative treatment. Also of interest are the **nine stone piers** supporting the railings at the front of the building.

Also by Shelmerdine is the **Regional College of Art, 250 Picton Road,** dated 1898-9, and originally built as the Technical Institute. It is of red brick with ashlar quoins and window mullions; the main entrance is particularly attractive with Ionic columns and a curved arch.

Set back from the main road and partly obscured by a petrol filling station are the remains of a nineteenth century terrace of cottages. **Nos. 199-201 Picton Road and 1 Sandown Lane.** They are brick built with stone round arched door cases; some original windows and doors remain.

Nos. 12-34 Sandown Lane are a particularly attractive terrace of nineteenth century houses, some of which have been altered by pebbledashing and the installation of new doors and windows. The original treatment of the terrace was stucco, the ground floor being deeply horizontally scored. The projecting end blocks of the terrace have moulded window cases on all floors; the remainder have moulded cases on the upper floor only. A very pleasing feature of the terrace is the incised and painted tympanum.

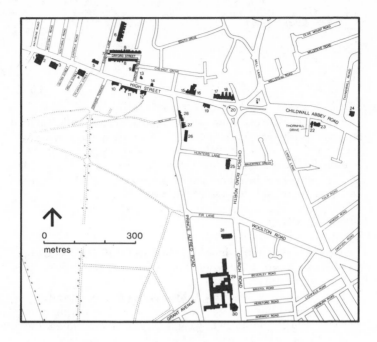

The Edinburgh Public House on the corner of Sandown Lane and Orford Street dates from the 1860s; it has a nicely panelled door set into a round arched doorway. Two windows on Orford Street have cast iron balconies. **Nos. 1-37 and 2-34 Orford Street** are two very pleasant mid-Victorian brick terraces, basically similar but differing in the treatment of door cases, some having Doric pilasters and others carved brackets. Nos. 2 and 4 Orford Street have attractively panelled doors and original windows.

No. 11 Grove Street is the return end of 34 Orford Street. It has stone bands and two original windows. **Nos. 1-9 Grove Street** is a terrace of small brick cottages; No. 9 projects and has a shop front and projecting stone bands. The terrace is greatly altered by the insertion of modern doors and windows, but Nos. 1 and 3 still have original doors.

Grove Street leads into High Street and almost directly opposite are **Nos. 16A and 16B (Barclays Bank) and 18 High Street.** This fine red brick building has a sandstone round arched doorway to the bank with pilasters and a small bay window above. Three gables face on to the main road and centrally placed on the facade is a sandstone plaque bearing the inscription 'Bank of Liverpool: Wavertree Branch.' The windows have stone mullions and transomes and are leaded.

Nos. 22-34 High Street are a row of late Georgian brick houses with stone bands, Nos. 22, 24 and 28 having Tuscan porches. No. 26 is a slightly smaller house with slender columns to the door case and a round arched traceried fanlight. No. 28 has curved labels over the ground floor windows, and No. 34 is stuccoed with, on the second floor, Tuscan pilasters supporting a triangular pediment.

Nos. 38-42 High Street is a late eighteenth century stuccoed building. The entrance to No. 38 is at the side of the house with the door set into a Tuscan porch decorated with wreaths. The windows are set into moulded cases.

Set well back from the main road is **No. 35 High Street 'Rose Cottage'** a very pretty late eighteenth century cottage with a flag roof and original windows. The charm of this house is enhanced by its well kept garden and attractively cut hedge.

The deeply incised stucco and heavy labels and bands of the **Prince Alfred Public House** and adjacent **chemist's shop** add character to this attractive early nineteenth century building.

Nos. 85 and 87 High Street are small early nineteenth century scored stucco cottages. They have both been modernised but No. 85 has original windows.

No. 89 High Street is the former **Wavertree Town Hall,**

102 High Street

Town Hall

126

dated 1872 by John Elliot Reeve. The Town Hall is a painted ashlar building with a rough rock faced basement. It is built in an amalgam of styles; the central porch is supported at ground floor level by Ionic columns and at first floor level by composite columns. A coat of arms is carved over the entrance and comprises a tree with the motto 'I flourish in the shade'. The windows on ground and second floors are also treated in different styles, the ground floor windows being set in moulded cases with decorated keystones over, while the first floor windows are set in architraves with ornately carved rosettes and consoles.

The Lamb Hotel, dating from the late eighteenth century is, by comparison with the Town Hall, a much more restrained building but aesthetically more pleasing. It is of red brick with stone dressings with a gable each side of the central portion of the building. One gable has a coach entrance and the other a sandstone bay window of later date. The central entrance has a Tuscan porch with a frieze of metopes and triglyphs.

Attached to the Lamb Hotel is a terrace of brick houses. **Nos. 113-127 High Street.**

Opposite the Lamb Hotel are **Nos. 98-102 and 102A High Street,** a brick terrace of late Georgian houses. The most outstanding property of this terrace is No. 102 which has early nineteenth century bowed shop windows flanked by Tuscan half columns. The door has a rectangular traceried fanlight and is also flanked by Tuscan half columns.

Situated on a traffic island at the junction of High Street and Church Road North is a **clock tower** designed as a memorial to Sir James Picton, the local historian and architect, dated 1879. It is a square stone tower with four clock faces and crowned by a dome. Around the base of the tower are four iron street lamps with dolphins entwined about their bases.

Set on the old Village Green is **Wavertree Lock-up** a small early nineteenth century stone building, octagonal with a pointed roof.

Just beyond the Village Green in Childwall Road are a group of stuccoed Victorian villas, **No. 1 'Thornhill'** being the finest. This house is 'L' shaped in plan, and has well proportioned windows and good mouldings including architraves and curved broken pediments on brackets. **Nos. 2 and 3** are semi-detached and similar in style to No. 1. **'Mossfield',** on the opposite side of Childwall Road, is a large villa with rusticated ground floor. Below the heavy cornice is a frieze with triglyphs and metopes, which contributes to the rather fussy appearance characteristic of some classical houses of the 1850s.

At the corner of Church Road North and Hunters Lane is the **Liberal Jewish Synagogue, No. 28,** formerly Wavertree

The Church of Holy Trinity

The Lock-up

The Bluecoat School Chapel

Rectory. This is a large eighteenth century house standing in its own grounds, brick built with stone lintels to the windows cut into voussoirs and the door set into a moulded case with a convex frieze and a traceried fanlight.

The 'listed' buildings in Prince Alfred Road are divided into terraces; the first, **Nos. 27-35** are early nineteenth century, stuccoed and horizontally grounted at ground floor level. All the upper floor windows are set into moulded cases, and No. 35 has a Tuscan porch.

Nos. 19-25 Prince Alfred Road are early Victorian brick houses. No. 19 is much altered with only the upper windows as original; Nos. 23 and 25 have round arched door cases with fanlights and No. 21 has original windows.

The final group are **Nos. 9-17 and 17A Prince Alfred Road** also early Victorian houses. No. 17A is set back from the rest of the terrace and has a robustly carved wooden porch and the original door and windows. Nos. 9-13 have moulded door cases and in addition No. 9 has original windows, also in cases. No. 17 has a small gabled dormer window.

Of special interest in this area is the **Liverpool Bluecoat School,** which started life in 1717 as the Blue Coat Hospital situated in School Lane, Liverpool. By the close of the nineteenth century the School Lane building had become too cramped and in 1903 the architects, Briggs, Wolstenholme and Thornley, were commissioned to design a new school building to be situated in Church Road North, Wavertree, and which was completed in 1906. The tower dates from 1915 and was the gift of Sir Charles Nall-Cain.

Nikolaus Pevsner considers that the Bluecoat School is 'without doubt the most spectacular building in Wavertree and one of the most spectacular half-dozen of its date in Lancashire'. It is of red brick with Baroque ashlar details to entrance and windows. The splendid 105 ft. high brick clock tower is topped with ashlar aedicules (the openings framed by pediment supporting columns) and an ogee roof.

The Chapel to the Bluecoat School is also by Briggs, Wolstenholme and Thornely and was built at the same time as the school. The chapel is of red brick with ashlar dressings and a balustraded parapet; there are stone swags over some of the windows, and the roof is domed and topped with a small domed lantern.

The Church of Holy Trinity, Church Road North, dates from 1794 and is by John Hope. It is ashlar with rusticated quoins and nicely carved window cases and brackets supporting pediments. The east end, dated 1911, is by Sir Charles Reilly, who also created a very fine chancel inside the building.

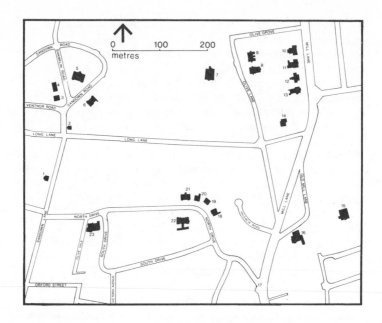

1 47 and 49
   Sandown Lane
2 87 Sandown Lane
3 66 Sandown Lane
4 7 and 9
   Shanklin Road
5 50 Sandown Road
   and 12 Shanklin
   Road
6 69 and 71
   Sandown Road
7 Sandown Hall
8 'Bloomfield House'
   and 'Eastgate'
   42 and 44
   Olive Lane
9 'Rooklands' and
   'Westfield' 46 and
   48 Olive Lane
10 7-8 Olive Mount
   Villas
11 5 and 6
   Olive Mount Villas
12 3 and 4
   Olive Mount Villas
13 1 and 2
   Olive Mount Villas
14 Methodist Church
   Mill Lane

15 Late Eighteenth
   Century House
16 'Newstead'
   Old Mill Lane
17 Monk's Well
18 37 and 39
   North Drive
19 35 North Drive
20 33 North Drive
21 29 and 31
   North Drive
22 18 and 20
   North Drive
23 St. Mary's Church
   North Drive

130

14 Sandown Park and Victoria Park

These Victorian residential parks contain a number of fine houses, although sadly many have fallen into a state of disrepair. **Nos. 35 and 37 Sandown Lane, and 47 and 49 Sandown Lane,** whilst not being part of the Park proper, are exceptional Georgian properties in a not very distinguished terrace. Both buildings are brick built with stone bands and pediment, and each has a Doric doorway with round fanlights. No. 35 has guttae carved under the metope and a triglyph frieze and No. 49 has a very nice panelled door and a traceried fanlight.

No. 87 Sandown Road is a small Victorian lodge with its stucco painted pink and the moulding around the windows picked out in white. Moulded into the frieze are laurel wreaths.

There is an interesting group of buildings at the junction of Sandown Road and Shanklin Road, the first being **66 Sandown Road** which is a two-storey stuccoed Victorian villa. A feature of this building is the Tuscan porch which has a balustraded parapet and a Greek key frieze. The windows are set in moulded cases.

Nos. 7 and 9 Shanklin Road are an identical pair of stuccoed Victorian houses, with moulded window cases and ornamental balustrades over the doorways. The doors appear to retain the original panelling.

The most attractive building of this group is situated on a triangle of land and is numbered **50 Sandown Road and 12 Shanklin Road.** The building is brick with the ground floor stuccoed and the upper windows set in moulded cases; there are quoins on the upper floors and a small round arched window set into each gable. A pleasing feature of the building is the ornamental balustrades over the ground floor windows and the carved bay leaves on the convex frieze above the windows. The doors are set in Tuscan porches at each end of the building. The fact that the building and grounds are well maintained add to the charm of this property.

The final building in this small group is **Nos. 69 and 71 Sandown Road** which is a stuccoed Victorian semi-detached house. The ground floor of each has a three-sided bay, and the windows and doors are set in moulded and decorated cases.

The most dominant building in the area is **Sandown Hall,** Olive Lane, an early nineteenth century villa set in extensive grounds. It is a pleasingly proportioned building and its simplicity contrasts with the rather more florid style of other buildings in the vicinity.

'Bloomfield House' and 'Eastgate', Nos. 42 and 44 Olive Lane, and 'Rooklands' and 'Westfield', Nos. 46 and 48 Olive Lane, are two pairs of early nineteenth century villas. They are of painted scored stucco with moulded window cases. 'Bloomfield House' and 'Eastgate' have very wide eaves with brackets and mouldings on the underside.

The properties known as Olive Mount Villas, Nos. 1-8 (consecutive) Mill Lane, are an interesting group of early Victorian houses in different styles. **Nos. 7-8 Olive Mount Villas** are stuccoed with classical details, a frieze of laurel wreaths with guttae carved under them and pilasters flanking the bay windows.

Nos. 5 and 6 Olive Mount Villas are also stuccoed but treated in the Gothic style with labels over the windows and barley sugar chimneys. No. 6 has a particularly attractive carved wooden gate.

Nos. 3 and 4 Olive Mount Villas are stuccoed with modillioned eaves which, together with the panelled and studded door of No. 4, gives them a Roman appearance.

The final building in this group, **Nos. 1 and 2 Olive Mount Villas,** are Gothic and stuccoed, with No. 2 having the remains of carved barge boards. Both properties have castellated porches.

The former **Independent Methodist Church,** Mill Lane, was once the home of Sir James Picton, whose work, *Memorials of Liverpool,* has been a valuable source of information whilst compiling this book. It is one of the finest buildings in this group, and is built of red sandstone with Dutch gables. The Jacobean strapwork doorway is now partly sealed and used as a window; the small ground floor windows have stone mullions. There is an octagonal stairway tower near to the Jacobean doorway and matching the tower is an octagonal pavilion once used as a library which was built by Picton and bears his coat of arms and motto. A modern extension is a continuation of the library and it is to the architect's credit that it does not unduly detract from the building.

The late eighteenth century house, now part of Olive Mount Children's Hospital, is a two-storey ashlar house with swags carved on panels on the second floor and a large fan carved panel over the door. The doorway itself is of interest; it has a porch with Adam type columns supporting an iron balcony with honeysuckle ornament.

Set in its own grounds in Old Mill Lane is **'Newstead'** a very

9 Shanklin Road

35-37 Sandown Lane

Newstead

39 North Drive

fine stuccoed Victorian villa. The more obvious points of the building are the octagonal castellated tower and the splendid two-storey verandah decorated with delicate iron leaves. Much of the charm of the building, however, lies in details such as the finely worked egg and tongue moulding around the door and window openings and the dentilled cornice which is continued into the **glass conservatory** — adjoining the building. **The sandstone gatepiers** are finely carved as are the wooden gates which are inset with Gothic cast iron ornament.

At the junction of Mill Lane and North Drive is the **Monk's Well;** this now comprises a red sandstone plinth with a blind pointed arch which is topped with a cross. The Latin inscription of the cross reads 'God gives, Man drinks' and on the cornice of the plinth 'qui non dat quod habet dorm . . . . anno 1414'.

North Drive leads once again into the Park. **Nos. 37 and 39** are a pair of brick semi-detached mid-nineteenth century villas with pointed windows set into two small gables at the front. The window and door arches are decorated with blue, cream and red bricks and the single storey bays have decorative cast iron balustrades.

No. 35 North Drive is a free-standing brick built villa with stone window cases. The doorway is particularly attractive having Corinthian pilasters and a nicely panelled door.

No. 33 North Drive is also a free-standing brick villa; it has a yellow, blue and red brick band at cornice level, and similar bands over the upper windows.

Nos. 29 and 31 North Drive are similar to Nos. 37 and 39, but have three-storey bays and moulded wooden barge boards. The doorways are set into each gable and are nicely panelled.

Nos. 18 and 20 North Drive are also brick semi-detached villas with single storey bays having cast iron balconies. The doors appear to be original and are set in the front of the building.

The final building in this walk is **St. Mary's Church,** North Drive, standing in well maintained grounds and dated 1874 on the west door. It is built of yellow stone rubble with pink sandstone ashlar door and window arches, and spire. The north doorway is decorated with Gothic carving and the spire has gryphons projecting from its base.

This walk starts at the **Public Library,** Kensington, which dates from 1890, enlarged in 1897, and is by Thomas Shelmerdine who designed other public libraries in Liverpool in a similar style. The library is a splendid red brick building with stone dressings, the central entrance is of stone with Ionic columns and iron lamp standards. There is a Dutch gable to the right of the entrance, a plain gable to its left, and stone arcading forming a balustrade around the upper part of the building. An attractive feature is the timber and glass octagonal lantern on the roof which is topped by an open dome.

Adjacent to the library is **Christ Church,** Kensington, dated 1870 by W. & G. Audsley. This is a rather overpowering Italian Gothic building in dark brick with stone dressings and window arches of red and blue brick. There is a carved frieze at ground floor level with grotesque masks and gargoyles.

At the junction of Kensington and Deane Road stands **Barclay's Bank,** formerly a Martins Bank building dated 1898 by James Rhind. As with other Martins banks of this period this is a very attractive and unusual building with a rusticated stone ground floor and red brick upper floors with stone dressings. The ground floor windows have Ionic columns and the doorway is set in the concave corner of the building with the stonework extending upwards above roof level. A lower wing of the bank, facing on to Deane Road, is brick with an octagonal tower having a frieze of swags and a bell-shaped roof.

A little way down Deane Road is the Jewish Cemetery set back from the road behind a **Victorian screen** in the Greek style. The entrance is a round arch with attached Doric columns, a frieze of triglyphs and metopes, and inscription 'Here the weary are at rest' and an inscription in Hebrew characters. **The railings** on Deane Road are cast iron set in a low stone wall.

Nos. 13 and 15 Deane Road, are two stuccoed Victorian villas; No. 13 is castellated with two bay windows in gables. The front door has Gothic carving, and is set in a moulded case with a label. No. 15 has Gothic arched windows and an oriel window set into a bay.

Beech Street runs parallel to Deane Road, and **Beach Mount** is a two-storey terrace of four houses dated 1861. They are brick

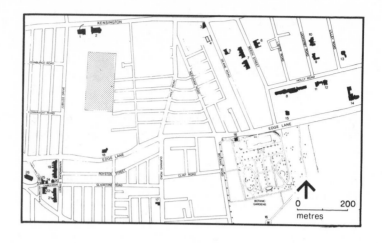

1 Public Library
Kensington
2 Christ Church
Kensington
3 Barclay's Bank
Jewish Cemetery
4 Victorian Screen
and Railings
5 13 and 15
Deane Road
6 Beech Mount
Beech Street
7 Oak and Elm
Terrace
8 University Hall
Holly Road
9 17 Lockerby Road
10 11 and 13
Lockerby Road
11 12 Holly Road
12 14 Holly Road
13 39 Lilley Road
14 309 and 311
Edge Lane
15 293 Edge Lane
16 Botanic Gardens
Lodge and Fountain
17 Fire Station
Durning Road
18 115 Edge Lane
Adelaide House
19 Clare Terrace
2-16 Marmaduke
Street and 12A
Edge Lane

20 16A Marmaduke
Street including
5 Church Mount
21 18-28 Marmaduke
Street
22 1 and 2
Holland Place and
2, 2A and 4
Church Mount
23 1 Church Mount
24 3 Church Mount
25 13 Towerlands
Street
26 Church of St. Mary

built with a stuccoed ground floor, each house has a single-storey bay window with cresting, and deeply recessed doorways in round arched moulded cases. The upper windows are set in moulded cases and the eaves cornice is supported by brackets. The whole terrace is nicely maintained and retains its Victorian charm.

Oak Terrace and Elm Terrace in Beech Street, are two identical groups of terraced houses. They are stuccoed with round arched windows on the ground floor and the doors set in round arched porches. Some of the houses have bay windows and Nos. 6 and 7 Oak Terrace have a balustrade over their porches.

Beech Street leads into Holly Road and the **University Hall,** the oldest portion of which, a Victorian classical villa, has now been absorbed into a more recent building. It is a fine stuccoed building with Doric columns to its entrance porch, windows set in simple moulded cases, a triangular central pediment and eaves cornice on brackets.

No. 17 Lockerby Road is, in comparison to the classical simplicity of the University, a more ornate building of deeply horizontal scored stucco. The central porch has Tuscan columns and a pediment; the ground floor bays have balustrades. The upper windows are in moulded cases, and the eaves cornice is broken by two half dormer windows set in deep round arched cases.

Nos. 11 and 13 Lockerby Road are semi-detached Victorian stuccoed houses similar in style to No. 17. Each house has a large gable with a single-storey balustraded bay window, and an entrance set in a side extension.

Returning to Holly Road, **No. 12** is a nicely maintained Victorian classical villa in painted stucco. The central entrance porch is pedimented with a window each side of the glazed front door. The central pediment has a window in moulded architraves and a cornice supported on ornamented brackets; other windows are treated more simply. This house is a fine example of restrained Victorian classical architecture and is in contrast to **No. 14 Holly Road,** which is a stuccoed Victorian Gothic villa. It has a gabled porch with a pointed arch and a label. A gabled wing has stone mullioned and transomed windows; a smaller gable has a pointed arch window with Gothic tracery. These two houses show the differences in taste of the Victorians and their interpretation on a modest scale.

No. 39 Lilley Road is a stuccoed Victorian villa with horizontal grouting and a round arched central doorway with a curved pediment. A large ground floor window has mullions with small carved lion heads; a round arched window over the

Public Library Kensington

293 Edge Lane

entrance has a flat pediment and the eaves cornice is broken by two round arched half dormer windows.

Nos. 309 and 311 Edge Lane were at one time two separate houses but are now joined into one property, they are both stuccoed and No. 309 Edge Lane has a horizontally scored ground floor.

No. 293 Edge Lane is a fine Victorian Gothic villa in brick with stone quoins and dressings. It has Dutch gables at front and side and a balustraded round arched porch with heavy scrolls at its base. There is a two-sided oriel window at first floor level above a stone mullioned and transomed window. It is interesting to note that the Gothic details of this house have been carried on around its sides away from the main facade.

The last buildings in this section of the walk are the **Lodge** to the Botanic Gardens, Edge Lane, and the **fountain** further in the gardens. The lodge is a two-storey stone building with a hipped slate roof behind a parapet, and four giant pilasters at the front. The fountain is cast iron with three shell basins supported on dolphins, Liver Birds and a tall lamp standard.

The next walk in this area is centred on Holland Place; however, it is worth making a brief detour to see the **Fire Station,** Durning Road. This is a splendid Victorian Gothic building in smoke-stained ashlar with two large arched entrances and also at ground floor level a row of small stone mullioned and transomed windows. The upper lights of the windows are circular and quatre-foil. There are four similar windows on the first floor but they are separate, each one having a label. The building has a castellated parapet with a crouching animal carved at each end, and a slate roof. Two carved stone chimneys are other attractive features of this building.

Adelaide House, No. 115 Edge Lane, is an early nineteenth century brick house with stone dressings; the bricks are alternate red and cream laid in a chequer pattern. There is a very attractive doorway with Doric columns and a round arched traceried fanlight; the windows retain their original glazing bars. The house is a restrained building which owes much of its charm to its pleasing proportions.

The buildings in the Holland Place area are a pleasant group of early nineteenth century houses; the walk commences at **Clare Terrace (Nos. 2-16 Marmaduke Street and 12A Edge Lane).** This is a stuccoed building with a central triangular pediment, the ground floor is horizontally scored and the doors and windows are set in moulded cases. The terrace appears to be converted into flats, but care has been taken to retain its original character. **No. 16A Marmaduke Street,** including **5 Church Mount,** is a brick building with stone

Fire Station, Durning Road

Barclay's Bank

dressings. No. 16A retains its original windows, while those of No. 5 have been altered. No. 5 has a very nice doorway with a panelled door, Doric columns and a frieze of metopes and triglyphs.

Nos. 18-28 Marmaduke Street is also an early nineteenth century two-storey terrace but in brick with stone dressings. A number of the moulded door cases have been removed but that of No. 20 is original with Ionic columns and cornice. No. 22 has original windows and No. 24 Marmaduke Street has an attractive door and frame with a rectangular fanlight. No. 28 Marmaduke Street is three storeys high, it has original windows and a doorway with Doric columns, a frieze of metopes and triglyphs and a traceried fanlight.

Nos. 1 and 2 Holland Place are attractive brick houses with stone dressings. The ground floor windows have attractive upper lights and the doorways have fluted Ionic columns with rectangular fanlights.

Nos. 2, 2A and 4 Church Mount are attached to Nos. 1 and 2 Holland Place and are also brick with stone dressings; Nos. 2A and 4 have Doric columns to the doorways. **No. 8 Church Mount** is the gable end of No. 18 Marmaduke Street and is in brick with stone dressings. The doorway to No. 8 is wider than those of the other houses; it also has Doric columns and an arched fanlight.

No. 1 Church Mount forms part of the facade on to Towerlands Street; it has a round arched doorway with simple pilasters. **No. 3 Church Mount** is free-standing, its windows and door are altered but it still retains Doric columns to the doorway. **No. 13 Towerlands Street** adjoins No. 1 Church Mount; it is brick with stone dressings as are the other houses in the group; it has original windows and simple pilasters to the doorway with a traceried fanlight.

The final building in this group is the **Church of St. Mary,** dated 1812-3. It is a simple brick building matching the other properties in the group. There are stone battlements and a square tower, and the windows have pointed arches.

The simple style of the buildings in and around Holland Place, including those 'unlisted' buildings in North View, make this a pleasant and architecturally restrained area in comparison to other more exuberant parts of nineteenth century Liverpool.

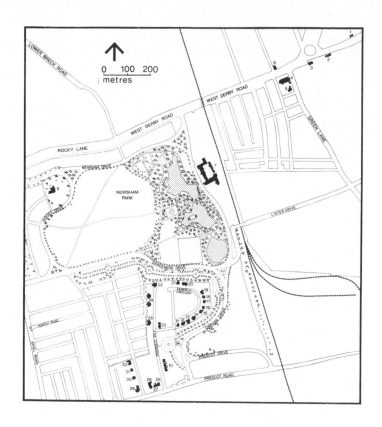

This walk starts at an early seventeenth century house, **No. 695 West Derby Road (Tue Brook House)** — at one time a farm house, this little building is dated 1615 and is built of whitewashed stone with red sandstone dressings and a stone flagged roof. The windows have stone mullions and leaded lights, and the doorway has a dated stone lintel. The narrow **cobbled forecourt** at the front of the building attests to its former rural charm.

On the opposite side of the road to Tue Brook House stands an attractive group of properties starting with **No. 358 West Derby Road,** a stuccoed late Georgian house with a round arched doorway having a keystone and traceried fanlight and a panelled door. **Nos. 354 and 356 West Derby Road** are two small cottages, with a stone built ground floor and brick upper floor. They may once have been thatched but now have slate roofs.

A more imposing group are **Nos. 340-352 West Derby Road,** a brick terrace built in the first half of the nineteenth century. No. 352 is now a garage but the remainder of the terrace is virtually intact with Nos. 340 and 348 in particularly good condition with stone sills and lintels to the windows, stone doorways with pilasters, fanlights and decorative cast iron balconies.

The finest building in this area is the church of **St. John the Baptist,** West Derby Road, which is listed as Grade 'A', the ecclesiastical equivalent of Grade I. It was built in 1868-71 by G. F. Bodley in pale sandstone with random bands of red sandstone, and red sandstone tower and buttresses. The interior of the church is outstanding and the restoration of the decorative stencil work won for the Vicar and congregation a 1975 Heritage Year Award of exceptional merit. The timber in the roof is painted white with red and green stencilled motifs and verses from the Bible; the black oak rood screen is also decorated, gold leaf having been extensively used. The overall effect is truly magnificent.

In the grounds of the church, but facing on to Green Lane, is the **Vicarage of St. John the Baptist,** which is also by Bodley. It is a grey brick building with random bands of red pressed brick and sandstone dressings. The windows have stone mullions and transomes with small leaded panes and the sandstone door frame has a fine panelled door.

Opposite St. John the Baptist Church is **Barclays Bank, 611 West Derby Road,** formerly Martins Bank, and thought to be by Francis Doyle. This is a splendid little bank building having a rusticated stone ground floor with round arched windows and a red brick upper floor. The mansard roof has dormer windows. The treatment of the entrance set in a chamfered corner is very attractive, with a convex frieze supported by Doric columns, stone sculpture of a Liver Bird and a round window surrounded by a wreath and carved swags.

Park Hospital is on Orphan Drive, one of the roads passing through Newsham Park. It was originally built as the Seamen's Orphanage in 1871-4 by Waterhouse and is a Gothic building in brick with stone dressings and a green slate roof. The windows have stone mullions and transomes with brick relieving arches over them, the roof having gabled dormers. There is a tall tower at the south end of the hospital with a steep roof and smaller tower attached to it. The entrance is of sandstone with, as a reminder of its former use, a sailing ship carved above the door.

At the other side of the Park is **Newsham House,** an imposing late eighteenth century villa set amongst wide lawns, around the perimeter of which Judge's Drive sweeps in a great curve. It was built by Thomas Molyneux, no relation of the Earls of Sefton, who owned the estate of 116 acres which was bought from him by the Corporation in 1846 and was later laid out as Newsham Park. In 1868 the house was altered and enlarged to accommodate the Judges and their staff when staying in Liverpool for the Assizes. Queen Victoria also stayed here in 1886 when visiting the Great Liverpool Exhibition. The drive is lined by elaborate cast iron lamps on stone plinths and leads to the main front which has a three-bay pediment and composite style porch. The rear wing is later, but beyond this are the **stables and coach house,** a long block with a first floor containing alternately square and circular openings.

Nearby, on the corner of Sheil Road and Huntley Road, is an 1863 **Post Office pillar box.** Sheil Road was named after Alderman Richard Sheil, the first Irishman to sit in the civic chamber.

The erection of private houses at Prospect Vale, Fairfield Crescent and the southern part of Elm Vale preceded the construction of Newsham Park itself, which commenced in 1866 to the designs of Mr. Tyerman. The gates and incidental buildings are unfortunately not of great architectural merit.

Nos. 6-16 Prospect Vale are, or were, three identical Victorian semi-detached houses. Nos. 14 and 16 Prospect Vale

Tuebrook House

Church of St. John the Baptist

are the least altered of the group and retain the original stucco and decorative features such as the wreaths moulded on the frieze over the joint doorways and the windows with straight and curved pediments. No. 10 Prospect Vale is worthy of note as it shows how expensive and well meaning 'improvements' can spoil the original character of a property. The stucco has been pebbledashed, the upper window has small 'Georgian' style panes of glass put in, and the lower Victorian window has been removed and replaced with a small 'Georgian' style bow window.

Fairfield Crescent, at right angles to Prospect Vale, comprises early Victorian houses and villas built in differing styles. **No. 2 Fairfield Crescent** is a large stuccoed house with adjoining **stable.** It is in the Gothic style with the door set into a steeply gabled porch, and with Gothic mouldings on a blind window just above the porch.

Nos. 4 and 6 Fairfield Crescent are a pair of semi-detached houses. They are stuccoed with bay windows on the ground floor and upper windows set in moulded cases. A distinguishing feature of the houses is a tall Gothic pilaster at each end of the building.

Nos. 8 and 10 Fairfield Crescent are also stuccoed semi-detached houses with carved barge boards and large bay windows. No. 8 is the least altered and has a round arched window in the gable; each house has a fretted cast iron porch.

Nos. 12 and 14 Fairfield Crescent are similar to Nos. 4 and 6, but having the end pilasters decorated with an egg and dart moulding.

No. 16 Fairfield Crescent is a detached Victorian villa set in its own grounds. It is of scored stucco with round arched windows set in moulded cases and a modillioned cornice. There is a square Victorian porch at the front of the building with a heavy cornice.

No. 18 Fairfield Crescent is a red brick villa set in its own grounds. The brickwork is decorated with bands of blue brick and the gables have carved barge boards.

No. 20 Fairfield Crescent is a brick and stucco villa with two-storey bay windows and a central balustraded doorway. There are cast iron lamp standards either side of the door.

No. 22 Fairfield Crescent is a later Victorian villa with a stuccoed and horizontally scored ground floor and brick upper floor with the cornice supported on ornate brackets. The entrance door is set in a round arched frame and is attractively panelled. A brick **stable** is attached to the house, and has a round arched entrance on its gable end with a round window above the entrance and a broken pediment.

30 Fairfield Crescent

611 West Derby Road

6-8 Prospect Vale

No. 24 Fairfield Crescent is a rough cast villa with a very attractive porch having Ionic columns, a moulded frieze and a cornice.

Nos. 26 and 28 Fairfield Crescent are semi-detached houses in scored stucco each having a bay window. Set in the gable of each house is a small pointed window with labels terminating in carved faces.

No. 30 Fairfield Crescent is one of the pleasantest houses in this group. It has two gables with fretted barge boards and labels over the windows. The nicely panelled door is set in a pointed arched case with a label over and the whole being in a castellated porch.

Returning to Prospect Vale **Nos. 18 and 20** are a pair of stuccoed semi-detached villas with labels over the upper windows and a bay window in each gable. An attractive feature is the ornamental Gothic frieze over the bays and central windows.

No. 51 Prospect Vale originally 'Prospect House' is the earliest building in the street. It is of scored stucco with the cornice supported on brackets, and windows set in moulded cases. There are bay windows at the front and the original entrance is set in a round arched porch at the left hand side of the building.

Nos. 47 and 49, and 43 and 45 Prospect Vale are two pairs of early Victorian semi-detached houses; originally all were stuccoed, although now some are pebbledashed. The windows are set in moulded cases with the entrances in square porches.

Nos. 35 and 37 Prospect Vale are early Victorian semi-detached stuccoed houses horizontally scored at ground floor level. There is a large pedimented gable centrally placed on the building with two pointed Gothic windows and, on the first floor, Venetian windows set in moulded architraves. The doorways are set in square balustraded porches.

No. 1 Prospect Vale, 'The Hollies', is a well kept house in scored stucco with bands and moulded and decorated window cases. The door is centrally placed and has a moulded architrave supported on brackets. The facade facing on to Prescot Road has a pedimented gable with an ornamental medallion.

Nos. 153-155 Prescot Road adjoin 'The Hollies' and are a pair of Victorian villas in scored stucco. There is a gable at each end with carved barge boards and the windows have labels over them.

No. 151 Prescot Road is a large detached house in scored stucco; the central portion projects slightly and is pedimented. The windows are set in moulded cases and there are two large bays at the front. At the side of the building is a single storey extension with blind round arched windows. **The boundary wall** to the property is in red sandstone.

On the opposite side of Elm Vale are **Nos. 147 and 149 Prescot Road,** a pair of Victorian stuccoed villas. No. 147 has a particularly fine doorway, with a frieze and cornice supported by Tuscan pilasters. The windows on a side wing have labels over them.

A rather more unusual building is **No. 5 Elm Vale,** a stuccoed Gothic villa. There are three gables at the front, two with heavy carved barge boards, the central one having a pediment and brackets and a ball finial supported by a column. The square porch is centrally placed and has three gables with ball finials. The windows are stone mullioned and some have labels.

No. 11 Elm Vale is a detached stuccoed Victorian villa with an attractive centre porch of Tuscan piers, frieze and cornice. All windows are set in moulded architraves.

The final building in this walk is **13 and 15 Elm Vale,** a pair of stuccoed Victorian semi-detached villas, with a gable each end and carved barge boards. There are labels over the windows and No. 13 has a gabled porch at the side with a well designed door and a label over it.

37 Prospect Vale

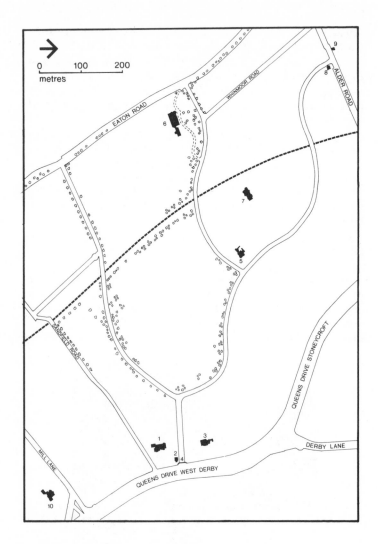

1 Basil Grange
2 Basil Grange Lodge
3 Gwalia
   Sandstone Villa
4 Park Entrance
5 St. Ives
6 Kiln Hey
7 The Old Hall
8 Park Keeper's Lodge
9 Alder Lodge
   Alder Road
10 162 Mill Lane

Sandfield Park was built in the mid-nineteenth century as a private estate of villas set in the palatial grounds of The Old Hall, an eighteenth century mansion. It retains a picturesque layout with winding roads lined by stone walls and hedges. Unfortunately, few of the original houses remain, and their replacement has generally been unsympathetic. There is, however, a large area of open parkland, and the surviving houses are set in fine mature gardens.

Flanking the Queens Drive entrance to the Park are two imposing villas, one with a lodge. The lodge belongs to **Basil Grange,** a two-storey Victorian Gothic villa in sandstone with tall octagonal chimneys.

Basil Grange Lodge has pedimented gables and an ornamented cast iron porch in the angle between these, supported on slender fluted columns.

Gwalia, the sandstone villa on the southern side of the Park entrance, is Italianate in style and stands amongst spacious lawns and shrubberies. An asymmetrically placed four-storey square tower surmounted by a pierced balustrade gives the design some grandeur. **The Park entrance** consists of six square stone piers with dentilled cornices. The gates have been removed, but a sign remains demanding a toll 'For daily use of Park Roads all vehicles 1 penny per wheel'.

In the centre of the Park at the point where the two roads join is **St. Ives,** a large sandstone house dated 1853. This building has much detail of interest, the first to be noticed being the carved timber entrance gates which display a heraldic panel with the optimistic motto 'I never forget'. There are heavy carved barge boards to gables and eaves, moulded and panelled architraves to windows, and plaster cartouches on the inner walls of the porch. There is a small conservatory adjacent to the entrance, and the secluded garden with its dense shrubberies, borders, lawns and fine trees is distinctly evocative of elegant Victorian domestic life.

The road off to the left of St. Ives leads to another mid-nineteenth century villa, **Kiln Hey,** which is situated on an eminence at the corner with Eaton Road. The house is approached by a pine tree lined drive, and is surrounded by extensive lawns. It lacks, however, the necessary architectural

'Gwalia', Sandfield Park

'St. Ives', Sandfield Park

distinction for its setting, and has been extended in a most prosaic manner. Of interest are the projecting eaves on curly brackets and the tall Venetian window in the entrance front.

It is now necessary to return to St. Ives where the adjacent house is **The Old Hall** in the grounds of which the Park was built. This is in origin an eighteenth century mansion but, due to extensive alterations, it is now scarcely recognisable as such. Lying close to the road are the lodge and stables to the Old Hall, a pleasant group of brick buildings around a courtyard.

The Park entrance in Alder Road is without its gates, but here is situated the **Park Keeper's Lodge,** a single storey sandstone cottage in Gothic style, with tall clustered chimneys and a porch with Tudor arched entrance. Across Alder Road is **Alder Lodge,** a Victorian Gothic cottage in brick, now colour-washed. It has an extremely steeply pitched roof and presents a picturesque side wall to the road with its pierced and ornamental barge boards and small windows.

Also within the area is **Fremont, 162 Mill Lane,** a good classical Victorian stucco villa. This is symmetrical, of two-storeys, and has a central porch supported on Ionic columns and flanked by lampholders.

'Kiln Hey', Sandfield Park

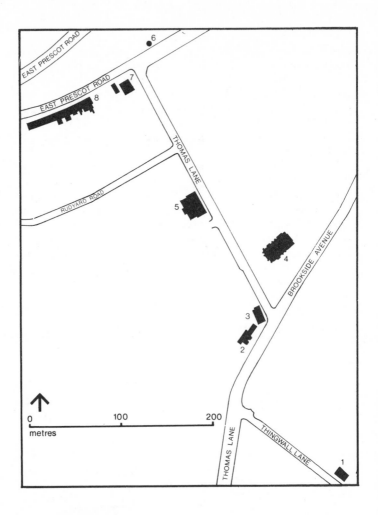

1 'The Cottage'
  Thingwall Lane
2 'Oak House'
  76 Thomas Lane
3 68-74 Thomas Lane
4 Church of St. John
  Evangelist
5 28 and 30
  Thomas Lane
6 Drinking Fountain
  East Prescot Road
7 256 East Prescot
  Road
8 204-240 East Prescot
  Road

154

The walk begins at **'The Cottage',** Thingwall Lane, at one time the stables to Dovecot Hall, now demolished. It is an early nineteenth century brick building, stuccoed and scored to give the impression of stone, with two large doors under the central pediment. The Gothic pointed windows have tracery in their upper portions which are blind, and the pitched roof is hidden behind a parapet.

'Oak House' (No. 76 Thomas Lane) is a small brick house dated 1784. It has the original twelve-paned sash windows on the upper floor and two gabled bays on the ground floor with a glass and timber porch between them. Attached to the house is a lower brick building which may at one time have been a barn.

Nos. 68-74 Thomas Lane are a small group of late eighteenth century cottages; the original brick has now been either painted or pebbledashed. No. 74 retains original windows and the remains of a moulded door case. Opposite Nos. 68-74 Thomas Lane stands the **Church of St. John Evangelist,** dated 1835-7. A red sandstone building with perpendicular style windows and Tudor style arches to the doorways and a clock tower topped with a slender spire. The chancel and south chapel were built in 1890 by Aldridge and Deacon.

Nos. 28 and 30 Thomas Lane date from the early nineteenth century and were once a brick farmhouse. No. 28 has a round arched doorway and segmental arched windows; the arches have been made up by bricks rubbed down to form voussoirs — slightly wedge shape so that they fit together.

No. 30 Thomas Lane is a smaller building with stone sills and lintels to its windows. Both properties retain the original windows.

Opposite Thomas Lane and set into the wall of the Knotty Ash Community Centre, East Prescot Road, is a **stone drinking fountain** inscribed 'Water's Best' 'RT 1887'.

Occupying the corner site at Thomas Lane is **No. 256 East Prescot Road,** a fine detached early nineteenth century brick house with stone sills and lintels to its original windows. The doorway is particularly fine with fluted Tuscan columns and cornice, round traceried fanlight and a panelled door.

The final properties in this walk are **Nos. 204-240 East Prescot Road,** a row of late eighteenth century cottages. This

Church of St. John the Evangelist

Entrance to Church

Stone Drinking Fountain

terrace is altered by the insertion of modern shop fronts and windows. Originally all the ground floor windows and doors were pointed with tracery in their upper portions, similar to 'The Cottage', Thingwall Lane, and the upper windows segmental arched. Now Nos. 224 and 250 are the least altered houses with original windows and plain panelled doors. Nos. 222 and 224 are set in a central gable with an open doorway between them allowing access to the rear of the properties.

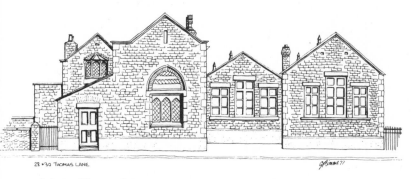

28 & 30 Thomas Lane

256 East Prescot Road

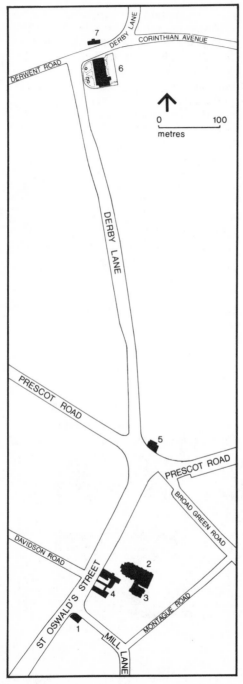

1 2 Mill Lane and 51
  St. Oswald's Street
2 St. Oswald's Church
3 St. Oswald's
  Presbytery
4 St. Oswald's Schools
5 Barclay's Bank
  Prescot Road
6 St. Paul's Church
7 75 Derby Lane

19 *Old Swan*

Old Swan was one of the fastest growing districts of Liverpool in the late nineteenth century. Its name probably derives from its once notable Inn, formerly called 'The Three Swans'.

The walk starts on the corner of St. Oswald's Street and Mill Lane. **No. 2 Mill Lane,** an early nineteenth century brick building, forms an effective curve to this corner and includes **No. 51 St. Oswald's Street.** At the mid point is a doorway with fluted Doric columns and a semi-circular fanlight. To the right, the late nineteenth century shop front with pilasters is now sadly boarded up and neglected. Leading on from this in Mill Lane is a terrace of mid-nineteenth century houses of three-storeys with projecting ground floor windows, mostly in poor condition. The sandstone wall opposite encloses the churchyard of **St. Oswald's Church** which is entered from St. Oswald's Street. Of the original church of 1842, by A. W. N. Pugin, only the west steeple remains. This has a slender broach spire and finely carved detail in the decorated style. It was, in fact, the first Roman Catholic Church in the North of England to have a steeple since the Reformation. The Relief Act of 1791, whilst allowing Catholics to have churches, forebade steeples and bells. The church itself was rebuilt in 1951-7 by Adrian Gilbert Scott, whose design, though necessarily simpler than the original building, nevertheless tries to match the scale of the steeple. The result, however, is rather dull. The interior space is dominated by a series of huge concrete parabolic arches which sit uncomfortably on squat sandstone piers. Immediately to the south of the nave is **The Presbytery,** a mid-nineteenth century Gothic stone building of two storeys with pointed arched windows. **St. Oswald's Schools,** built in 1855, are attributed to A. W. N. Pugin, though there is much doubt expressed about this. Certainly the picturesque layout of the school buildings, with cloistered entrance, lawns, hedge-lined walks and gardens, all under the shadow of the church spire, are reminiscent of Pugin's ideal of a medieval Christian community life. Unfortunately, a large part of the grounds are now disused.

Also defaced and suffering neglect is the Old Wesley Chapel built in 1845 and situated adjacent to the school buildings on St. Oswald's Street.

On the other side of the street is a large corporation housing

St. Oswald's Schools

Barclay's Bank

St. Paul's Church

160

development of the 1930s inspired by the then fashionable work of the modern Dutch architect, Dudok, and reminiscent of the great liners lying at berth in the River Mersey. Across Prescot Road, on the corner of Derby Lane, is a splendidly elaborate **Barclays Bank** — again a one time Martins Bank building by the prolific local architects, Grayson and Ould. Here they displayed their virtuosity in all the major architectural styles within one building. It has a Dutch gable to Prescot Road with Renaissance window surrounds, and a plain gable to Derby Lane with a two-storey stone mullioned oriel. The entrance is set between these at an angle, with a Gibbs doorway surround and open pediment. Above this is an octagonal turret with machicolations, surmounted by a concave roof and timber lantern. The whole building is striped in bands of white Portland stone and bright red brick, and whether one approves of such stylistic extravagance or not, it certainly commands attention.

A short distance up Derby Lane on the right is **St. Paul's Church,** Stoneycroft, by Sir Giles Gilbert Scott, built in 1916. This is a highly original and convincing building designed during the time when Scott was engaged on radically changing his design for Liverpool Cathedral. It is built of pale grey brick in a severe style with massive central tower and pyramidal roof. The interior, which has recently been well restored, has three high square groin-vaulted bays supported on large internal piers which are hollowed out to form low passages, a constructional device used in certain medieval French churches.

No. 75 Derby Lane, formerly called Moss Cottage, situated opposite the church, is an eighteenth century cottage which has now been roughcast rendered and painted.

In Derwent Road are some attractive 'unlisted' early Victorian buildings, notably Nos. 3-25, a two-storey terrace of stuccoed houses each of three bays with a central doorway. The three-storey terrace opposite is of a slightly later date, but the street is unified by low sandstone walls, standard gateposts and good front gardens with many trees. Derwent Square with large semi-detached Italianate houses on one side is also of interest.

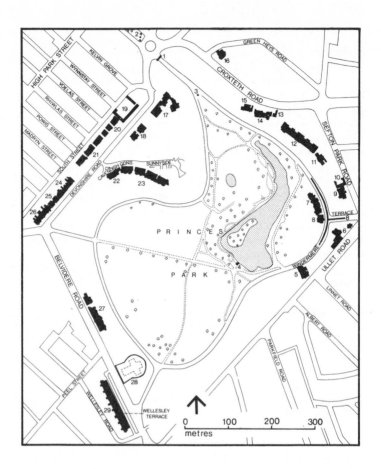

1 Main Entrance	**11** 12 Sefton Park Road	Devonshire Road
2 Statue of	and Coach House	**22** Cavendish Gardens
Hugh Stowel Brown	**12** Princes Park	**23** Sunnyside
3 Richard Vaughan	Mansions	**24** 38-52, 54 and 56
Yates Memorial	**13** 18A Croxteth Road	Devonshire Road
4 Boathouse	**14** 16 and 18	**25** 58 and 60
5 Parkside	Croxteth Road	Devonshire Road
9 Ullet Road	**15** 14 Croxteth Road	**26** 62-72 Devonshire
6 Bellerive Convent	**16** 7 Croxteth Road	Road
and Lodge	**17** St. Edmund's	**27** 13-17 Belvedere
7 1-4 Windermere	College	Road
Terrace	**18** 3 and 5	**28** Site of
8 Windermere House	Devonshire Road	St. Paul's Church
and Iron Street	**19** Livery Stables	**29** 44-74 Belvedere
Lamps	**20** 12, 14 and 16	Road
9 16 and 18	Devonshire Road	
Sefton Park Road	**21** 18 and 20, 22	
10 14 Sefton Park Road	and 24, 26 and 28	

20 Princes Park

Princes Park and its residential surroundings are together a fine example of nineteenth century development. The land was bought in 1843 from the Earl of Sefton by Richard Vaughan Yates, a prominent citizen of Liverpool, who commissioned Sir Joseph Paxton to design a park of approximately 90 acres with residential development in and around it.

This was Paxton's first independent commission and it was followed immediately by one for the design of Birkenhead Park. The ideas that Paxton incorporated in his design for these parks, such as ornamental lakes, artifically mounded hills, curving paths, along which the gentry could parade, and subtly contrived views and vistas established the pattern for all future Victorian park design in Britain, America and on the Continent.

Although the present residential layouts vary to some degree from the original designs, they are, if anything, built to a more interesting pattern. The residences include elegant stucco and brick terraces, individual classical houses of great merit and charm and exuberant late Victorian villas with every degree of intricate detail imaginable.

The appropriate starting point for a visit to Princes Park is the **main entrance,** at the corner of Croxteth Road and Devonshire Road, probably designed by Pennethorne. It consists of two concave walls about five feet in height with an open panelled parapet and end square piers with cornices in ashlar. The main features are the two large stone piers with dentilled cornices and the four distinctive ornamental gates. Opposite the gate, at the start of the Boulevard, is the **statue of Hugh Stowell Brown,** a stone figure standing on a red granite plinth facing the Park.

Inside the Park, facing the main entrance, is the **memorial to Richard Vaughan Yates,** who was the founder of Princes Park. It takes the form of a red granite obelisk on a square base incorporated in which are two round urns forming drinking fountains.

The most noteworthy of the park buildings is **The Boathouse,** at the south end of the lake, probably designed by John Robertson in 1842 under the direction of Paxton. It takes the form of a timber chalet, with overhanging eaves, on a stone base. Distinctive features are the ornamental fretting to the balcony and stair rail.

Princes Park Gate

Princes Park Mansions

164

Leaving the Park at the gate leading to Windermere Terrace is **Parkside, No. 9 Ullet Road,** a mid-nineteenth century villa with its main facade overlooking Princes Park. A good example of its style it is finished in stucco with a variety of sash windows with interesting architrave and cornice details.

On the corner of Windermere Terrace and Ullet Road is **Bellerive Convent and Lodge,** originally a villa of mid-nineteenth century date. Of irregular plan its most significant feature is the pyramid-roofed staircase tower. The lodge is stuccoed, like the main building, with a hipped roof and curved bow window.

The most significant group of buildings in this area is **Nos. 1-4 Windermere Terrace,** four houses of mid-nineteenth century date of symmetrical design with one continuous roof. Distinctive features include the balustrade parapet and moulded string courses as well as the projecting porches.

Windermere House has the most impressive setting, facing the entrance to the terrace from Sefton Park. It is a detached Victorian villa, stuccoed, with a large projecting porch of classic design featuring four Ionic columns, a round arched entrance flanked with round headed windows, finished off by a bold cornice.

Before leaving Windermere Terrace mention must be made of the distinctive Victorian **iron street lamps.** There are nine in number each with fluted stems, cross arms and lantern tops.

Proceeding northwards along Sefton Park Road on the left can be seen **Nos. 16 and 18,** a pair of stuccoed Victorian villas with typical round-arched windows, bands, and sash windows.

No. 14, adjoining, was probably originally the stable block to No. 16 and is now a dwelling. It is single storey in height and the main elevations look out on to an attractive courtyard.

Built in the late Victorian cottage style, **No. 12,** with its **coach house** attached, is a good example of a two-storey stone built residence of that time. A distinctive feature is the projecting, castellated, mock tower in the middle of the facade.

Princes Park Mansions occupy an important site at the corner of Sefton Park Road and Croxteth Road. The south front, facing on to Princes Park has a basement and four storeys with an added fifth storey thus making it the largest Victorian building in the area. Designed as flats in 1843 by Wyatt Papworth the most distinctive features of this stuccoed building are the iron balconies and the central Doric entrance with cornice and balustraded parapet.

Adjoining is **No. 18A Croxteth Road,** formerly a coach house but now converted to a cottage with 'round eye' windows and gabled half dorme.

Nos. 16 and 18 Croxteth Road are semi-detached Victorian villas of stuccoed finish. Typical features are the moulded string course and top cornice with brackets.

Alongside is the detached villa, **No. 14 Croxteth Road,** which is constructed of stone to a symmetrical design. The central door, with its flanking windows, set in pilasters with decorative frieze and cornice, is the most distinctive feature.

Opposite is **No. 7 Croxteth Road** another detached mid-nineteenth century villa. It is stuccoed with rusticated ground floor and projecting eaves cornice. The large two storeyed bay window with sash windows and moulded architraves gives the building a distinctive look.

Proceeding past the Park Gates, on the south side of Devonshire Road, is **St. Edmund's College,** the middle portion of which was designed by Waterhouse in 1863. A wing in the same style was added in 1903 and there is a later extension to the right. The original building is of brick construction with bands of blue brick and stone. The doorway has a pointed arch with a decorative timber and slate porch culminating in a weather vane. A stained glass window in the stairway commemorates the date of the building.

Nos. 3 and 5 Devonshire Road are two detached Victorian villas, stuccoed and three storeys in height. The former has, as a central feature, a round-arched porch with clustered pilasters which is raised five steps from ground level and No. 5 features a projecting top cornice on brackets.

On the opposite side of Devonshire Road is a large square courtyard block of **livery stables** in brick and dressed stone. The main facade to the road is in the form of a heavily moulded segmental stone arch and this design feature is repeated several times in 'blind' form on either side. The rear of the courtyard contains the former stables now garages with 'round eye' windows above.

No. 12 Devonshire Road is a three-storeyed stuccoed Victorian villa with a central Ionic porch and is identical with its neighbour, **No. 14.**

Also in the classical Victorian style is the villa **No. 16 Devonshire Road** which, together with the neighbouring semi-detached villas, **Nos. 18 and 20, 22 and 24, 26 and 28,** in similar style, are three-storey buildings with typical window and moulded cornice details.

Cavendish Gardens on the opposite side of Devonshire Road at this point is a terrace of eight houses built for the Yates family in the mid-nineteenth century. They are stuccoed, three-storeys in height and symmetrical in design. Particular attention has been paid to the first floor windows which are emphasised by

Windermere Terrace

'Sunnyside', Princes Park

entablatures and central cast iron balconies. The end elevations have fluted Corinthian columns whilst the facade to the Park has one central pediment supported by giant Corinthian columns at the first floor.

Adjoining is **Sunnyside** which is a three-storey curving terrace, consisting of four pairs of semi-detached Victorian villas. All the details are particularly good with particular reference to the Tuscan style porches and the windows with their Gothic style geometric glazing bars.

Continuing along Devonshire Road is the terrace of stuccoed mid-Victorian houses, **Nos. 38 to 52,** notable for their variety of porch designs, some with Ionic columns and iron balconies. **Nos. 54 and 56** and the adjoining **Nos. 58 and 60** are identical mid-Victorian villas, stuccoed three-storeys in height notable for their steep gables and wavy-edged barge boards.

The last block on this side, **Nos. 62 to 72 Devonshire Road,** is symmetrical in design with three storeys and basement. Notable features are the common porches with cornices, the pierced balustraded balconies, the moulded architraves, and cornices on ornamented brackets.

Turning left into Belvidere Road, **Nos. 13 to 17** are three almost identical villas now used as a school. They date back to the 1840s and are of brick dressed with stucco and stone. Each has a central door with two round-headed lights and No. 17 has an Ionic porch. Of particular merit are the **iron railings** and the **two iron lampholders** in front.

Nearby is the site of **St. Paul's Church,** a once notable landmark in the area which was unfortunately recently demolished in spite of a Pastoral Measure which sought to retain the tower and its flanking wings.

At the end of Belvidere Road, on its west side, is the impressive long Victorian terrace, **Nos. 44 to 74,** fronting on to its own private road. Brick-built, of three-storeys and basement, with stuccoed ground floor, it shows consistency in design and detail. Of note are the unfluted Tuscan porches on the projecting centre and end blocks, and the variety of window details where these relate to different floor levels.

21 Toxteth

This walk contains a small number of buildings which are situated some distance apart. Toxteth is an area of some interest, being traditionally one of the more deprived areas of Liverpool and much evidence of this fact, both of a historical and current nature, is all too visible. This is in striking contrast to the nearby Princes Park area.

In the Middle Ages the area was a deer park, and the earliest building of any significance was probably the **Toxteth Unitarian Chapel.** Situated on the corner of Ullet Road and Park Road, this was formerly Presbyterian and dates from 1618. It was largely rebuilt in 1774, and the porch was added in 1841, and former porch being on the opposite side. The Chapel stands in a small churchyard and is now very confined by the busy road and surrounding buildings. Inside there are three galleries, the connecting one being added at the time of the rebuilding, and box pews. On the opposite corner of Ullet Road is **The Turner Memorial Home** built in extensive grounds in 1881-3 as a memorial to Charles Turner and designed by Alfred Waterhouse, the architect of the Prudential Building in Dale Street. It is a huge rambling building in Tudor Gothic style, basically of two-storeys, but given increased scale by a third storey in the irregular gables and a tall staircase turret with tiny windows and a conical roof set in an angle of the building. The Chapel at the south end has a perpendicular east window and inside a high timber roof and aisles. In the entrance is a white marble statue of Charles Turner and his son seated looking at a plan of the building. **The Lodge** has four wings and a central chimney.

Beyond the Toxteth Chapel in Park Road there are three pairs of Victorian semi-detached villas, one having an elaborate balcony, and one pair with classical mouldings. All are in very poor condition. No. 357, the butcher's shop, has an attractive early twentieth century shop front with an original glass name sign and a dentilled cornice with projecting heads of cows. **The Public Offices** in High Park Street, now housing a branch of the Ministry of Health and Social Security, was built in 1865-6 to a design by Layland. It is a heavy and imposing ashlar fronted block with a three bay pedimented centre and venetian window.

The Reservoir alongside with its sloping walls and round angle tower was built in 1855. On the corner of Mill Street and

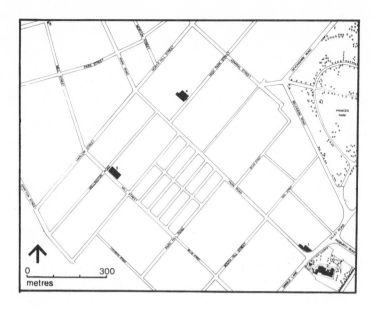

1 Toxteth Unitarian
  Chapel
2 Turner Memorial
  Home
3 Lodge to Turner
  Memorial Home
4 Public Offices
  High Park Street
5 Florence Institute
  for Boys

Wellington Road (across Park Road) is situated **The Florence Institute for Boys,** an interesting and attractive building. It is interesting as a piece of social history, having been built as a youth club in 1889, a function which it still performs. On the corner there is an octagonal turret, to Wellington Street, three Dutch gables with a large window of cusped lights, and to Mill Street a series of shallow canted two-storey bays with mullioned and transomed windows and ornamented terracotta friezes. Further along Mill Street, on the corner with Northumberland Street is a **Post Office pillar box** of the hexagonal type erected in Liverpool between 1866 and 1879.

Toxteth Unitarian Chapel

Turner Memorial Home

171

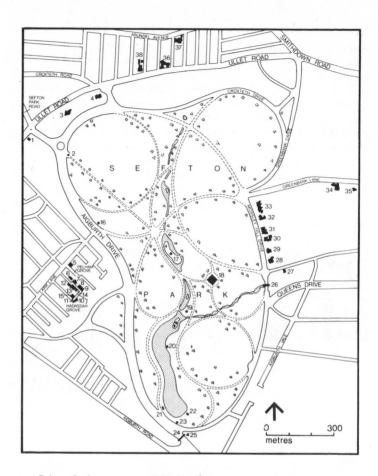

1 Princes Lodge
2 Samuel Smith M.P.
Monument
3 Rankin Hall
4 Sefton Court
Mansions
5 Albert Public House
Lark Lane
6 7 and 9
Hadassah Grove
7 11 and 13
Hadassah Grove
8 15 Hadassah Grove
9 17 Hadassah Grove
10 19 Hadassah Grove
11 Stone Arch
12 2 Hadassah Grove
13 4 and 6
Hadassah Grove

14 8 Hadassah Grove
15 14 Hadassah Grove
16 Drinking Fountain
17 The Bandstand
18 The Palm House
19 William Rathbone
Statue
20 East Shelter
21 West Shelter
22 The Boat House
23 Drinking Fountain
24 Aigburth Road
Entrance Gate
25 Fulwood Lodge
26 Mossley Hill Drive
Iron Bridge
27 'The Bridge'
28 'Bridge House'
7 Mossley Hill Drive

29 'Duffus'
6 Mossley Hill Drive
30 5 Mossley Hill Drive
31 3 and 4
Mossley Hill Drive
32 2 Mossley Hill Drive
33 'Gladhill'
1 Mossley Hill Drive
34 'Greenbank House'
Greenbank Lane
35 Greenbank Lodge
36 Unitarian Church
and Hall
37 Roman Catholic
Church of St. Clare
38 St. Agnes Church
Hall and Vicarage

22 Sefton Park Area

In 1866, the Corporation of Liverpool announced an international competition for the design and layout of a public park to the south of the City centre. The winning design was submitted by M. Andre of Paris and Mr. Hornblower of Liverpool, and resulted in the creation of Liverpool's largest public park, covering approximately 233 acres. The park was named after the Earl of Sefton, from whom the land was originally purchased, and was opened to the public in 1872. The site was originally composed entirely of agricultural land, devoid of trees or plantations. The transformation of this land into the present magnificent park illustrates the magnitude and quality of both the concept and its achievement.

As a means of securing a financial return, building sites were provided within the park. A number of villas, of which some eighty-four remain, were erected as an integral part of the design, being neither a rigid boundary to the park nor intrusions into it. Although some of the villas are of great architectural merit, the majority are more of interest for their eccentric style and solid craftsmanship so exuberantly created in the Victorian period.

Adjacent to the fine park entrance, where Sefton Park Road, Aigburth Drive and Croxteth Drive meet, is **Princes Lodge,** one of the typical lodge buildings in red brick and half timber sited at each formal park entrance, and, immediately facing, in the park itself, is the **monument to Samuel Smith, M.P.,** who died in 1906. It takes the form of a tall granite obelisk on a square plinth with sculptured panels and bronze inscription. The sculptor was C. J. Allen and the architects, Willink and Thicknesse.

To the left of the entrance is **Rankin Hall,** a tall Victorian Gothic mansion built of brick and red sandstone. A large tower with an octagonal vice ending in a turret dominates the entrance front. The high gables have ornamented bargeboards and are filled in with terracotta patterns. A projecting stair window on the right has elaborate Tudor Gothic tracery, and the garden front has an arcaded wooden balcony on the top floor overlooking the park, and a balustraded terrace lower down over a basement.

Nearby is **Sefton Court Mansions** an imposing three-storey late nineteenth century stucco house situated at the corner of the Croxteth Drive entrance to the Park. The elevations are asymmetrical and boldly composed, particularly the entrance facade with its porch of unfluted Doric columns and the large pedimented second floor window with richly moulded architraves. The entrance front has an elegant bow window supporting a balustraded balcony which looks out over spacious lawns and the park.

On the west side of Aigburth Drive and through the Lark Lane gate to the park is Hadassah Grove entered through a private street with stone gate piers. The buildings in this quiet cul-de-sac with the **Albert public house** form an outstanding group probably dating back to 1840.

Nos. 7 and 9 Hadassah Grove are a two-storey brick pair each with a central doorway with panelled pilasters. The many paned sash windows on the ground and first floors are distinctive features.

The adjoining **Nos. 11 and 13** have similar design details but are stuccoed and **No. 15** has been pebbledashed.

No. 17 is a brick villa with deep overhanging eaves and sash windows with shutters. Of particular note is the iron verandah. Of similar style is the neighbouring **No. 19.**

Between Nos. 19 and 14 is a **stone segmental arch set within two pairs of pilasters and a cornice.** Although now blocked it probably led to the stables which served this private estate.

On the opposite side from No. 11 is **No. 2 Hadassah Grove** a free-standing brick house with interesting window details and a centre panelled door with flanking pilasters topped with a frieze and cornice.

Nos. 4 and 6 are a brick pair with typical central doors and window details, whilst **No. 8** is similar in many ways to No. 2 with, in addition, a stone cornice.

The last house of the group is **No. 14** which adjoins the gateway at the far end of the street. It has a distinctive central doorway with fluted columns and a round fanlight in a brick arch. The facade has four brick pilasters.

In the park, a short way from Lark Lane, is a **drinking fountain** which is a replica of Alfred Gilbert's Eros from the Shaftsbury memorial in Piccadilly Circus. It was made in 1932 and is signed A. B. Burton.

Proceeding south, in the centre of the lake is the **bandstand,** octagonal in plan, consisting of a brick base and slender iron columns supporting a red-tiled pagoda roof finished off with a domed lantern and ornamental wind vane.

The most significant park building is the **Palm House**

Sefton Park Lodge

Albert Public House

175

opened in 1896, designed and built by Mackenzie and Moncur. It is also octagonal in plan with three tiers of glass domes on arcading. The interior has tall slender iron columns and a central spiral iron stair leads to an upper level catwalk.

South of the Palm House is the **statue of William Rathbone,** a grey granite plinth with a standing white stone figure on top. The reliefs, by T. Brock, 1876, represent the philanthropic activities of this well-known Liverpool family and the figure is the work of the sculptor, T. Foley, 1877.

A number of small buildings around the boating lake are of interest. These include the identical **shelters** on the east and west sides. They date from 1870 and are thought to be the work of the park designers, Andre and Hornblower. Square in plan they are, typically, of timber construction with an overhanging slate roof.

The boathouse, at the south end of the lake, is of similar date and construction — also thought to be the work of Andre and Hornblower, as is the **drinking fountain** at the junction of Aigburth Drive and Mossley Hill Drive. It is built of sandstone in the Gothic style with entwined dolphins, under an open canopy supported by marble columns, as a central feature.

Opposite is the **entrance gate** from Aigburth Road, which consists of six red granite piers surmounted by lanterns with an ornamental central arch bearing the City's coat of arms. Alongside is **Fulwood Lodge** a typical Andre and Hornblower design in red and blue patterned brick and stone with steep slate roof and carved bargeboards.

Following the carriage drive northwards is the **iron bridge** on Mossley Hill Drive built in 1870 and, once again, by the park designers. It is a cast iron bridge over a ravine landscape feature and consists of brick end piers with stone cornices each finished with an iron ornamental lamp. The roadway is supported by an iron trellis set in round arches and iron piers and completed with iron railings.

Overlooking the iron bridge is a Victorian cottage called **'The Bridge'.** This has a variety of picturesque details such as floral patterned plasterwork in gables, partly timbered walls, bay windows, and an oriel on scroll brackets over the entrance.

Adjacent to the bridge is the first of a number of detached Victorian villas, **'Bridge House', No. 7 Mossley Hill Drive,** of red brick construction with matching red tiled roof. Among its notable features are the tall chimneys, the stone balustraded balcony and the inset arched doorway flanked by stone Ionic pilasters.

The neighbouring **'Duffus', No. 6,** is of red and brown brick with terracotta ornament culminating in a red tiled roof with

Hadassah Grove

The Palm House

tall chimneys. **No. 5** introduces red sandstone along with red brick and is unusual in that one gable is of timber whilst the other is terracotta. An additional feature is the two-storey stone canted bay window.

Nos. 3 and 4 are semi-detached Victorian villas but not identical. Although No. 4 has the usual mixture of brick with red tiled roof, No. 3 has an octagonal turret with an octagonal spirelet roof on the angle and a Tudor doorway.

The detached villa, **No. 2** Mossley Hill Drive, is of similar materials but differs in that its sash windows have segmental arches. The last house is **'Gladhill', No. 1,** a long detached villa in red brick and timber. It has small 'cottage' type casement windows some of which have stone mullions and transoms. The gables are covered with 'fishscale' patterned tiles and this house also has a Tudor doorway.

The two stone gate piers at the Greenbank Lane entrance to the house are of particular note. They are square in plan with carved panels of oak leaves and acorns finished off on top by iron lampholders.

'Greenbank House' on Greenbank Lane, was the home of the Rathbone family from 1787. The main block is a marriage of Georgian and Gothic styles but the most distinctive feature — a lace-like cast iron screen on the garden facade — is a later addition (about 1815) and is typical of the decorative cast iron work in Liverpool about this time, a style which, in turn, spread to the Colonies and America with Liverpool's shipping trade to these countries. The building is now used as a club for University staff and students.

Returning into the park and proceeding the length of Greenbank Road can be found the third of the entrance lodges, **Greenbank Lodge,** somewhat larger than the others it is nevertheless typical Andre and Hornblower design with red brick, steep slate roof and decorated bargeboards.

Turning left and along Ullet Road on the right hand side can be found the **Unitarian Church and Hall,** 1896-1902, designed by Thomas and Percy Worthington who were Manchester Unitarians, and represents the strongest period of this Church in Liverpool linked as it then was with famous families such as the Roscoes, Rathbones, Holts and Booths. The church is one of the most ambitious Unitarian churches in the country and makes an excellent group with the hall and linking Memorial Passage. Built in red brick with stone dressings and interior it has a large clerestorey but no tower. The west doorway has beaten copper doors in the Art Nouveau style, by Richard Rathbone, and the library and vestry contain frescoes by Gerald Moria, 1902. Other internal features of note are the Art Nouveau light fittings, stained glass by Morris & Co., a bust of Roscoe by Gibson dated 1834 and a monument to William Rathbone by Foley, 1874.

The Roman Catholic Church of St. Clare in Arundel Avenue was built in 1888-90, only three years later than St. Agnes. Designed by Leonard Stokes, one of the most inventive of late Victorian architects, it is a strikingly original building, and was illustrated in the inter-war edition of the Encyclopaedia Britannica as an example of modern architecture. It is still Gothic in style, but it is so freely adapted that it could not be said which period is responsible for its inspiration. Note the turret and spire, and on the south side the confessionals with irregularly placed windows. The interior has deeply projecting wall piers or buttresses forming side chapels, with aisles running behind an arcade of lozenge shaped piers placed transverse to the nave. The presbytery of the same date and also by Stokes adjoins the east end of the church and is similarly free in composition. The entrance with a pointed stone arched opening is surmounted by a label, the carved head stops of which are a remarkably early example of Art Nouveau decoration.

St. Agnes Church, Ullet Road, was paid for by Douglas Horsfall, a wealthy City stockbroker and benefactor of a number of churches. Built in 1883 in red brick externally and stone internally and making skilful use of architectural massing it is considered to be the most impressive Victorian church in Liverpool. Designed in the thirteenth century style by John Pearson, the architect for Truro Cathedral.

Connected to the church by a passage is Norman Shaw's **St. Agnes Church Hall** built in 1887 in simple Gothic style.

This fine group of buildings is completed by Norman Shaw's **St. Agnes Vicarage,** 1887. Built in brick with stone mullions and leaded windows it relies on the careful handling of scale and detail for architectural effect. Although small it is considered to represent a significant step in the development of the modern domestic style.

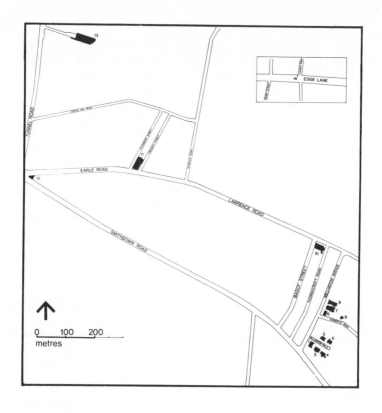

23 *From Smithdown Road to Edge Hill Station*

Near to Sefton Park and just off Smithdown Road, (opposite Sefton General Hospital) are situated a surprising group of 'listed' buildings. These are centred around Wellington Avenue where unfortunately four 'listed' Victorian semi-detached houses have recently been demolished. There remains, however, **No. 2 Wellington Avenue,** which is attached to **No. 2 Wellington Field,** and with which it forms an identical pair of plain stuccoed villas. Wellington Field is a small private road of semi-detached houses set in gardens and lined with large trees. **Nos. 3 and 5** have a centre gable with cusped barge boards. **Nos. 4 and 6 and 8 and 10** are similar, but have moulded architraves and curious carved barge boards. **Nos. 7 and 9** are of brick with stone lintels and labels.

No. 1A Wellington Avenue is an amusing three-storeyed brick house carrying applied stucco decoration which is obviously far too elaborate for its size. Consequently the full entablature over the first floor window clashes with the moulded architraves surrounding the pointed arched window above, whilst on the ground floor the exaggerated projecting doorcasing competes with the stuccoed bay for room. **Nos. 12 and 14 Wellington Avenue** are a good pair of early Victorian houses faced with roughcast render. The doorways have fluted Doric half-columns and attractive semi-circular fanlights with glazing bars intact.

The Methodist Church and Sunday School form an interesting pair of buildings set side by side facing the road. Built in 1904 of red brick with bright yellow terracotta dressings, one is virtually a dimutive version of the other. Details of the two are, however, different and show the vast range of ornamentation obtainable in tiles at that time. The church has some Art Nouveau glass in the west window. Behind the church is **No. 3 Garmoyle Road,** a scored stucco Victorian villa with wide eaves and a large two-storey stone bay to one side.

Two blocks away on the corner of Lawrence Road and Bagot Street is the **Church of St. Bridget** by E. A. Heffer. This was built in 1872 and is very unusual for its date in taking the pure form of a basilica. There is a very high plain campanile at the north-west corner and an entrance niche at the west end surmounted by a carved medallion containing the head of God. Two other medallions have figures of saints, the one at the base of

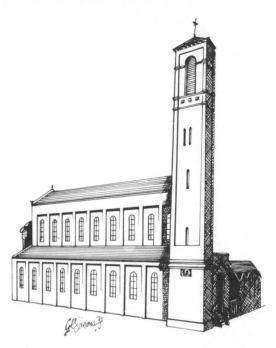

Church of St. Bridget

Church of St. Dunstan

the campanile is perhaps St. Bridget. The inside is basilican also, even having a free-standing altar in the apse, but the large pulpit has Gothic detail. The mosaic reredos of the Last Supper is by Salviati of 1886.

Nearby in Earle Road is a church of a very different nature, the **Church of St. Dunstan** of 1886-9 by Aldridge and Deacon. This has a tall west front with two flanking angle turrets all built in a very harsh red Ruabon brick. A moulded brick window of five stepped lancets is set in a large pointed arch with the tympanum containing the attenuated carved forms of Christ and angels. The porch is crowned by a statue of St. Dunstan in a niche with the gable filled in with patterned red tiles. The interior is all of brick apart from round stone piers. On the sharp corner of Earle Road and Smithdown Road is a fine former **Martins Bank** building. This is of ashlar with a rusticated basement and three-storeys above. There is a corner entrance with one window on each upper floor flanked by coupled Doric, Ionic and Corinthian columns.

Edge Hill Station in Tunnel Road, is the oldest passenger railway station in the world still in operation. The twin two-storey pavilions opposite one another alongside the north and south platforms are the original buildings of 1836 built by Stephenson when the Liverpool to Manchester railway was extended to the new Lime Street terminus. The first terminus had been at Crown Street which was then given over to goods and coal traffic. The original pavilions are of seven bays; these were extended in 1848 in matching style but of single storey only. A square brick engine house with boldly modillioned cornice was built behind the north extension in 1848. The whole station is at present in a depressing state of disrepair, but it is hoped that the main buildings will be restored for the 150th anniversary in 1980 of the opening of the world's first passenger railway line.

A **Post Office pillar box** on the corner of Edge Lane and Church Road is of the type in use in Liverpool in 1863.

Edge Hill Station in 1836, from a contemporary print by Ackermann

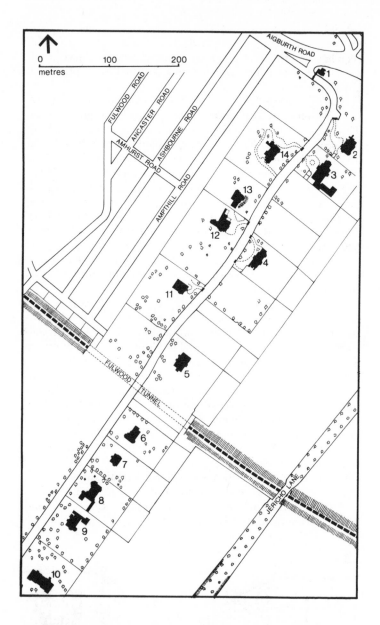

1 The Lodge and four entrance piers
2 3 Fulwood Park
3 5 Fulwood Park
4 9 and 9A Fulwood Park
5 Osborne House
6 15 Fulwood Park
7 17 Fulwood Park
8 19 Fulwood Park
9 21 Fulwood Park
10 23 and 25 Fulwood Park
11 8 Fulwood Park
12 6 Fulwood Park
13 4 Fulwood Park
14 2A and 2B Fulwood Park

Fulwood Park is a private residential estate, similar to that at Grassendale and Cressington, situated alongside the River Mersey between St. Michael's Hamlet and Otterspool Park. It dates back to about 1840 and is of a simple layout with a carriageway entered off Aigburth Road by way of a gate lodge and entrance gates. Some very large detached and semi-detached houses, of stucco finished Italiante style, line both sides of this road.

The Lodge, No. 1A, is of stone, two-storeys high with distinctive octagonal chimneys and labels to each window. The single storey wings are in consistent style.

Beside the lodge are the **four entrance piers** of red sandstone, two of which are square in plan and two octagonal, each with matching cornice and capping. The gates have been removed.

The large house, **No. 3,** now converted into flats, was built around 1840. It is two-storeys in height, stuccoed, with Italianate features such as the Tuscan porch, cornice with modillions, and pierced balconies. The round arched windows in rectangular moulded architraves are distinctive.

No. 5 is a house in similar style but of three-bay symmetrical design with, in this case, an Ionic style doorway and pediment. More recent additions to the south and north are in matching style. The octagonal, panelled sandstone gatepiers to this property are of particular note.

On the same side of the access road are **Nos. 9 and 9A** built originally as a single house in 1840 with a symmetrical facade two-storeys in height. Features of note are the small shallow porch and glazed window above in moulded architraves, Venetian windows on each floor with triple sashes in moulded architraves surmounted by cornices supported on scroll brackets, the cornice strings and top moulded cornice. The two pairs of square gatepiers in front with their Gothic panelling and modillioned cornices are worthy of note.

No. 11, is also circa 1840 in similar style, stuccoed with distinctive moulded architrave and cornice features. The side facade is more unusual with its five windows and rectangular porch with Tuscan pilasters.

The adjoining **No. 15** is asymmetrical, with a two-storey, five-

Entrance Lodge, Fulwood Park

15 Fulwood Park

17 Fulwood Park

11 Fulwood Park

sided, bay window, but nevertheless of similar style to its neighbours. The doorway, which is glazed and pedimented, and the nearby open portico on three square piers are of particular interest.

No. 17 continues the style but with a more unusual projecting wing whilst the main block has a portico of two square piers with moulded capitals and three round-arched windows. The dormers are a later addition.

Another facade which incorporates a two-storey bay window is that of **No. 19,** which like its neighbours, dates back to 1840. The multi-paned sashes on each floor are a distinctive feature as is the wide portico on square piers with its frieze and cornice continuing along most of the front.

No. 21 completes the group 15 to 21 which are similar in style and probably the work of the same architect containing, as they do, architectural features of consistent style.

The last building on this side, **Nos. 23 and 25,** is a pair of mid-nineteenth century semi-detached villas in the Gothic style, two-storey, and stuccoed. The gables with their distinctive barge-boards, the gabled porches and the twelve-paned sash windows with labels and carved headstops are of particular note.

Returning in the direction of the main entrance gate is **No. 8** which is a detached two-storey house in the typical stuccoed style of the Park. It differs in that its main elevation looks towards the river and has as its main features an asymmetrically placed bow window with moulded cornice and balustraded balcony. The gatepiers surmounted by sculptured lions are of particular note.

The adjoining **No. 6** is L-shaped in plan with a symmetrical front of three windows and a projecting central bay. Of interest are the two pairs of gate piers of tapering design with recessed panels and the two lamps surmounting them.

No. 4 is asymmetrical with its main facade once again facing on to the main entrance road. It has two projecting bays on the ground floor, one of which is over a large semi-circular bow. Of note is the eaves treatment with its deep projection on brackets.

The last building on this side contains **Nos. 2A and 2B,** originally one villa dating back to 1840. This is larger than its neighbours having three floors plus a basement. Its facade is symmetrical with five-windowed bays, stretching over two storeys, flanking the central three windows. Notable features are the continuous string course between ground and first floor, the first floor iron balconies and the parapets with inset balustrades. The gate piers to No. 2A with their Gothic arrow-slit detail are good examples of their kind.

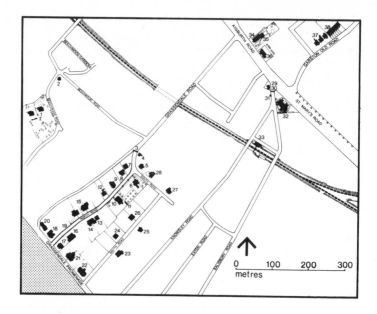

1 'The Dell' and
  'The Chestnuts'
2 16 Beechwood Road
3 Four Gate Piers to
  Grassendale Park
4 1 North Road
5 'Arcadia'
6 'Ormiston'
7 2 North Road
8 'Daylesford'
9 'Norton'
10 11 North Road
11 The Coach House
12 Angorfa'
13 21 North Road
14 'Langdale' and
  'Holt House'
15 'Wested' and
  'Woodside' and
  'Riverdale House'
  and No. 26
16 'Norwood' and
  'Grange House'
17 'Stapley'
18 'The Old House'
19 Iron Street Lamps
20 1 Grassendale
  Promenade
21 9 and 11
  Grassendale
  Promenade

22 'Fairholme' and
  'Scarletts'
23 39 and 41
  South Road
24 'Whitehouse'
25 'Mitford Lodge'
26 12 and 14 South
  Road ('Southwood')
27 17 South Road
28 'Beechville'
29 Cressington Park
  Lodge
30 Gate Piers
31 Iron Street Lamps
32 St. Mary's Church
33 The Station
34 Church of St. Austin
35 Presbytery
36 563 and 565
  Aigburth Road
37 33, 37 and 41
  Garston Old Road
38 St. Mary's Terrace

188

25 Grassendale and Cressington Parks

Grassendale and Cressington Parks were laid out in the early to mid nineteenth century as a private speculative venture. A network of roads leading to an elegant riverside promenade was constructed and lined with sandstone plinth walls and cast iron railings. Restrictive covenants relating to the size of plots, building lines, external materials and other features of design were, and still are, administered by Trustees of the Parks. The whole area consequently achieves a unity, which is greatly enhanced by the large gardens with their wealth of planting and mature trees.

The walk starts outside the Parks, at the south end of Beechwood Road, where there is a good group of Victorian Gothic buildings. **'The Dell'** and **'The Chestnuts'** are a pair of mid-nineteenth century semi-detached stucco villas situated amongst trees with their own drive. They have curious timber finials at the base and ridge of their gables, and, on the garden side, 'The Chestnuts' has an attractive cast iron verandah with traceried spandrels and barley-twist columns. 'Beechwood' is built of rock-faced sandstone and has a large projecting chimney which is pierced with a lancet window and incised with a cross. The coach house to 'Beechwood' has arrow slits and round openings in the first floor. **No. 16 Beechwood Road** is a small mid-Victorian cottage with richly patterned Gothic barge-boards and pointed arched windows.

Finally, in this group is a very large multi-gabled stuccoed house, No. 22 Beechwood Road, which has an interesting single-storey extension with roof lantern and stone mullioned windows. 'Grassendale House' recently stood on the land now occupied by the Beechwood Gardens housing estate. Of this property, only 'Woodlea', an early Victorian stuccoed house in Grassendale Lane, now remains.

The entrance to Grassendale Park, which is at the south end of Grassendale Road, is marked by **four gate piers** of sandstone. These are pilastered and have Tuscan capitals, the middle two supporting iron lamps on voluted bases. The gates have been removed as have virtually all iron railings throughout both parks. All the listed buildings within this park date from the 1840s, and most are stucco faced. **No. 1 North Road** was the former lodge, and is of small and simple proportions. **No. 3**

('**Arcadia**'), which is situated at the corner with South Road, has a fine cast iron porch and balcony supported on fluted colonnets. **No. 5** ('**Ormiston**') is an impressively scaled classical villa. Particularly splendid is the large Ionic porch, and other details of interest include cast iron balconies, window cornices on consoles, and the overhanging roof cornice in which the gutter forms part of the moulding. **No. 2** opposite is more plain and suburban with its lean-to roof and glazed entrance canopy. **No. 4** ('**Daylesford**') has the upper parts of the gables panelled to imitate half-timbering. **No. 10** ('**Norton**') is again classical. A dentilled cornice continues across the whole front of the house including ground floor bays and porch, with an acroterion over the centre. The large porch, situated centrally, has two fluted Ionic columns in antis. **No. 11** is Gothic in some of its details, including a pointed arched doorway and lancet adjacent, but other windows are segmental headed and have keystones.

The **coach house** at the rear of No. 11 is of painted brick, and has an attractive wind vane in the form of a fox. **No. 14** ('**Angorfa**') is less interesting than other houses that are 'listed', gaining distinction only from its stuccoed front and fine setting. The three houses opposite are an example of the poor type of infill that has occurred in recent years. Grassendale and Cressington Parks were designated a Conservation Area in 1968 with the intention of protecting the original park character. It is evident that further unsympathetic development would greatly erode the arcadian nature of the area. **No. 21** was formerly a stable and coach house, but is now converted into a dwelling. Next come a fine group of three similar pairs of semi-detached villas.

'**Langdale**' and '**Holt House**' differ from the others in that the ends have panelled pilasters and the seven windows facing the road on each floor, of which some are blank, have hood moulds. The cast iron balconies to upper windows are particularly notable. '**Wensted**' and '**Woodside**' opposite, and '**Riversdale House**' and **No. 26** are identical and again have splendid ironwork balconies. All three have small end wings containing the entrance, thus leaving the front as a severe and symmetrical window and wall composition. **Nos. 33 and 35** ('**Norwood**' and '**Gage House**') are another impressive pair of semi-detached classical villas. These have end wings with open pediments, and each contains a rectangular Venetian window on the ground floor with panelled pilasters and a frieze containing wreaths. The centre portion has two french windows on the ground floor set under a Tuscan porch in antis.

No. 37 ('**Stapley**') is one of the most splendid houses in the Park, the design and detailing being particularly bold and self-

Riversdale House

The Esplanade (Grassendale Promenade)

assured. Note the details of moulded eaves on brackets, dentilled window cornices on consoles, and balustraded balconies, and compare the strength of design of the North Road facade with that of **'The Old House'** opposite. This latter has a wide vocabulary of classical details such as moulded eaves on modillions, window architraves and fluted pilaster jambs to the doorway, but the composition of these elements lacks unity. Also of particular note in North Road are the **cast iron street lamps.** These are nineteenth century and of a type once used all over Liverpool.

On The Esplanade, in front of The Old House, can be seen some of the original railings with signs of where others were cut off at the base for use in the war effort. **No. 1 ('River Bank'),** The Esplanade, situated just beyond The Old House is somewhat crude in its detailing, but has large two-storeyed bays overlooking the river. All the houses on The Esplanade are set high above the road to obtain the best views.

Nos. 9 and 11 are a pair of plain semi-detached houses with end gables facing the river. 'Fairholme' and 'Scarletts' are similar to No. 1 and are similarly crude in detailing. The stucco surface, recently repaired, is heavily scored, but lacks other enrichments.

In South Road, No. 51 has Gothic gateposts with gabled cappings and incised quatrefoils. No. 28 shows the classical style debased by ungainly proportions and crude details. In contrast, **Nos. 39 and 41,** despite additions to the rear, display great elegance and refinement in their use of classical forms. The three first floor windows have bold dentilled cornices on consoles, and sills supported on brackets. The centre one is blank and has a curved pediment, and the outer two have iron balconies. The ground floor windows are contained within pilastered architraves and dentilled cornices. **No. 22 ('Whitehouse')** is less pure in form, the proportions of three-light windows and canted bay being strictly unclassical. **No. 31 ('Mitford Lodge')** is distinguished by a hipped roof with deep overhanging eaves on brackets and heavy dentilled cornices to chimneys. **Nos. 12 and 14 ('Southwood')** are similar to Nos. 39 and 41 but lack the detail refinement, and No. 12 has unfortunately lost some of its stucco mouldings. **No. 17** has splendid neo-Greek cast iron balconies over the two canted bays to each side of the central shallow pedimented doorway. Note also the four full height pilasters dividing the front into three equal bays. No. 19, which is similar in form, has suffered from unsympathetic alterations. **No. 7 ('Beechville')** is of good quality and robust details. It has an irregular plan, the entrance being on a side wing, whilst the front has two different bays on the ground floor, one with a

The Lodge, Cressington Park

Cressington and Grassendale Station

balustraded balcony. The fine gateposts are of the same design as others in the park, including No. 5 North Road opposite (which was described earlier).

It is now necessary to continue up Grassendale Road to Aigburth Road in order to enter Cressington Park. Cressington, although laid out at the same time as Grassendale, did not develop as early or with equal architectural distinction. The individual houses did not follow the classical stucco pattern and, since they adopted no other stylistic discipline, lack unity. The plots were large, however, and the same restrictions on building lines and roadway treatment as adopted at Grassendale were imposed, achieving a common frontage, and allowing for lavish planting between the houses and the roads.

The entrance to Cressington Park is impressive. **The Lodge** is set obliquely to Aigburth Road and, though only single-storey, makes a striking impression in marking the entrance. It is built of sandstone, and has nicely cut mouldings including a scroll frieze and bracketed eaves. In the centre, and approached by steps, is a Tuscan porch in antis with two square piers. There are **four original gate piers** to the park entrance, two being new. The old ones are square, built of stone, and have cornices and fluted capitals. Just inside the park, near the lodge, is a **cast iron street lamp** of original design.

Also marking the entrance to the park is **St. Mary's Church** of 1853-4 designed by A. H. Holme in the decorated style. Inside, a feature of interest is the laminated beams supporting the roof, which form a cross of flying arches over the central space between the transepts.

The residents of these two private parks had their own railway station — **Cressington and Grassendale Station** built by the Cheshire Lines Committee in the 1840s. It is a splendid complex of buildings with elaborate details such as pierced bargeboards, half-hipped roofs, and curious eaves brackets, and has recently been restored by British Rail for the re-opening of the Garston line. The best view of the station is to be obtained from the bridge on Knowsley Road.

Though none of the original houses in Cressington Park are 'listed', mostly being late Victorian and Edwardian, many are of interest, and a perambulation via the Cressington Promenade may be considered worthwhile. In any case, some houses close to the station should be noted. No. 18 (The Vicarage), Knowsley Road, is very similar to many in Grassendale Park, as also is No. 5, except that the first floor is not stuccoed. Nos. 22 and 24, and 26 and 28, are two pairs of fine semi-detached brick villas with heavy panelled end pilasters, and projecting ground floor windows with moulded stone cornices and architraves. No. 3

opposite is a large and imposing late Victorian house with half-timbering to gables and elaborately constructed bargeboards.

The walk now continues to Aigburth Road, where a small group of 'listed' buildings are centred on the **Roman Catholic Church of St. Austin.** This was built in 1838 and is a plain rectangular building with large octagonal west pinnacles. The west front faces the road, where a large rose window with Gothic tracery is set high in the gable above a steeply roofed west porch. Inside there is a gallery supported on iron columns. Attached to the north-east end of the church is **St. Austin's Presbytery** a simple three-storey brick building. **Nos. 563 and 565 Aigburth Road** are a semi-detached pair of Victorian Gothic houses to the south of St. Austin's Church. These are faced in stucco, and each has a projecting central bay with pointed arched doorway, and Gothic door and fanlight in ogee arched architraves.

Nearby, in Garston Old Road, is another interesting group of houses. **Nos. 33, 37 and 41** are three similar detached mid-nineteenth century Victorian villas (Nos. 35 and 39 do not appear to exist). Each has bracketed eaves, moulded barge-boards and other typical picturesque details.

St. Mary's Terrace (Nos. 45-47) of 1852 is in contrast more formal. This is a particularly fine three-storey terrace of brick houses with a continuous iron balcony to the first floor. Each house has a round arched doorway with fluted Doric attached columns and moulded cornice, and is approached by a flight of stone steps with railings.

Cast Iron Street Lamp

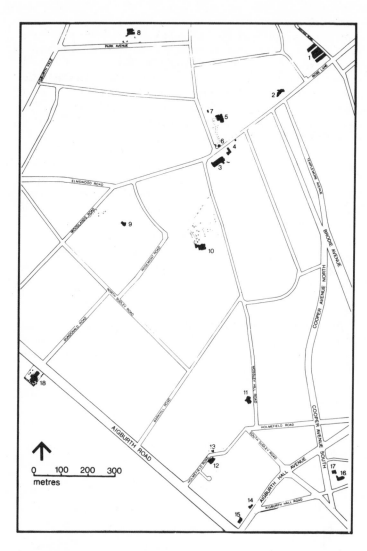

1 Stanley Terrace and
  Gordon Place and
  brick paving
2 1 and 3 Rose Lane
3 Church of
  St. Matthew and
  St. James
4 Vicarage and parish
  boundary stone
5 St. Saviour's
  Convent and stone
  balustrading

6 South Lodge and
  entrance gates and
  gate piers
7 North Lodge
8 Mansion now part of
  Mossley Hill
  Hospital
9 'Kelton'
10 Sudley Museum and
  Art Gallery
11 'Holmefield'
12 Grange Hotel

13 27 Holmefield Road
14 Stanlawe Grange
15 1 Aigburth Hall
  Avenue
16 'Oak House'
17 'Oak Cottage'
18 St. Anne's Church

In the nineteenth century Mossley Hill was probably the most exclusive residential area of Liverpool. Merchants and ship-owners built individual villas in large grounds on sites with fine views over the slopes down to the River Mersey, privacy being assured by the high sandstone walls which are a notable feature of the area. Most of the remaining villas are now occupied by institutions or have been converted into flats, though the majority are maintained in good condition.

The walk starts at Mossley Hill Station, adjacent to which there is a group of Victorian terraced houses which are in striking contrast to the general opulant nature of the surrounding area. These are **Stanley Terrace and Gordon Place** which both lead off Bridge Road and form narrow pedestrian streets between simple two-storey terraces of eight or nine dwellings each. They would not have satisfied early twentieth century bye-laws requirements, and it is remarkable that they have survived to this day. Details of doors and windows are different in the two streets, Gordon Place being wider and probably a little later in date. Gordon Place has vitreous blue **brick paving** set in diagonal patterns raised above the level of Bridge Road and separated from it by a stone sill.

At the base of the hill in Rose Lane are **Nos. 1 and 3,** a pair of semi-detached stucco villas of the 1840s, typical of many such speculative developments carried out at that time in Liverpool. Further up on the left is a **parish boundary stone** set against the stone wall at the edge of the road. Although badly worn, a vertical line is visible in the centre with 'W' on the left for Wavertree and 'G' on the right for Garston.

Splendidly situated on the brow of the hill at the junction of the four roads is the **Church of St. Matthew and St. James** by Paley and Austin of Lancaster and built in 1870-5. This is one of Liverpool's landmarks, and it is amongst the finest of the churches designed by this prolific but always competent firm of architects. In this case it is the scale which is impressive, particularly the monumental crossing tower, the interior of which is open to the inside with a narrow wall passage behind two-light openings. All stained glass, including some by Morris & Co., was destroyed during the war, but in the vestry porch is an interesting Art Nouveau memorial to the South African war.

Immediately to the east of the church is the **Vicarage,** dated 1873, and probably also by Paley and Austin. It is a very free design in a simple domestic style containing elements of the Arts and Crafts movement. It also has geometric traceried windows and a pointed arched doorway.

Opposite the church in North Mossley Hill Road is **St. Saviour's Convent,** previously 'The Homestead', a large private house. The original house is early Victorian Tudor, possibly by Cunningham and Holme, with a 'High Victorian' addition. The later part includes the entrance with carved spandrels, balustraded balcony to upper window, and tower above with oriels and steep roof. Also added is the large iron and glass conservatory. The interior contains many ornamented ceilings, the drawing room having one which is finely panelled. The extensive **stone balustrading to the terraced garden** on the south and west sides is carved with quatrefoils. The outbuildings which were built with the original house include the **North and South Lodges.** The South Lodge presents an interesting face to Rose Lane, with paired octagonal chimneys, gables, and an oriel window rising above the high boundary wall. At this corner are a pair of richly ornamental **entrance gates and two octagonal stone gate piers** with iron finials. Nearby in Park Avenue is Mossley Hill Hospital which includes a **mansion** built by Alfred Waterhouse in 1868-9. This has a skilfully composed asymmetrical front (now ruined by a profusion of pipework) enriched with much decorative use of brickwork, such as machicolated eaves cornice and dog tooth string courses. The west side is symmetrical and lacks equal interest, contributing to the overall harsh character of the house.

Another large private house now in institutional use is **'Kelton'** (House of Providence), situated in Woodlands Road. The original house (the only 'listed' portion) is surrounded by unsympathetic Victorian Gothic and recent additions, and is only visible from the north and east sides. It is an early nineteenth century stuccoed villa with an Ionic porch of two double columns. Returning to Mossley Hill Road, the next building of note is **Sudley Museum and Art Gallery,** bequeathed to the City in 1944 by Miss Emma G. Holt. This was the residence of George Holt, the shipowner, from 1883 until his death, during which time he formed a remarkable collection of contemporary paintings and sculpture. It is these that are on show, and the house and its contents form a splendid example of Victorian artistic good taste. The house itself actually dates from the 1830s, but was altered and extended by Holt in the 1880s. The original part is of five bays and is of low proportions. On the garden front has been added an iron Ionic verandah from where

Stanley Terrace

South Lodge and Gate Piers to St. Saviour's Convent

there is a good view of the river, and a conservatory with 'Chinese' glazing. Inside, the fine staircase with tiered columns and dome above, is part of the original house, but later features of interest include the 'aesthetic' tiled fireplaces and inlaid mahogany bookcases. The lodge is in a plain style similar to the main house, but with a Doric porch and circular bay.

Off Holmefield Road at the bottom of Mossley Hill Road is another large mansion, **'Holmefield'**, now part of the I.M. Marsh College of Physical Education. This is a square stuccoed classical villa of the 1830s with an Ionic portico. Another similar mansion, this time with the Doric order, forms the nucleus of the College, but this has been extended and altered many times. Further along Holmefield Road is the **Grange Hotel,** formerly a Victorian Gothic villa with a gabled porch and Tudor-arched entrance leading directly off the street. Of interest are the steep gables with their ornamented barge boards and brackets in the form of fantastic carved and painted beasts. On the garden side is a 'lean-to' conservatory with a dentilled cornice on foliated cast iron columns. Opposite the hotel is **No. 27 Holmefield Road,** a delightful 'cottage orné' well sited for visual effect at the bend in the road. The plan is in the form of a cross with equal arms, each with a curved Queen Anne gable with amusing animal heads at eaves and pinnacle. On one gable is a coat of arms and a niche containing a statue. Unsympathetic additions and modern windows have unfortunately affected the symmetry of the building.

This whole area below Mossley Hill is now chiefly characterised by modern suburban houses, but there is an interesting early survival, **Stanlawe Grange** in Aigburth Hall Avenue. It was a grange belonging to Stanlawe Abbey and is said to be a late thirteenth century cruck frame building. There is, however, evidence of alterations in the fifteenth, sixteenth and seventeenth centuries and it has again recently been completely modernised. The recent work has been carried out with much sensitivity and the result is attractive, though giving little idea of the original date of the building, the oldest external fragment being the three-light mullioned window to the left of the front.

No. 1 Aigburth Hall Avenue, the adjacent house, is of a very different nature, being a large pleasant Edwardian house in Queen Anne revival style. It is roughcast with a brick string course and has curved Dutch gables, shallow bay windows and Venetian windows above. The entrance front is symmetrical with two gabled wings and a central Tuscan porch in antis.

A further grand house in Aigburth, now surrounded by modern development, is **'Oak House'** at the junction of Cooper Avenue South and Aigburth Hall Road. This was built for

Alderman Cooper, a local ironmonger, in 1842, and is a large sandstone mansion of idiosyncratic irregularity. There are almost no two elements the same, and all manner of window, door and roof details are used for picturesque effect. **'Oak Cottage'**, the former lodge, is much simpler by comparison, and has deep sash windows to each side of the central entrance. At the rear is the stable with a loft above.

A final building worth visiting in this area is **St. Anne's Church** on Aigburth Road, designed by Cunningham and Holme. Built in 1836-7 this is a curious and interesting church, being an early example of the Norman revival. The nineteenth century journal, *The Ecclesiologist* called the squat west tower 'laughable'; however, some of the Norman features are convincing, and the style is used consistently, with many corbelheads and head-stops both inside as well as out, and even the gatepiers are Norman.

27 Holmefield Road

St. Anne's Church

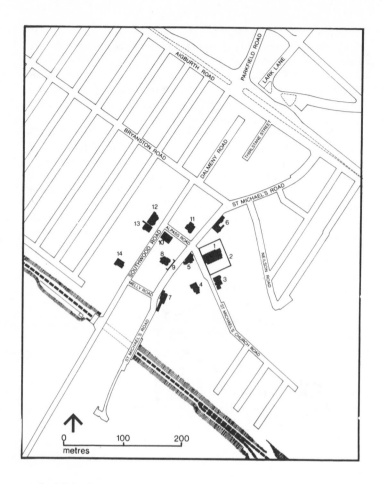

1 St. Michael's
   Church
2 Iron railings and
   two gate piers
3 1 (The Friary)
4 The Hermitage
5 Carfax
6 Holly Bank
7 The Cloisters
8 6 (The Vicarage)
9 Garden wall and
   four gate piers
10 4 (Arnewood)
11 3 Southwood Road
12 16 and 18
   Southwood Road
13 20 Southwood Road
14 24 Southwood Road

27 St. Michael's Hamlet

John Cragg, proprietor of the Mersey Iron Foundry, settled in St. Michael's Hamlet in the early nineteenth century and built a group of five houses and the church. These buildings are of considerable interest for their early and extensive use of cast iron for a variety of structural and decorative purposes. The area also includes a number of attractive detached, semi-detached and terraced properties, some set in spacious gardens with mature planting, and all reached by narrow and leafy lanes. St. Michael's Hamlet was designated a Conservation Area in 1968 and retains a secluded and most peaceful character, despite being in the middle of a densely populated housing area.

St. Michael's Church is the focus of the settlement with its broad squat tower visible from most of the surrounding roads. The church was designed by Thomas Rickman, a scholarly architect, whose published work had a very important influence on the great nineteenth century Gothic revival. He had met Cragg in 1812, and between them they developed the use of cast iron for church design, the remarkable church of St. George, Everton, being the supreme achievement of this collaboration. St. Michael's was built in 1814-5, and everything possible is made of iron, including the high plinth, cladding to the clerestory, parapets, copings, finials and, of course, window tracery, door and window surrounds and crestings. The walls are filled in with red brick which was formerly stuccoed. Inside, slim iron columns support arches and carry the roof with its delicate iron tracery panels. The small churchyard is closed off from the street by **iron railings and two gate piers** with crocketted finials.

Alongside the church is **No. 1 (The Friary),** St. Michael's Church Road, one of the five houses built by Cragg. These houses were constructed shortly before the church, but Rickman was probably involved in their design. All have romantic names and are designed in a free Tudor style, faced in stucco, but with iron used for door frames, cusped and latticed windows, fireplaces, staircases and balustrading, etc. The Friary has an irregular and asymmetrical front to the road, with gabled wings, a two-storey bay, and a buttressed porch with Gothic panelled door. **The Hermitage,** which is situated opposite, is smaller in scale and set back from the road. Ironwork details include an attractive delicate verandah with cresting where it reaches the garden front. **Carfax,** on the corner of St. Michael's Road and St. Michael's Church Road, and formerly called The Nunnery, has now been pebbledashed. On the garden side is a tall projecting battlemented porch. Windows have been altered and removed on the St. Michael's Road side, but of interest are the small diamond shaped opening lights set in the original latticed windows. **Holly Bank,** the large house with its stables and coach house stretching along St. Michael's Road, and garden adjoining the churchyard, was John Cragg's own house. The garden entrance is marked by elaborate Gothic gate piers with open decorated tracery. Also of iron is a canopy with cresting over the side entrance to the house. The main house has two wings at right angles, with overhanging eaves supported on curved cast iron brackets. The coach house entrance, now blocked up, is marked by a round 'eye' in the gable projection above, and beyond is the original stable entrance. The church initially served a wide area and many of the congregation coming long distances, they left their horses in spacious stables during the service. The fifth of the houses built by Cragg is **The Cloisters,** situated further up St. Michael's Road. This, like Holly Bank, presents a long stuccoed elevation to the road. An iron Gothic traceried trellis porch shields the entrance, and on the garden side is a delicate verandah with trellis supports. Inside, an eliptical iron staircase with Gothic balustrading leads out of the hall, and even door panel beadings are of iron.

Besides John Cragg's houses, a number of others were built in St. Michael's Road and Southwood Road at about the same time. Though these do not display the same fanatical use of ironwork, they are of complementary architectural quality, and add to the distinct character of the area. **No. 6 (The Vicarage),** St. Michael's Road, is in a Gothic style, though it is essentially classical in form. The walls are stucco faced and the panelled pilasters with trefoiled heads and leaf capitals are particularly good. Other Gothic details include the door, hood moulds, and quatrefoiled balustraded parapets above the bays. **The garden wall with four square Gothic gate piers** is also of note.

No. 4 (Arnewood) is a distinguished classical villa with panelled pilasters, string course, frieze and eaves cornice. The porch with fluted Doric columns and pediment is of fine quality. The side elevation on to Alpass Road presents a three-bay front with sash windows in moulded architraves. Matching this facade is the side elevation of **No. 3 Southwood Road;** however the front to Southwood Road itself, with its blind windows and crudely detailed porch, is much less distinguished. Connected to this house is a stable block with depressed coach entrance and

St. Michael's Church

Holly Bank

small window above, and at the rear is a nice verandah with iron trellis work. Opposite No. 3 are **Nos. 16 and 18 Southwood Road,** a pair of semi-detached stuccoed villas with boxed eaves on modillions and a curly iron trellis between bays. **No. 20** is a small plain three-bay stuccoed villa of rectangular form. **No. 22** is a large eccentric Gothic style villa now used as the Norwegian Seamen's Church. All windows have pointed arched heads, and most retain the Gothic iron glazing bars. The separate stable block at the rear has similar details. **No. 24** is again classical, having a rectangular central porch with a frieze and cornice, but has unfortunately had a modern glazed canopy added. At the end of Southwood Road is St. Michael's Station, and opposite are two small cottages which are also of interest.

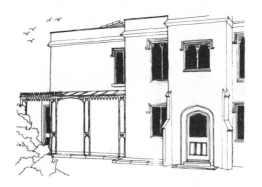

The Hermitage

22 Southwood Road

4 St. Michael's Road

The 'listed' buildings in this area are too distantly spaced to form
a walk. The whole area was rural until the 1930s when Liverpool
Airport was built and the large Speke Housing Estate was begun
under Sir Lancelot Keay, the City Architect and Director of
Housing. This housing lacks the variety of the earlier estates such
as Norris Green, and an absence of landscaping means that the
area is chiefly characterised by the bland industrial estates that
surround it.

Speke Hall (Grade I) has suffered greatly by this development. An airport runway now encircles the house and the drive
is shared with an industrial estate. It remains, however, one of
the finest examples of timber framed building in Britain. It was
built by the Norris family and is dated 1558, 1605 and 1612
(though there are medieval fragments) and remains otherwise
unaltered. The house has an inner courtyard and a moat crossed
by **two stone bridges.** Also of stone are the base, chimney
breasts and porches. Otherwise all is black and white with bold
herringbone bracing and decorative features such as lozenges
and quatrefoils. Internally there is a Great Hall extending
through two floors and a series of rooms leading off corridors
running around the sides of the courtyard. There is much good
panelling and plasterwork and fine Elizabethan fireplaces in
many of these rooms. Of special interest are the hiding places
and observation holes, including a main escape shaft in the north
wing, for the Norrises were a staunch Royalist family during
the Civil War. **The North Lodge** to Speke Hall is a Victorian
half-timbered cottage with steep roofs, decorated barge boards
and finials.

There is no longer a village of Speke, but a small nucleus
around **All Saints Church** at the junction of Hale Road, and
Speke Church Road marks the original village and retains some
village character. The church was designed by Pearson and built
in 1876 in a flamboyant decorated style. It is more straightforward than his vigorous design for St. Agnes, Ullet Road, and
relies for effect on simplicity and correctness. The south-west
tower with its broach spire makes a valuable contribution to the
skyline of this flat and featureless area. **A lychgate** of red
sandstone with a timber shingle roof leads into the churchyard.
The Village School is probably of a similar date and presents a

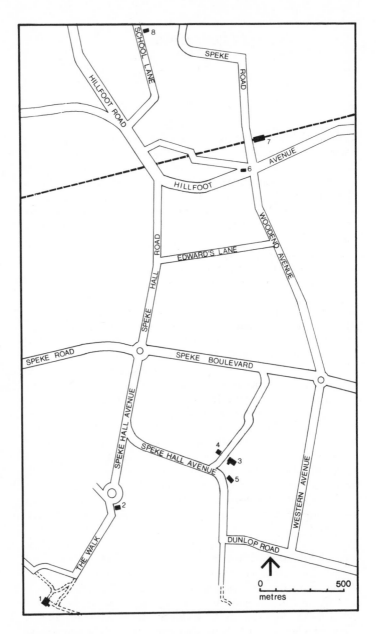

1 Speke Hall and two stone bridges
2 North Lodge
3 All Saints Church and lychgate
4 Village School
5 30-34 Hale Road
6 The Hunts Cross
7 Hunts Cross Station
8 Golf Lodge

Speke Hall

The Courtyard, Speke Hall   East Wing, Speke Hall

The Village School

30-34 Hale Road

Hunts Cross Station

well composed Gothic asymmetrical face to the church. It is a small sandstone building with a timber spired bellcote and tall stone chimney panelled with Gothic tracery.

On the other side of the church is a terrace of late eighteenth century cottages, **Nos. 30-34 Hale Road.** These have an attractive symmetrical front, No. 32 being larger and forming a central feature with a pediment and large round arched doorway.

The extension of Hale Road, Oglet Lane, formerly led down to the river and to Yew Tree Farm. This has, however, been severed by an airport runway, and the only access is via Dungeon Lane. Yew Tree Farmhouse is a modest Georgian house of three-storeys with a central doorway and small segmental headed windows. There is a group of early nineteenth century brick farm cottages in Dungeon Lane, but most are in poor condition or altered; however, this hamlet still possesses the remoteness and fine river views that must have characterised this whole estuary until recent years.

The Hunts Cross marks another old rural settlement, now vanished. All that remains of the medieval cross is the stump of the shaft on a stone cube base sitting on two square stone steps. It is situated at the junction of Hillfoot Avenue and Hillfoot Road. Nearby in Speke Road is **Hunts Cross Station** built by the Cheshire Lines Committee. It is an ingeniously planned building in a simple Victorian Gothic style. The street entrance is at an upper level with the station master's house above. A staircase leads down to a balcony and the principal rooms, the platform being further below. Windows are paired, with pointed heads, and the second floor has a row of dormers containing pointed arched openings.

In the nineteenth century large houses were built off School Lane on the edge of Woolton Village in generous grounds. The Golf Club House is one of these houses, and **The Golf Lodge** half way up School Lane is one of a pair of stone lodges marking the entrance. The other lodge has been pebbledash rendered and altered into a shop, but the Golf Lodge retains its original twelve paned sash windows, boarded door and moulded stone cornice.

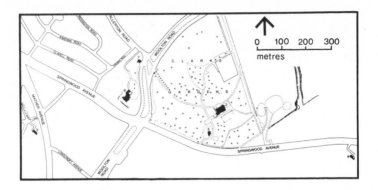

Main staircase detail, Springwood House

The walk starts at Allerton Hall.

The Allerton estate predates the Commonwealth and records show that it was sold to the Hardman family in about 1735 for £7,700. William Roscoe, Liverpool's celebrated poet, historian, statesman, banker, botanist and Unitarian, bought the estate from the family in 1799. It is said that his father was once the butler there and Roscoe may have purchased the estate for sentimental reasons. He added to the Hall and whilst living there carried out farming experiments. He was forced to sell the estate in 1816.

The North Gate Piers to Allerton Hall, Woolton Road. The ensemble comprises four square stone piers with horizontal deep joints connected by a low stone wall with iron railings above between the piers. It was probably built circa 1810 when Roscoe was completing the Hall.

Allerton Hall in Clarke Gardens, Woolton Road, is now a banqueting suite for Liverpool City Council; this red sandstone mansion was mainly built in the eighteenth century. It was extended and finished about 1812. The centre and west wing date from the eighteenth century, the east wing has a rainwater head dated 1810. It is a classical house of three storeys with a rusticated ground floor, advanced wings and central pediment, the latter with Roman unfluted giant columns. The entrance is plain with a large lion mask over the original panelled door. The interior has some eighteenth century panelled rooms and plaster-work. William Roscoe's room has a back screen of fluted Ionic columns.

Also situated in Clarke Gardens is **The Cottage.** The building, of two storeys with a semi-basement, is dated 1639 above the main door but there are a number of later additions. The main building material is squared and coursed stone with a gable end slate roof with saddle stones and small shaped kneelers. Certain of the roofs have been altered at a later date and bricks have been inserted. Several of the original iron casement windows remain.

Despite being lined with cemeteries and a crematorium, Springwood Road is not depressing as there are plenty of trees and greenery. The open farmland round Oak Farm gives a small hint of what south Liverpool must have been like before the

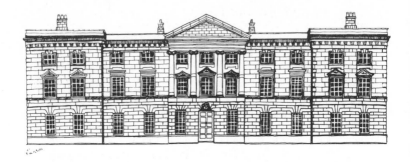

Allerton Hall

Springwood Cottages, Brocklebank Lane

Springwood

twentieth century arrived.

Oak Farmhouse, Springwood Avenue, dates back to the seventeenth century but has been altered since. The two-storey house is of red sandstone partly painted white with a roof of old flags and slates. Two old windows are now blocked up — a lower one of five lights and an upper one of ten lights with stone mullions and transoms. The south front has the remains of a mullioned window but later windows have been inserted. Later additions, perhaps of the eighteenth century, are of red sandstone with small paned sliding sashes.

Longcroft Avenue and Danefield Road leading to and from Springwood Cottages respectively, are lined by inter-war neo Georgian City Council housing exhibiting the high design standards of Sir Lancelot Keay, the then City Architect. Alas in 1976 many of the houses and flats were in the process of having their small paned windows renewed, the replacements taking the form of 'picture windows' completely destroying the original character of the buildings.

The red sandstone cottages, known as **Springwood Cottages, Brocklebank Lane,** are of two low storeys and dated 1684. They have slate roofs and stone chimneys. There is a coat of arms on the front wall, a drip mould and a stone porch with a curved roof. The windows are three light casements with small panes with the exception of a 'cross' window on the ground floor and a ten light stone mullioned and transomed window above the gabled wing.

Springwood House, Woolton Road, was started by the plantation owner, William Shand, and completed by 1839 by the shipowner, Sir Thomas Brocklebank; it is now a Cheshire Home. It is a wholly classical mansion and very characteristic of its date. Of grey ashlar, the house is visible from all sides. The main facade has plain giant pilasters, a cornice and parapet and five sash windows. A pair of semi-circular bay windows and a stone conservatory are located on the ground floor of the garden front. The interior has a noble inner staircase hall with a balustrade and columns in the Regency manner with contemporary plasterwork and marble mantlepieces.

Springwood Lodge, Woolton Road. Again built in 1839, the house is of ashlar, single storey and square in plan. It has clustered central chimneys and a central vertically panelled door in a moulded case with a fanlight.

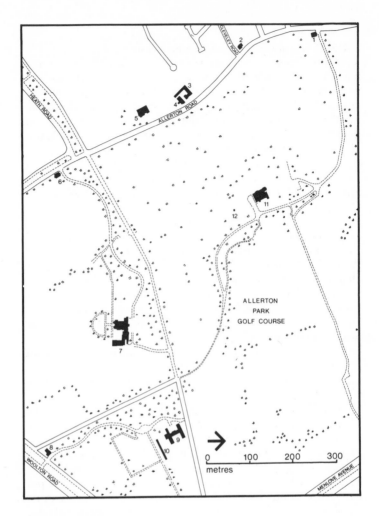

1 Lodge to Allerton
  Park Golf Course
2 Hoarwithy
3 Stable Block
4 Cleveley Cottage
5 New Heys
6 Lodge to
  Allerton Priory
7 Allerton Priory
8 Lodge and
  gate piers
9 Laundry and stables
10 Orangery
11 Golf Club House
12 Obelisk

This walk, starting at the main entrance to Allerton Park Golf Course in Allerton Road, covers 'listed' buildings and artifacts associated with four nineteenth century private estates. To the west of Allerton Road are the remaining buildings of the Cleveley estate and to the east of the road are buildings belonging to the Allerton Park, Allerton Priory and Allerton Towers estates. These estates bear witness to the incredible wealth that came into the hands of Liverpool entrepreneurs in the nineteenth century. The estates at the time of their creation were in open countryside some five miles from Liverpool City Centre. Normal transport for the owners of the estates and their families would be by horse and carriage but the London railway line and its stations is not far away and the use of the railway would have speeded up movement into the City centre for the members of the families working there or visiting it.

The Lodge to Allerton Park Golf Course, Allerton Road, was most probably designed in 1815 by Thomas Harrison of Chester. It is a stuccoed single-storeyed cottage in the Greek Doric style with a portico of four columns. The hipped roof is of slate with tall centre clustered chimneys.

On the west side of Allerton Road lay the Cleveley estate, built for Sir Joseph Leather, a cotton merchant, in 1865. The estate has now been built over and the mansion demolished but a number of associated buildings adjacent to Allerton Road remain. The architect for all the buildings was Sir George Gilbert Scott (1811-78), the architect for the buildings fronting St. Pancras Station in London and the grandfather of the architect for the Anglican Cathedral in Liverpool.

The first of these buildings is **Hoarwithy, Allerton Road,** which was the lodge to the former Cleveley mansion and was built in 1865 and designed by Sir George Gilbert Scott. It is a single-storey stone cottage with a steep gabled roof and tall stone chimneys. The stone mullioned windows have delightful 'Chinese' glazing bars.

Also originally part of the Cleveley estate is the **former stable block to Cleveleys, Allerton Road,** by Sir George Gilbert Scott, and built in 1865. It forms three sides of a courtyard to the north of Cleveley Cottage. The whole complex is of stone with quoins. The coach house wing is on the shorter arm, the longer

Cleveley Cottage, Allerton Road

The Lodge to Allerton Tower

Gate Piers to Allerton Tower

wing has a louvred and pinnacled clock tower and spire. There is a pyramid roofed portico over the yard and low single storey stabling at the rear.

Cleveley Cottage, Allerton Road, built in 1865 by Sir George Gilbert Scott, is of stone with quoins and a steep slated gabled roof with a gabled half dormer. The windows have 'Chinese' glazing bars.

Now used as part of a school is **New Heys, Allerton Road,** built in the 1860s in the Alfred Waterhouse style. It is red brick with blue brick bands in the Gothic style with steep gables, patterned slate roofs, projecting chimneys and pointed arches. Obviously built to last.

Allerton Priory, on the east side of Allerton Road, was built for J. Grant Morris, a colliery owner, in 1867-70. The lodge is visible from the road but the mansion is not. The architect for all the buildings was Alfred Waterhouse who was born in Liverpool in 1830 but later moved to London to establish a national practice. His buildings include Manchester Town Hall, Liverpool and Manchester Universities and many buildings for the Prudential Assurance Company, including that in Dale Street. **The lodge to Allerton Priory, Allerton Road,** is a two-storeyed cottage of red brick with blue bricks and sandstone bands; it has casement windows and tall clustered centre chimneys. The timber porch supports a prominent half-timbered upper storey. **Allerton Priory, Allerton Road,** has red and blue brick bands and red sandstone dressings. It has three storeys in a simple Gothic style. The distinctive tall tower over the porch has a roof in the form of a truncated spire and the entrance below has foliated capitals to clustered columns. Gables, pinnacles and an oriel with a conical roof complete the composition. The motifs are mainly those of the thirteenth century but details from other Gothic styles and periods are employed when usefulness pointed to them. The inventiveness of Waterhouse and similar Victorian architects in reinterpreting Gothic styles is never ending.

Woolton Road, adjacent to Clarke Gardens and Allerton Tower, is one of the loveliest dual carriageways in any British city. Mature trees and stone cottages have sensibly been allowed to remain in the centre reservation.

The buildings on the Allerton Tower estate were all designed by Harvey Lonsdale Elmes (1814-1847), the brilliant young architect who designed St. George's Hall when he was only 25 years old. His work at Allerton Tower and other domestic work in Liverpool is most disappointing when compared to the skill and originality shown in the design of St. George's Hall.

The lodge and gate piers to Allerton Tower, Woolton

Road, designed by Elmes in 1847, is a painful mixture of debased early Victorian and classical motifs. The stuccoed round temple-like lodge has a dome enriched with a frieze and swags. The two main gate piers are pierced by arched openings and are rusticated. There are two smaller side piers with curved connecting walls.

The laundry and stables at Allerton Tower, again designed by Elmes in 1847, are of brick and sandstone arranged in an 'H' plan form. The centre front has a large round concave arch with a round 'eye' in the gable/pediment above and a vaulted roof underneath leading to a rear cobbled yard. There is round arched arcading on the end of the laundry wing.

The Allerton Tower orangery, is a long stuccoed single-storey building with fourteen glazed bays divided by Doric half columns. Designed by Elmes and built in 1847.

The two buildings on the Allerton Road Golf Course that are 'listed' are by Thomas Harrison of Chester. He was an accomplished architect and his works include the Lyceum Club, the parish church of Liverpool in Chapel Street, of which only the spire remains of his work, and the former Portico Library in Manchester.

Allerton Golf Club House, Allerton Road. This rather sad building is the remains of a stone faced mansion built in 1815 by Harrison of Chester. The rest of the building was destroyed by fire. Just enough of the building remains to make one mourn. It was built for Jacob Fletcher, the son of a highly successful privateer. Part of the ground floor remains with eight Greek Doric columns and a frieze to a portico over a moulded doorway and six former windows. A wide shallow bow window with Greek Doric columns is located on the return side.

On the lawn in front of Allerton Golf Club is an eighteenth century **obelisk** built as a focal point in the landscape as seen from Allerton Hall. It is of red sandstone, square in plan and tapering upwards. It was probably erected by the Hardman family of Allerton Hall. Its angles face the points of the compass and it is exactly five miles from Liverpool Town Hall.

Allerton Golf Club House

31 In and Around Calderstones Park

The walk starts in Calderstones Road which borders Calderstones Park, one of the many open spaces in this area which in
the nineteenth century were the private parks belonging to the
mansions of the wealthy. Although many of the private estates
have been built upon, particularly between the first and second
World Wars, large areas of open space, many now public,
remain.

The entrance to Calderstones Park, at the corner of
Calderstones Road/Harthill Road was previously the entrance
to the Harthill estate owned by John Bibby, the mansion of
which has since been demolished. It takes the form of two square
ashlar pillars with gigantic atlantes supporting impost blocks
and cornices. Four feet high walls run at each side carrying four
statues representing the four seasons. The statues were taken
from Brown's Buildings in the City Centre when they were
demolished. They were designed originally in 1861-3 by J. A.
Picton.

Harthill Road, which curves and slopes slightly, is of great
charm; former mansions of the wealthy are occasionally visible
above the Woolton sandstone walls and through the mature
trees planted in the nineteenth century to embellish the large
private grounds.

One of these mansions is now **Calder High School** (original
building only), built in the nineteenth century and of two high
storeys, mainly of stucco with red sandstone features. The
sandstone porch is made up of four composite columns with a
frieze, cornice and balustraded balcony. There is a delicate iron
verandah on the right hand side with barley sugar columns and
a tall sandstone rooftop look-out tower with arcading and a
balustraded parapet.

Originally a private mansion built in 1866, **Quarry Bank
House, Harthill Road,** is now part of a school. Built in the
Gothic style of red sandstone it is of two high storeys with tall
windows and projecting high chimneys. The carved arched
entrance porch includes granite columns and leads to a rich
Gothic interior. The entrance hall is square with an oak panelled
staircase, an octagonal balcony over the stairwell and a panelled
ceiling with a shallow dome.

North Lodge, Harthill Road, is a fanciful building of red

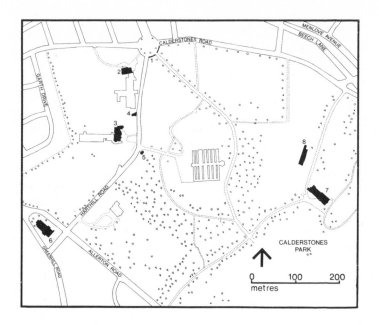

1 Entrance to
  Calderstones Park
2 Calder High School
3 Quarry Bank House
4 North Lodge
5 Harthill Lodge
6 All Hallows Church
7 Calderstones House
8 Stables

sandstone built in 1867 as the lodge to Quarry Bank House. It is of two-storeys with an eight sided hipped roof and a gabled porch at an angle at the side.

Harthill Lodge, Harthill Road, is a Victorian lodge to the former mansion of the Bibby family. It is of two-storeys with a stucco finish and with deep fretted bargeboards.

Of special interest in this area is **All Hallows Church, Allerton Road,** which is located on an island site. It was built between 1872-6 by John Bibby of Harthill in memory of his first wife hence the size and care shown. His wife was the daughter of Jesse Hartley, the engineer who built Albert Dock and much of the early dock system in Liverpool. The architect was G. E. Grayson and the building is of red sandstone in the perpendicular style, with a mighty square buttressed tower of the Somerset type. Inside there is a nave with lower aisles and a chancel all in ashlar. Fourteen out of the fifteen windows were designed by Sir Edward Burne Jones and executed by William Morris. The best windows are on the west and east ends, the latter depicting the Adoration of the Lamb. The colouring of these two windows is exquisite with white and brown predominating. The white marble statuary monument to Mrs. Bibby is by Federigo Fabiana and she is shown rising heavenwards — an angel with spread wings hovering over her.

Allerton Road in the nineteenth century was bordered exclusively by the parks and mansions of the wealthy. Many of the parks still remain on the east side of the road, mostly in the ownership of the City Council, but the parks have disappeared on the west side. Opposite the Allerton Road entrance to Calderstones Park may be seen a charming brick and tile hung building (not 'listed'). This was originally the stables to Allerton Beeches, a mansion now demolished. The mansion and stables, built in 1884, were designed by Norman Shaw, the architect of Scotland Yard in London. Shaw also built another mansion adjacent to Allerton Beeches in 1884 named Greenhill, again demolished. They were the works of one of Britain's finest nineteenth century architects.

Standing in the middle of Calderstones Park is **Calderstones House (The Mansion House),** built in 1828. It is assymmetrical and of two-storeys in the Georgian tradition. It is entirely of painted stones with the exception of the projecting stone portico which consists of four fluted Doric columns and an entablature. The front has ten sash windows each with twelve panes. The internal staircase is top lit.

The stables to Calderstones House are now used as a cottage and stores, and were probably built in 1828. They are of red sandstone with a top cornice. The centre has three

North Lodge, Harthill Road

The entrance to Calderstones Park

Calderstones House

symmetrical arches (the middle one an entrance, the other two for coaches) with semi-circular lunettes over. The former stables are at the rear.

Calderstones Park is named after the prehistoric Calderstones which are now housed in the County Museum. Six of the stones were previously set up in the circle outside the Menlove Avenue entrance to the Park, after the destruction of the original monument in the nineteenth century. The six stones appear to have formed components to a passage grave covered by an earth barrow. The stones are of interest for the carving on their surfaces which include cup and ring motifs, spirals and representations of human feet.

Harthill Lodge, Harthill Road

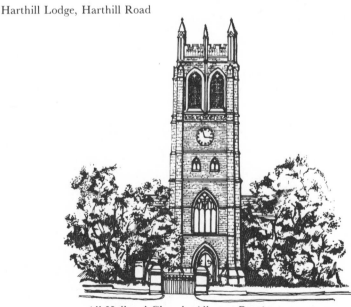

All Hallows' Church, Allerton Road

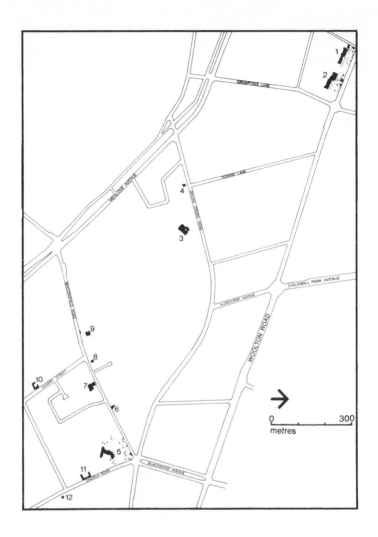

1 St. Joseph's Home
and Lodge
Woolton Road

2 Bishop Eton
Monastery and
Lodge

3 Druids Cross House
Druids Cross Road

4 14 Druids Cross
Road

5 St. Gabriel's
Convent and Lodge

6 Beaconsfield House

7 'Stoneleigh'
48 Beaconsfield Road

8 37 Beaconsfield Road

9 'Abbotsleigh'
Beaconsfield Road

10 'Newstead Farm'
Quarry Street

11 'Knolle Park Mews'
Church Road

12 Reynolds Lodge
Church Road

This walk is through a very pleasant residential area of Liverpool where the 'listed' buildings have been maintained to a high standard.

The first of these buildings is **St. Joseph's Home, Woolton Road,** which was built as a private mansion by A. W. N. Pugin in 1845-7. The house presents a stark asymmetrical face to the road with a small porch and irregularly spaced windows. The garden side is more elaborate, having cross-gables, one with an oriel supported on a buttress. This side, however, is dated 1866, and with much internal work including an elaborate fireplace, is probably by E. W. Pugin. **The Lodge** is characteristically Puginesque and has 'H.S.' in a panel on the projecting chimney. Also Gothic is the **stables and coach house** which has an intriguing tall louvre on the roof with a conical capping.

Adjacent to St. Joseph's Home on Woolton Road is a group of interesting Roman Catholic Institutions, formerly two Victorian mansions and their grounds. **Bishop Eton Monastery** is a large house with attached chapel. The chapel was begun in 1851 by A. W. N. Pugin and completed by his son, E. W. Pugin, in 1858. The simple exterior is in the thirteenth century style probably by the father, whilst the more extravagant interior is characteristic of the son. Stained glass in the west window is by Kempe. The original house is of 1858 by E. W. Pugin and is curiously plain. The four-storey tower with painted timber louvres to the belfry was probably added in 1889, and the east wing by Sinnott, Sinnott and Powell is also of that date. **The lodge** has a large gable on to the road with a mullioned window and round 'eye' above. The adjoining gateway is topped by a stepped parapet containing the figure of a saint and 'B.S.' in two shields.

A sad exception to the high standard of maintenance of buildings in this area is **Druids Cross House, Druids Cross Road,** at one time St. Catherine's Roman Catholic Children's Home, it now stands empty and has been extensively vandalised. The house, an Italianate villa, is in painted ashlar, dates from 1847 by Harvey Lonsdale Elmes, and is a disappointing building from the architect of St. George's Hall. The dominating feature at the front is its large square entrance porch with massive Doric columns and smaller Ionic columns supporting a barrel vault;

The Lodge to St. Joseph's Home

14 Druids Cross Road

windows are set in moulded cases with a cornice on consoles over them. There is a fine contemporary conservatory at one side of the main entrance. At the rear of the house there is a large three-sided bay with french windows flanked by Ionic columns supporting pediments.

No. 14 Druids Cross Road was the lodge to Druids Cross House, and dates from the same time. It is thought that it too is by Harvey Lonsdale Elmes. This is a fine single-storey house in local red sandstone, the doorway has a cornice supported by brackets, and the mullioned and transomed windows have sills also on carved brackets. There are rusticated quoins, a slate roof and sandstone chimney stacks.

Similar in concept to 'Druids Cross House' is **St. Gabriel's Convent** (formerly 'Knolle Park') situated at the junction of Beaconsfield Road and Church Road. This house too is of painted ashlar. Again its dominant feature is a very fine portico of four Corinthian columns supporting a decorated architrave. The ground floor windows are very simply treated while those in the first floor are set into moulded cases.

The convent has a very attractive Greek style **lodge,** also in painted ashlar. It has a pediment supported by fluted Doric columns, a nicely panelled door set in a moulded case and windows also in moulded cases. There are **four stone gate piers** at the entrance to the drive with **iron railings and lamps.**

Returning to Beaconsfield Road, **'Beaconsfield House'** is a splendid Victorian Gothic villa in red sandstone with two pointed gables to the front of the house, three at each side and steep slate roofs. Typical Gothic features are the labels over the stone mullioned windows, the ogee arch over the doorway, and the tall octagonal chimneys. The presence of ivy on the front of the house adds to the 'antique' charm of this restrained example of Victorian architecture.

In contrast **'Stoneleigh'** and the attached **No. 48 Beaconsfield Road** is a large classical villa in red sandstone ashlar dating from the mid-nineteenth century. There is a large square porch at the front of the house, supported by square Doric columns, and a balustraded balcony. The windows are set in moulded cases; between the ground and first floors there is a moulded string course. To the left of the building there is a lower wing with a single storey bay window.

No. 37 Beaconsfield Road, a smaller sandstone villa, is now divided into two dwellinghouses. Attractive features of the building are the octagonal chimneys, the stone mullioned windows and the finial topped gables. At the side of the house is a square porch with Tudor arches.

Set in its own grounds and now used as a school lies **'Abbotsleigh',** a large Victorian Gothic mansion in sandstone. The windows have stone mullions and transoms, and to the side is a two-storey bay. The entrance porch is steeply gabled with a Tudor arched doorway and a large glazed outer porch.

'Newstead Farm', Quarry Street, a reminder of Woolton's one time rural setting, is now used as a dwellinghouse. The building is of 'snecked' sandstone rubble with a pointed arch facing on to Quarry Street. There is an open courtyard behind the street frontage and the main house portion of the building has small gables with barge boards.

'Knolle Park Mews', Church Road, as the name suggests, was originally the stable block to 'Knolle Park' and was built in 1828. It has been converted into dwellinghouses. The mews is of red sandstone with a round arched entrance flanked by panelled pilasters.

The final property in this walk is **Reynolds Lodge, Church Road,** dated 1883 on a gable. It is of brick construction with a red tile roof and decorative tile hanging on the upper part of the gables. There are decorated tiles on the chimney stacks and the lower windows have stone mullions. A very attractive feature of the building is the open porch, at the side, which has carved balusters.

Reynolds Lodge, Church Road

The first written record of Woolton appears in the *Domesday Book*, 1086, from which the following is a translated extract 'Uctred held Ulventune (Little Woolton). There are two carucates of land and half a league of wood. It was worth 62 denarii'. Nothing from this time remains, and the walk starts at the oldest building in Woolton, the **Old School, School Lane,** which dates from the early seventeenth century (the inscription 1610 should not be taken as historically accurate). The unusually large blocks of sandstone that form the outer walls and the Gothic windows give rise to speculation that the building could date from an earlier time, possibly being the oldest elementary school in Lancashire.

A little way along School Lane, tucked into a cul-de-sac is **Ashton Square** a terrace of cottages built for the estate workers of Woolton Hall and dating from the late eighteenth century. Brick built, local sandstone has been used for the Gothic arches over the doors and windows; No. 3 Ashton Square still has its original latticed lights with the Gothic curve used as a decorative feature. Much of the original **cobbled footpath** survives intact.

A narrow alley leads to Speke Road and **Woolton Hall,** a grade I building, which is built of sandstone ashlar. This building dates from 1704 and at that time was the home of the Molyneux family who had had a house on this site for many years. The Hall was purchased by Nicholas Ashton in 1772 and in 1774 Robert Adam was employed to remodel its interior and exterior. The facade is much as Adam designed it, apart from the massive Victorian *porte cochere* at the front and the single-storey apse to the 'New Drawing Room' at the rear. The four medallions on the front depict classical scenes. The building was latterly used as an extension to Notre Dame College; however, internally Mrs. Ashton's sitting room on the first floor and the Octagon room on the ground floor have survived and Adam's original decorative ceilings and fireplace surrounds can still be seen in them. The cantilevered main staircase is also by Adam.

The red brick terraces, **Nos. 35A-51 Woolton Street,** date from the nineteenth century and have sandstone dressings. Nos. 35 and 41 Woolton Street still have original fanlights.

At the end of the terrace are the **Corporation Offices,** built at the same time as the rest of the buildings; the brick has a stucco

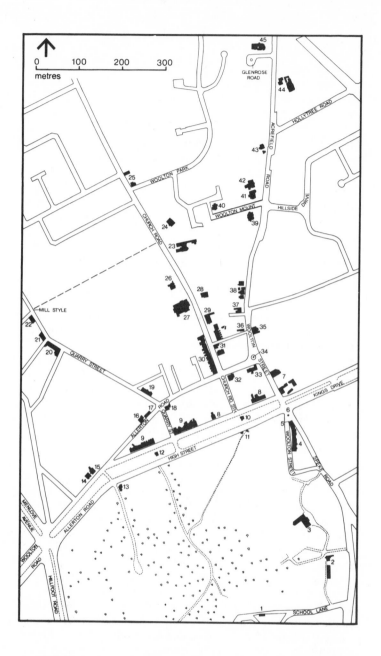

1 Old School
2 Ashton Square and cobbled footpath
3 Woolton Hall
4 35A-51 Woolton Street
5 Corporation Offices
6 Village Cross
7 Dairy and cobbled yard and buildings to Salisbury Farm and 'Coffee House'

finish. Facing the Corporation Offices is the restored **Village Cross.**

Woolton Street continues after being broken by High Street/ Kings Drive and **Salisbury Farm Dairy,** together with the **cobbled yard** at its rear and **old farm buildings,** form an interesting late eighteenth century group. A little further along Woolton Street is the early nineteenth century **'Coffee House'** public house with its painted rough cast front and quoins. The date stone of 1641 has been reset on the left hand side wall.

High Street comprises a variety of semi-detached and terraced brick houses **Nos. 2-16 and 20-58,** some with stone quoins and mouldings; Nos. 56 and 58 have particularly attractive doors, porches and windows. On the spacious central reservation stands the former lodge to Woolton Hall, **'Woodleigh',** built of red sandstone in the classical style with unfluted Greek Doric columns. Particularly noteworthy is the carved frieze with swags (a festoon of fruit, leaves and flowers) and urns. Opposite 'Woodleigh' is the original **gateway to Woolton Hall Park.**

Also on the central reservation is **'Woolton Wood Lodge'** a Victorian brick building with stone Dutch gables.

'Heaton Lodge' at the junction of High Street and Allerton Road is more obviously a gate house than its neighbours as it stands in the grounds of the Liverpool Nurses' Home. The lodge is a fairly substantial building in comparison with the other lodges in the vicinity being two-storeys of rusticated sandstone with stone chimneys.

Woolton Hall

Coffee House, Woolton Street

234

Almost directly opposite 'Heaton Lodge' is **No. 120 Allerton Road,** a Regency house now converted into two dwellinghouses. The stucco has been scored to give the impression of ashlar. At the front is a Gothic timber and glass porch flanked by shallow bay windows with cornices and parapets.

Nos. 116 and 118 Allerton Road are a pair of rubble masonry red sandstone houses inscribed '1904 Woolton District Nursing Society Nurses' Home'.

Woolton Library, Allerton Road, was originally the Methodist Chapel built in 1834. The entrance, now sealed with matching sandstone blocks, faced on to Allerton Road and has a round arched doorway.

Nos. 82-86 Allerton Road is a terrace of early nineteenth century brick houses of which some still have the original twelve paned sash windows and No. 82 has a low segmental brick arch to the back yard and warehouse loading bays above.

At the junction of Allerton Road and Quarry Street South stands **Nos. 61 and 61A Allerton Road,** a nineteenth century building of red sandstone ashlar blocks.

The name Quarry Street derives from the nearby sandstone quarry, the stone from which has been used to construct many of the buildings in the area and is still being used on Liverpool's Anglican Cathedral. One half of a block of terraced houses, **Nos. 2-8 Quarry Street,** is built of sandstone, the remainder, **Nos. 10-14 Quarry Street,** are of brick with sandstone sills and lintels.

The terrace, **Nos. 55-67 Quarry Street,** comprises the sandstone former Black Horse Hotel, now used as a sculptor's workshop and a terrace of brick fronted cottages with stone quoins. The window openings of the terrace are unusually large and have stone lintels and sills.

Nos. 69-75 Quarry Street is a brick terrace with sandstone rubble gables and sandstone lintels. No. 75 has the original door and windows.

If sandstone is incorrectly laid it has a tendency to flake and this can be seen in the terrace, **Nos. 81-87 Quarry Street,** which is built of ashlar blocks. Some original windows still exist and Nos. 81-83 have stone chimneys.

Woolton Quarry can be crossed by means of the 'Mill Stile', the entrance to which is opposite Castle Street and brings the more intrepid walker out in Church Road opposite the **Archbishop's House,** the one time residence of the Roman Catholic Archbishops of Liverpool. This is an early nineteenth century Greek style building of red sandstone ashlar and built by a local miller, James Rose, who was responsible for much of the building and road making in the area.

Beech Corner, Church Road

30 Allerton Road

Adjacent to 'The Archbishop's House' lies **'Churchfield'** a mid-nineteenth century sandstone ashlar building having a square porch with a round arched window.

Further along Church Road is **'Riffle Lodge'** and adjoining **stables.** 'Riffle Lodge' is an ornamented Tudor style cottage with a sandstone ground floor and timber and plaster upper storey with oriel windows. The bargeboards are pierced and highly decorated. The stables are a single storey sandstone building with a wood octagonal louvre topped by an iron weathervane.

Returning to Woolton Village along Church Road, **'Beech Corner'** is situated to the north of St. Peter's Church. This house, formerly 'Rosemont', built by James Rose, has a Greek Doric portico.

St. Peter's Church, dated 1886-7, by Grayson and Ould, replaces an earlier classical building. Once again local red sandstone has been used in the construction of this Victorian Gothic perpendicular style church.

Almost directly opposite the church is **'Yewfield'** a stuccoed Regency house with an attractive iron verandah over the ground floor.

Adjacent to 'Yewfield' is **St. Peter's Village School,** brick built and dated 1825 on a round sandstone plaque, the sash windows are original. Church Road continues on the odd numbered side **(Nos. 7-35)** as a continuous terrace of brick houses. Nos. 21, 23, 25 and 27 have latticed wood porches and No. 17 has an original door and fanlight. This terrace terminates at **No. 30 Allerton Road,** which has a shop front and canted doorway.

The even numbered side of Church Road, **Nos. 2-26,** is divided into shorter groups of stone terraced houses. **No. 8** Church Road is a larger house with a gable/pediment and forms the return of **Nos. 2-6 Church Road,** which face on to the 'Lodes Pond'.

Church Road leads once more into Allerton Road. **Nos. 25-27 (Lake House), Allerton Road,** are brick nineteenth century houses. Lake House has a particularly attractive doorway with flanking lights and a plain fanlight. **Nos. 3-11 Allerton Road** are early nineteenth century mock-Tudor with No. 11 Allerton Road being still used as a private dwellinghouse, the remainder being shops.

On the small roundabout at the junction of Allerton Road and Woolton Street stands a large **iron street lamp** dated 1873. At the end of Woolton Street is situated the **Elephant Hotel,** which was once a private house. The re-sited date stone of 1772 is not accurate as the present building dates from the

8 Church Road

Lake House, Allerton Road

238

early nineteenth century with later additions. The carved elephant's head leaves no doubt as to the building's name and together with the iron balconies is an attractive feature of this public house.

No. 1 Mason Street, just off Woolton Street, is a late Georgian house with a stone base, the remaining three storeys being of hand made brick with stone quoins. The sash windows and round arched fanlight are an original feature of the house.

Acrefield Road is a continuation of Woolton Street, the first house being **'Greenbank' (No. 2)** an early nineteenth century brick built house with some original windows. **Nos. 8-20 Acrefield Road** are a group of early nineteenth century houses; one is detached the others being paired. **'Bankside',** Acrefield Road, stands at the entrance to 'Woolton Mount' and is a Victorian Gothic villa with a castellated porch and elaborate bargeboards; the stucco has been scored to resemble ashlar.

The private roadway known as **'Woolton Mount'** is worthy of note as it has been paved with red sandstone blocks. At the top of Woolton Mount stands **'The Mount',** another scored stucco Gothic villa with the windows having labels over them. The final house in Woolton Mount is **'Acrefield Kindergarten'** a classical early Victorian villa of scored stucco and quoins; the porch is in the Greek Ionic style.

Returning to Acrefield Road, **'Hillciffe',** a Regency villa in scored stucco has two shallow gables at the front and a cast iron verandah. The wooden canopy of the verandah is supported by slender iron columns and extends over the door to form a porch. Although simpler than its more ornate Victorian neighbours, 'Hillcliffe's' pleasing proportions make it a very attractive house.

'Acrefield Cottage', Acrefield Road, is also simple in style, having only a finely moulded eaves cornice for decoration. **The lodge to 'La Casita', Acrefield Road,** is now so greatly altered that it hardly merits inclusion in this walk. All that remains of its classical facade is a Greek pediment.

'Aymestry Court', Acrefield Road, is dated 1891 and is in red brick with a red tiled roof and tall ornamented chimneys. There is a large black and white half timbered gable at the front with small dormers to one side. Attached to the house is the **coach house,** dated 1887, in red brick with the upper storey projecting and hung with red tiles. There is a black and white gabled half dormer. **The lodge to 'Aymestry Court'** is a more ornate building dated 1884, and also built of red brick having a red tiled roof with a pyramidal louvre topped by a weather vane. There is decorative tile hanging on the gable with the remainder being black and white half timbering. An attractive feature of this building is the decorative 'pargetted' panels.

The final building in this walk is a splendid late Victorian house now divided into three separate dwellings, **'Strawberry House', 'Mossdene' and 'Crawsfordsburn',** in Glenrose Road.

This house is a fine example of the exuberant Victorian approach to architecture. It is in scored stucco with quoins and has a moulded cornice supported on brackets. The centre portion has a porch with pilasters and a balustrade, and is flanked by Venetian windows. Most of the windows have small leaded panes forming decorative patterns.

1 Mason Street

This walk starts some way outside Gateacre Village in Grange Lane, where in the angle created by its junction with Gateacre Park Drive lies **The Lodge,** a mid-nineteenth century sandstone house consisting of two parallel gabled blocks. Opposite, also in Grange Lane, is **The Gorsey Cop Hotel,** a square stuccoed villa of the 1840s, now much altered and extended, and surrounded by a tarmac car park. The house has a hipped roof, in the middle of which is a glazed roof light enclosed by decorative iron railings in a square. The nearby **Grange Hollies** is a house of similar date and style, but with more architectural distinction. Note the Venetian windows with curved pediments, and the pierced balconies to upper windows. The tight grouping of the buildings that make up the Gateacre Village area is a striking contrast to its larger neighbouring village of Woolton.

Grange Lodge, Grange Lane, is the first building in Gateacre Village. The sandstone front of the building, facing away from the road, has a seventeenth century stone mullioned window on each floor; the round arched doorway and fanlight date from the eighteenth century. The return wall, facing on to Grange Lane, is of brick.

'Soarer Cottages' and 'Paradise Cottages', Grange Lane, are two interesting groups. 'Soarer Cottages', dated 1896, are built of red brick to form an open courtyard at the front in the Tudor style. All have stone mullioned windows with small leaded panes. 'Paradise Cottages' probably date from the early eighteenth century and are built of rough sandstone with ashlar lintels over boarded and studded doors. Some owners have over reacted to living in buildings of such antiquity by embellishing their homes with modern cottage furniture.

Gateacre Riding School, Grange Lane, now occupies stables built in 1895 for Lord Wavertree's polo ponies. Also part of this group are **'Polo Cottage', 'Polo House' and 'The Cottage'.** The stables are in a long Tudor style building with a brick base and half timbered upper walls; there are three pyramid roofed louvres along the roof.

Set back from Grange Lane are two rows of small terraced houses known as **'York Cottages'.** Built of brick in the early nineteenth century these cottages have round arched doorways

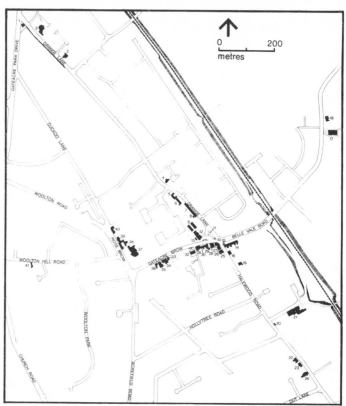

1 Lodge Gateacre Park Drive	**13** 'Lynton' Gateacre Brow	**28** Clegg's Factory
2 Gorsey Cop Hotel Grange Lane	**14** 1-9 Belle Vale Road	**29** 38-42 Gateacre Brow
3 Grange Hollies Grange Lane	**15** 1-1A Halewood Road	**30** 34 and 36 Gateacre Brow
4 Grange Lodge Grange Lane	**16** 5-9 Halewood Road	**31** 28A, B, C and D Gateacre Brow
5 'Soarer Cottages' Grange Lane	**17** Church of St. Stephen	**32** Unitarian Chapel
6 'Paradise Cottages' Grange Lane	**18** Church Cottages	**33** 10 and 12 Gateacre Brow
7 Riding School Grange Lane	**19** 'Kingsley' Halewood Road	**34** 6 and 8 Gateacre Brow
8 'Polo Cottage' 'Polo House' and 'The Cottage'	**20** Gateway to Hotel	**35** 4 Gateacre Brow
9 'York Cottages'	**21** Gateacre Hotel	**36** 2 Gateacre Brow
10 'Wilson Memorial Fountain'	**22** 78 and 80 Halewood Road	**37** Virgo Potens Hospital
11 'Jubilee Memorial'	**23** 82 and 84 Halewood Road	**38** Lodge and Stable Block, Rose Brow
12 'Black Bull' Public House	**24** Knotty Cross	**39** Red Sandstone House Rose Brow
	25 'Brown Cow' Public House	**40** 1A and 1-5 Rose Brow
	26 2-8 Halewood Road	**41** Cliff Cottage Woolton Hill Road
	27 44 Gateacre Brow	

with blind fanlights and sliding sash windows.

The landscaped triangle of land at the junction of Grange Lane and Gateacre Brow forms the nucleus of the Gateacre Village area. Situated on this triangle are the **'Wilson Memorial Fountain'**, **1883**, and the **'Jubilee Memorial'**, **1887.** The 'Wilson Memorial Fountain' takes the form of a small open-sided octagonal building with a pyramid roof; there is a large carved gargoyle on its northern side. The 'Jubilee Memorial' is a red granite column supporting a bronze bust of Queen Victoria signed 'Gleichen fecit 1887'.

Facing the 'Jubilee Memorial' is the **'Black Bull' public house,** a half timbered building in the picturesque style; the windows and timbering having been treated in a very decorative manner. **The cobbled forecourt** adds to the charm of the building. Adjacent to the 'Black Bull' are **'Lynton', a chemist's shop and post office;** all three buildings are built in the same manner as the 'Black Bull' and make this a most attractive group.

The group of houses, **Nos. 1-9 Belle Vale Road,** date from the first half of the nineteenth century and are built of red sandstone ashlar blocks with nicely proportioned doors and windows. Large sandstone slabs have been set into the ground end-on to form garden walls. **Nos. 1 and 1A Halewood Road** form the corner to Belle Vale Road and are also built of ashlar blocks. In contrast, the cottages **Nos. 5-9 Halewood Road,** are brick built with stone dressings.

The Church of St. Stephen in Belle Vale Road was built in 1872-4 by Cornelius Sherlock. It is thirteenth century in style and constructed of red sandstone, with a battlemented tower and octagonal spire. The stained glass in the west window is by Morris and Co., and was inserted in the 1880s. Grouped alongside the church are **Church Cottages,** a group of brick and half-timbered cottages with tall clustered diagonally set chimneys.

Returning to Halewood Road, **'Kingsley'** is a mid-nineteenth century brick villa standing in its own grounds; the centrally placed doorway has a round fanlight with glazing bars and in set in a pilaster doorcase. The windows have stone sills and lintels.

Further along Halewood Road is a free standing **gateway** to the Gateacre Hall Hotel situated at the edge of the pavement. Though now disused, this was the former garden entrance and survives from the late seventeenth century. It has broad proportions and a pediment on rusticated pilasters. **The Gateacre Hotel** itself is mid-eighteenth century but has had extensive nineteenth and twentieth century alterations. The interior has a panelled hall and staircase. **Nos. 78 and 80, and**

The 'Black Bull' Public House

Clegg's Factory and Jubilee Memorial

244

82 and 84 Halewood Road are two pairs of early nineteenth century cottages. Nos. 78 and 80 are built of sandstone, though the front of No. 78 has been painted. Nos. 82 and 84 are of brick, but are of different heights and have different window proportions. **Knotty Cross** is a large stucco house of similar date to these nearby cottages, but due to alterations and its present condition, it retains little original character.

Returning to the Village, and opposite 'Kingsley', stands the **'Brown Cow'**, a late Victorian Tudor style public house, having a gabled porch and iron hanging sign, and is a smaller version of the 'Black Bull'. **Nos. 2-8 Halewood Road** are a row of early nineteenth century brick cottages; the bricks have been laid alternately red and cream producing a chequered effect. All the houses have stone sills and lintels. No. 2 Halewood Road has an attractive round arched doorway with a traceried fanlight. **No. 44 Gateacre Brow** forms the end of this terrace.

Turning into Gateacre Brow **Clegg's Factory** is a good example of a picturesque factory building that would be associated with a Victorian village. It is brick built with decorative panels in blue and yellow brick. The roof is 'fish scale' slated and has a louvre topped with ornate iron cresting and a weather vane.

Nos. 38-42 Gateacre Brow are late Georgian brick cottages with typical round arched doorways and small paned windows. Adjoining are the early nineteenth century brick cottages, **Nos. 34 and 36 Gateacre Brow.**

Of particular interest in this area is the building **Nos. 28A, B, C and D (including No. 28) Gateacre Brow.** This late Victorian building has a red sandstone ground floor with its timber and plaster upper storey supported on brackets in the manner of Tudor buildings. The corner has an octagonal turret with a bell shaped roof. The plaster is decorated with a frieze of moulded panels depicting Biblical scenes.

Standing in its own grounds on Gateacre Brow is the eighteenth century **Unitarian Chapel,** a simple building of local red sandstone with tall segmental arched windows, and a small bell turret on the roof.

The early nineteenth century cottages, **Nos. 10 and 12 Gateacre Brow,** form a small corner group with an added Victorian shop front. It is interesting to compare the enectiveness of the scored stucco finish of this building with the sandstone ashlar of **Nos. 6 and 8 Gateacre Brow,** built in the mid-nineteenth century. Both groups have similar details, with Nos. 6 and 8 having timber bay windows.

No. 4 Gateacre Brow is a small nineteenth century stuccoed villa with stone side walls. The details of the doors and window

28A, B and C Gateacre Brow

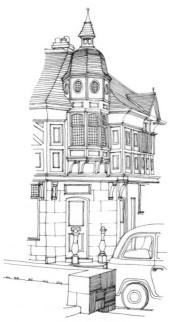

Detail of 28 Gateacre Brow

are similar to that of its brick built neighbour, **No. 2 Gateacre Brow,** both having twelve paned sash windows and round arched door cases with fanlights.

At the junction of Gateacre Brow and Rose Brow and standing in well maintained grounds is the old **Virgo Potens hospital** now used as a home for retired seafarers. This is a red sandstone mansion with stone mullioned and transomed windows, and a fish scale slate roof. Forming an open courtyard are the **lodge and stable block** built of red sandstone with the street facade rusticated; this also has a fish scale roof. Adjoining the stable block is a two-storey **red sandstone house** with a date stone inscribed 1787 and a rainwater head dated 1837.

Nos. 1A and 1-5 Rose Brow, a small terrace of early nineteenth century brick cottages with sandstone lintels and sills to the windows. The end house of this group is a very pretty sandstone building; the window openings and mullions, and the door frame are made of carefully finished stone blocks with sandstone labels. The roof is of fish scale slates and has four louvres; the ridge of the roof and louvres are topped with ornate fleur-de-lis cresting tiles.

This walk terminates at **Cliff Cottage, Woolton Hill Road,** a small red sandstone house built on the edge of a now disused sandstone quarry. Attractive features of this house are the Tudor arched doorway and a panelled stone chimney.

Unitarian Chapel

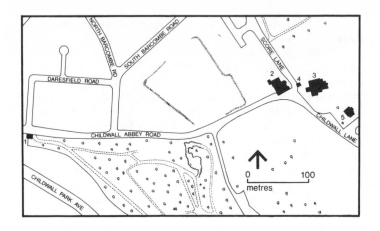

1 Lodge Childwall
  Abbey Road
2 Childwall Abbey
  Hotel
3 All Saints Church
4 'Hearse House'
  Score Lane
5 'Elm House'
  and Stable Block
  Well Lane

248

35 Childwall Abbey Area

The settlement at Childwall dates from Norse times; indeed, the name 'Childwall' derives from the Norse word *'Keldaville'* meaning a spring or well in a field. After a thousand years Childwall still retains its fields and the following description of Childwall surprisingly written in 1910 by a local author still holds true today:

'Childwall will retain its beautiful old world character for many years, but in an age when the aeroplane and the motor are annihilating time, space and distance, it is delightful to know that beautiful places like the Childwall Abbey Inn are reserved in all their beauty to keep before us a splendid stately picture of the days, manners and architecture amidst which the great ancestors and leaders of the English people were cradled.'

Childwall Hall is sadly now demolished, but the **Lodge, Childwall Abbey Road,** which may also be by the Hall's architect, John Nash, remains. This is a small fortress like building in ashlar sandstone with a castellated parapet, lancet windows and arrow slits. A two-storey wing has a round arched doorway and a small Gothic window on each floor.

The Inn, now known as **Childwall Abbey Hotel,** appears from records to be the renovated chapel of St. Thomas the Martyr dating back to 1484. In its time it has been the favourite stopping place of many famous actors appearing in Liverpool; included in the names scratched on the windows are those of Ellen Terry and Henry Irving. The most noticeable features of this red sandstone building are its castellations and its ogee curved windows, each of which has a grotesque mask carved on its keystone.

There has been a church at Childwall since the fourteenth century and much of the stonework of **All Saints Church** dates from this time although the church itself was altered in the eighteenth and nineteenth centuries. When in 1810 the tower of St. Nicholas' Church, Liverpool, fell and killed 21 persons it was considered that Childwall's sixteenth century tower may also have been unsafe and it was demolished and rebuilt in 1810-11 to the original design. Some of the old stones have been used on the face of the tower.

The windows in the north and south walls of the chancel are reputed to be original fourteenth century although the glass

All Saints Church

250

dates from 1854. Facing on to the main road and built as part of the boundary wall of the church is the early nineteenth century castellated **'Hearse House'**, once a resting place for hearses; it is now disused. A detailed account of the history of All Saints Church can be found in a booklet written by the Rector and on sale in the church itself.

The final building in this group is **'Elm House', Well Lane.** This early nineteenth century red sandstone house is set in its own grounds behind a high wall and has an embattled parapet. The window on the gable end has Gothic tracery. The **stable block to 'Elm House'** has oval windows on both gables.

Childwall Abbey Hotel

Detail of Childwall Abbey Hotel

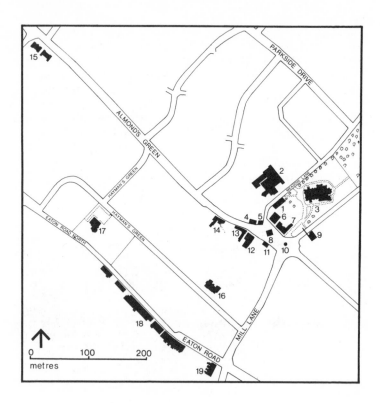

West Derby Village is an ancient settlement, noted in the *Domesday Book* as the Derbei Hundret, and, having the vast estate of Croxteth Park to its north-east, it still retains much of its rural village character.

The walk starts at a row of brick built cottages, **Nos. 6-16 Meadow Lane,** which date from around 1800; most have been altered, but No. 14 is virtually intact. Opposite the cottages is the **West Derby Church of England Primary School,** dated 1860. This is a most unusual sandstone building resembling a church more than a school house with its tower, stubby stone spire and decorated Gothic windows.

St. Mary's Church was built in 1853-6 by George Gilbert Scott for Lord Sefton. The church is in the decorated Gothic style which was so popular during the nineteenth century. On the south wall is set a sundial dated 1793 and taken from a previous church on that site.

Returning to the village centre, **No. 10 Almonds Green** is a yeoman's cottage dated 1660, the oldest building in the village and occupied until a few years ago. The sandstone walls have been covered for decades, if not centuries, with whitewash and the interior is lit by small stone mullioned windows. Nearby are the **village pound and stocks,** and this area was planted as a garden to commemorate the coronation of Edward VII.

The West Derby Public House, No. 8 Almonds Green, is a good example of a Victorian public house designed to fit into the rural surroundings of nineteenth century West Derby. The round arched doorway is in stone and has a traceried fanlight. It is interesting to compare the understated architecture of this pub with the earlier, and grander, **'Hare and Hounds'** on the opposite side of the road. This stuccoed pub was built with two blind lights flanking the first floor windows on the double gables facing Almonds Green. The iron balcony is an attractive feature of the building as are the two round arched doorways with rope mouldings and traceried fanlights.

Nos. 2-6 Almonds Green are a group of three red brick Victorian cottages, dated 1861-70 by Eden Nesfield. Attractive details of this group are the boarded doors and the ornamented red tile cresting to the slate roof. Nesfield also designed the

Village Cross of the same date which is situated in the roadway.

The Lodge to Croxteth Hall is a large Victorian Tudor cottage of red sandstone. The Victorian passion for detail and the grotesque can be seen in the diamond paned stone mullioned windows and the crouching beast on the rainwater head. The arms of the Earls of Sefton are carved over the doorway. **The gate piers,** supporting the **iron gates** to the driveway, are topped by stone lions holding iron pennants.

In the centre of the road is a **stone drinking fountain** dated 1894. Presumably at that time the use of the fountain was less hazardous than it would be today, even though it bears the exhortation 'Water is Best!' The fountain is topped by an ornate iron street lamp and was the gift of R. R. Meade-King and designed by Arthur P. Fry.

Opposite the Village Cross is **The Old Court House** dating from 1662, built of red sandstone with a stone roof; the stone mullioned windows have small leaded panes with wooden shutters. The interior has timber court room furniture including a high chair for the Steward.

Just beyond the 'Hare and Hounds' public house are **Nos. 11, 11A and 13 Almonds Green,** a group of early nineteenth century houses built of hand made bricks with stone roofs, and still retaining some original sash windows.

Nos. 15 and 17 Almonds Green are early nineteenth century brick houses, with the larger building **Nos. 19 and 19A** a later extension and having a late Victorian shop front.

At the extreme end of this road are **Nos. 97-103 and 105-109 Almonds Green,** an interesting architectural phenomena. Nos. 97-103 are a group of charity cottages in sandstone, presumably built in 1863 by J. P. and A. M. Heywood, whose names and date appear on a shield above the doorway. **Nos. 105-109** are late nineteenth century imitations in brick. The proportions and details are basically the same, but the later buildings differ in the central treatment of the addition of a two-storey gabled porch with Tudor arched doorway.

The houses in Haymans Green are good examples of Victorian villas and **Nos. 2 and 4 Haymans Green** are particularly noteworthy. They are scored stucco semi-detached villas. Each square porch has a round arched doorway and windows; the upper storey has triple lancet windows with moulded round arches.

'Lowlands', Haymans Green, now used by the West Derby Community Association, is a splendid scored stucco Victorian villa standing in its own grounds. The building is richly ornamented with swags and carved mouldings and a balu-

Lol Baxendale

St. Mary's Church

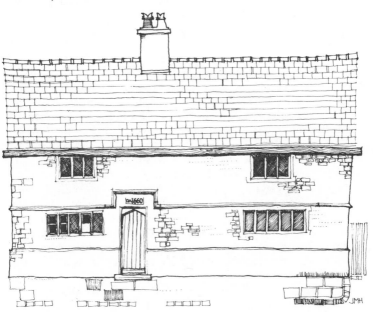

10 Almonds Green

straded stone balcony over the porch.

The late eighteenth and early nineteenth century cottages, **Nos. 17-93 Eaton Road North,** brings the walker back to reality after the extravagance of 'Lowlands'. Nos. 65-71 Eaton Road North are stone built, the remainder of this group being of brick. No. 69 has the original doors and windows, and the shops, Nos. 47 and 49 Eaton Road North, have shop fronts with a pierced iron grille above the windows.

Nos. 76-82 and 92-98 Mill Lane are two groups of late Georgian brick terraces. These attractive houses have stone bands, original doors with traceried fanlights and original windows. No. 92 Mill Lane is in particularly good condition.

There are a number of 'listed' buildings in the West Derby area which are too far removed to form part of a walk. One of them, **Leyfield House,** set back from Honeys Green Lane in generous grounds, is an elegant 1830s stucco villa. It is of three bays and well proportioned, having a central porch with dentilled cornice and Tuscan columns and pilasters.

Nearby, in Yew Tree Lane is **Broughton Hall,** a High Victorian Gothic house of 1856 built in rock faced sandstone. The entrance front is symmetrical, but the details of the two wings are deliberately different. The whole face is elaborately ornamented with castellated parapet eaves, flamboyant window tracery, tall chimneys with clustered octagonal stacks, turrets and oriels; however, in spite of all this extravagant decoration, the total effect lacks conviction. A splendidly elaborate conservatory is attached to the south-east corner of the house. This has a hipped roof and central lantern supported on iron columns with foliated capitals and traceried spandrels. The main rooms of the house have carved timber wall panelling and carved timber or moulded plaster ceilings. **The lodge to Broughton Hall,** which is situated beside the road, is in the same style, though being less grand in scale and more simple in decoration, it is rather more architecturally successful. A little further along Yew Tree Lane is **Rice House,** an early nineteenth century house, still Georgian in style. It is distinguished by a wide shallow curved central bay having large sash windows on each floor with Tuscan half-columns. The house is connected by a depressed brick arch to **Rice Farmhouse and its attached farm buildings.** These simple nineteenth century vernacular buildings extend along the roadside, the south end wall having a blind roundel in the gable.

Close to Spring Grove in Town Row is **St. Paul's Roman Catholic Church** of 1880 designed by Pugin and Pugin. It is built in rock faced sandstone with a tower and steep pyramidal roof and four cross-gables to each aisle. The interior is simple in scale, with the curves of the apse and timber barrel vault roof creating an agreeable space.

Nos. 52-56 Town Row are a group of late Georgian brick houses. Nos. 52 and 54 are of cottage scale and have been painted. No. 56 is larger and later in date, and has more architectural distinction.

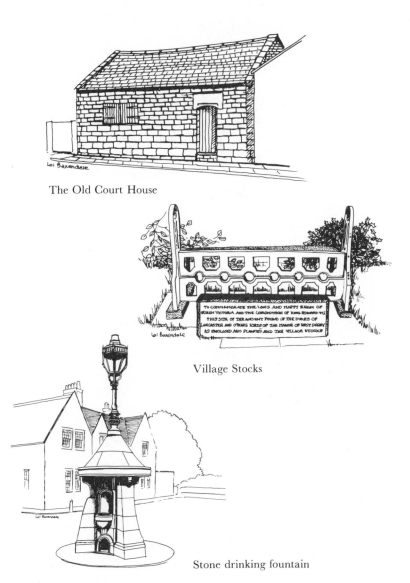

The Old Court House

Village Stocks

Stone drinking fountain

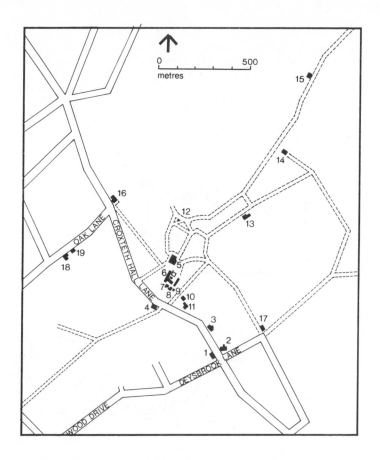

1 1, 3 and 5   14 Stand Farmhouse
    Croxteth Hall Lane   15 Stand Lodge
2 283 and 285   16 Aintree Lodge
    Deysbrook Lane   17 Finch Lodge
3 Old School House   18 Oak Farmhouse
    Croxteth Hall Lane   Oak Lane
4 Farm Lodge   19 Wildmere Cottage
5 Croxteth Hall   Oak Lane
6 Stables, gate piers
    and cottages to
    Croxteth Hall
7 The Dairy
8 The Home
    Farmhouse
9 The Bull Box
10 The Laundry
11 The Cottage
12 Bantam House
13 The Kennels
    and Keeper's Lodge

37 Croxteth Park

The association of the Molyneux family with Liverpool dates back to early Plantagenet times. They formerly lived at Sefton Old Hall, a moated house long since demolished, but in 1446 Sir Richard Molyneux acquired Croxteth Park. The area had previously been part of the forest of West Derby, which was used as a game reserve, and the estate always continued to be associated with sport and the rearing of bloodstock. It now contains a mixture of high quality agricultural land with grazing and cropfields, and thick belts of woodland to afford shelter for game and wild life. On the death of the seventh Earl of Sefton in 1973, Croxteth Park was donated to the City of Liverpool and later transferred to Merseyside County Council. It is now largely open to the public as a country park and run by the Merseyside County Museums Service. There remain a wide variety of estate buildings, which, besides being of great architectural interest, give a fascinating insight into the history and way of life of the estate community.

The existing approach to Croxteth Hall from the City is via Princess Drive and then Croxteth Hall Lane. At the junction with Deysbrook Lane on the boundary of Croxteth Park there are two terraces of late eighteenth century brick cottages. On the left, **Nos. 1, 3 and 5 Croxteth Hall Lane,** include a small shop and form an attractive corner block with a curved facade and conical roof. On the right, **Nos. 283 and 285 Deysbrook Lane** are partly concealed behind a curved brick wall. They are typical examples of the local cottage vernacular, with segmental arched doorways and window heads, and base courses of sandstone. These cottages would probably have been occupied by estate workers.

A high stone wall to Croxteth Hall Lane encloses the Park, but it breaks where **The Old School House,** surrounded by trees, fronts the road on the right. This is a single-storey Victorian red brick building with a central porch surmounted by a low-pitched pediment. In its simple form and character it is highly evocative of the days of the small village school. Further on, **Farm Lodge,** a single-storey brick cottage with small gables and a projecting porch supported on carved brackets, marks an entrance to Croxteth Hall on the opposite side of the road. On the right of this approach, the high wall conceals a vegetable garden and Rose Cottage, a gardener's whitewashed nineteenth century house. This present access to the Hall was originally the entrance for the stables and home farm, but it also leads on to the south side of Croxteth Hall where the gatehouse is situated. The principal approach was from West Derby, through the landscaped park, under Croxteth Hall Lane via a tunnel, and then ultimately to the north front of the Hall.

Croxteth Hall was built in 1575 by Sir Richard Molyneux, but the only visible evidence of this Jacobean house is two gables with mullioned windows now situated to the left of the gatehouse. This was probably neither a large nor elaborate house, and in 1702 the spectacular west front was added by William, fourth Viscount Molyneux, marking the time when Sefton Old Hall was demolished and Croxteth Hall became the main family seat. The west front is of an unusual Queen Anne design, the ground floor being brought forward to form a terrace and entrance at the level of the first floor principal rooms. The two floors above the terrace are of eleven bays, the main floor windows having pediments alternately triangular and segmental. The large and splendid doorway has coupled Corinthian columns supporting an open segmental pediment with central cartouche of a shield embossed with the Molyneux cross, Earl's coronet and supporters (two lions). The large vertical panel above has further trophies, surmounted by a keystone containing the Sefton Crest.

The east and south ranges including the gatehouse were built in 1874 in a gabled Tudor style, and in 1902 the north range was added, thus forming a central courtyard. The design of the latter is by J. McVicar Anderson, and is in a style corresponding with the west front, though lacking its distinction and fine proportions. The interior of the Hall is less successful and lacks unity. The extensions have not been well related spatially, and, apart from some carved oak fireplaces and imitation seventeenth century stucco, there are few architectural features of interest. The most impressive space is the grand staircase of 1902.

The Hall is surrounded by lawns, shrubberies and fine landscaped vistas. Hidden behind a bank of trees to the southwest are the **stables.** The entrance from the Hall, now blocked up, has **two square stuccoed gate piers** with an acanthus cornice and urns, and leads into a cobbled yard. Around the yard are an irregular grouping of stables, with **cottages for stableman, butler and grooms,** built in 1678 and extended in 1706. The single-storey block to the east and dated 1849 contains a riding school, and to the south is a cock-pit with a small balcony and fireplace. In the centre of the yard is a cast iron pump and large stone trough set under an attractive arcade.

Farm Lodge, Croxteth Park

Croxteth Hall

The Stables, Croxteth Park

This was probably used for washing the carriages. To the west of the stable block is the **dairy,** built in 1861-70 and designed by Eden Nesfield, partner of Norman Shaw, and a most original Victorian architect. On country estates the dairy was nearly always treated as an ornamental building because butter making was considered to be a polite art and a suitable occupation for young ladies. The dairy at Croxteth is no exception. It is a small striped brick building with a steep overhanging roof on bracketed eaves. Inside, the walls are tiled, although the nice original blue and white tiles have been replaced below the stone dado. The ceiling beams and timber brackets are charmingly painted with crosses and daffodils, emblems of the Sefton crest, by Albert Moore, a popular Victorian artist, many of whose finest paintings can be seen in the Walker Art Gallery. Originally there was a mosaic floor with a fountain in the centre of the room. **The Home Farmhouse** alongside the dairy has a Gothic extension also by Nesfield with small paned windows and a round chimney. This farmhouse, the home of the farm manager, is a straightforward two-storey Victorian cottage in the vernacular tradition.

In the adjacent paddock which is surrounded by a sandstone wall is a **bull box,** a small Victorian brick building with pyramid roof. Further to the south-east, and set amongst trees, some 150 metres from the stables, is the **laundry.** This was designed by John Douglas, an interesting and little known Victorian architect from Chester, who designed a large number of buildings for the Duke of Westminster on his estate near Chester. It is a picturesque design with tall clustered and ornamented chimneys and incorporates a cottage at the north end with gables, a bay window, and panels of pargetting with motifs of crosses and sunflowers. Beyond is the **cottage,** an eighteenth century building with later additions. The older part is of handmade brick with a deeply overhanging roof, tall chimneys and small paned windows. The later additions form a separate wing facing a secluded garden.

It is now necessary to return to the Hall and follow the long south-east wall of the vegetable garden beyond the estate manager's office. On the right is the gardener's cottage, and then the road crosses the River Alt. Shortly after this, in a clearing amongst the trees to the left of the road, is the **bantam house.** This is a delightful early Victorian six-sided brick building with rustic timber posts at the corners and a timber shingle roof. The pointed door and window openings also have rustic timber surrounds, and the general picturesque effect is characteristic of the romantic view of agriculture adopted by some nineteenth century landowners. **The kennels** by John Douglas are also picturesque, and Gothic in inspiration, but they do not display the same blatant rusticity. The kennels are situated some way distant on the lane leading to Stand Farm, and are designed as a rectangular building with an iron enclosure to the south with the kennels doors opening into it. The kennel-keeper's cottage is at one end, and has a country church-like entrance porch with timber benches built within it, and a pump and stone trough. The gable end is plastered and has pargetting in the form of pies and zig-zag ornament. The gamekeeper's cottage adjacent to the kennels is an attractive single-storey Victorian building with tall coupled cylindrical chimneys and bands of coloured brick-work.

Stand Farmhouse is set back from the lane and hidden behind a collection of barns. It is Victorian and has a symmetrical front with an unusual stepped gabled entrance porch. **Stand Lodge** is situated further on beside Croxteth Brook and is a typical small two-storey estate worker's cottage in a position away from public view. All the entrances to the Park have a lodge, each of which is different in design. **Aintree Lodge,** at the west boundary of Croxteth Lane, is in a more prominent location and is consequently more consciously architectural. Based on a Greek cross in plan, it has a hipped slate roof with central chimney, and nicely carved labels over the windows. **Finch Lodge** on Deysbrook Lane is situated at a bend in the road. It is, however, largely hidden by a curved stone wall, over which the deeply overhanging eaves of the cottage roof project. This hipped slate roof is dominated by tall clustered chimneys. Between Finch Lodge and Croxteth Hall Lane are two groups of brick farmworkers' cottages, one terrace of six and one diminutive pair.

Of the final original group of buildings of architectural interest on the estate only one remains. This is **Oak Farmhouse** on Oak Lane. Now surrounded by new housing, this farmhouse until recently formed a cluster of old buildings with Wildmere Cottage and associated stables and barns. It is an eighteenth century house with a stuccoed front and large casement windows, the upper ones given distinction by heavy moulded labels. Further towards West Derby, off Meadow Lane, there is another stuccoed building, Grove House, a large Victorian villa with a stable block attached. It is set within the Park, and is typical of nineteenth century West Derby, once a fashionable area of mansions and fine houses.

Glossary of Architectural Terms

Acanthus A plant with thick fleshy scolloped leaves used as a carved ornament on Corinthian and Composite capitals and other mouldings.

Acroteria The plinths for statues or ornaments placed at the apex and ends of a pediment.

Architrave The lowest of the three main parts which make up an entablature, also the moulded frame surrounding a door or window.

Ashlar Stone with an evenly dressed surface.

Atlantae A support in the form of a carved male figure.

Baluster A short pillar supporting a rail or coping and used to form a Balustrade.

Bargeboards The projecting boards placed against the incline of a gable of a building to conceal the ends of horizontal roof timbers. They are often highly decorated.

Brackets Small supporting pieces of stone or other material to carry a projecting weight.

Capital The head or crowning feature of a column.

Caryatid A support in the form of a carved female figure.

Classical Relating to Greek or Roman architecture.

Corinthian Column A column having a capital decorated with acanthus leaves.

Composite Column Ionic and Corinthian Columns combined in the Roman style.

Console An ornamental bracket, ogee shaped in outline.

Cornice The top projecting section of an Entablature or any ornamental moulding along the top of a building or wall.

Cupola A small dome crowning a roof or turret.

Cusp The projecting points formed at the meeting of the circles or arches in Gothic tracery.

Dentil A small block repeated to form a band along a classical entablature.

Doric Column A column having a simple capital.

Dressings Smooth or moulded stones set round an angle, window or any feature of a building.

Entablature The horizontal upper part of an Order. It consists of an architrave, frieze and cornice.

Finial A formal ornament at the top of a gable, pinnacle or spire.

Foliated Carved with leaf ornament.

Fleche A slender spire rising above a roof.

Fluting The shallow concave grooves on the shaft of a column, pilaster or other surface.

Flying Buttress An arch or half arch transmitting the thrust of a vault or roof from the upper part of a wall to an outer support or buttress.

Gable The triangular upper part of a wall at the end of a pitched roof.

Gothic The name generally given to the pointed style of medieval architecture prevalent in Western Europe from thirteenth — fifteenth Century, but may also refer to the Gothic Revival of the nineteenth Century.

Guilloche A pattern of inter lacing bands forming a plait.

Acanthus

Atlantae   **Caryatid**

Bargeboards

Corinthian Column

Cusp

Doric Column

264

Hipped Roof A roof having sloped instead of vertical ends.

Impost Block A projecting bracket-like moulding, on which the end of an arch rests.

Ionic Column A column having a capital decorated with a volute (a spiral scroll).

Keystone The central stone or brick of an arch or rib vault, sometimes decorated.

Label A projecting moulding on the face of a wall to throw off the rain; usually above an arch, doorway or window.

Machicolation A gallery or parapet built on the outside of towers or walls — in medieval times with apertures in the floor to enable defenders to drop missiles on attackers.

Mansard Roof A roof with a double-slope; the lower part being steeper than the upper.

Moulding Three-dimensional ornamentation.

Mullion A vertical post or other upright dividing a window or other opening into two or more lights.

Neo-Gothic The nineteenth century revival of Gothic architecture.

Neo-Greek A return to the principles of Greek architecture.

Obelisk A tall tapering shaft of stones.

Ogee A double curved line made up of a convex and a concave part.

Order In classical architecture a column with a shaft, capital and entablature. See Composite, Doric, Ionic, Corinthian.

Oriel Window A cantilevered upper floor bay window.

Pagoda Originally built as a temple in the Far East but often used in Britain as a feature in a garden or park.

Parapet A low wall, sometimes battlemented, placed to protect any area where there is a sudden drop.

Pediment A low gable over a portico, door or window.

Pedimented Portal A large doorway with a pediment above.

Pilaster A shallow pier or column attached to a wall.

Plinth The projecting base of a wall or column pedestal.

Podium A continuous pedestal on which the remainder of the building rests.

Portico A roofed space, open or partly enclosed, forming the entrance of a building.

Quoins The dressed stones at the corners of buildings, usually laid so their faces are alternately large and small.

Sash Window A window frame with sashes, i.e. sliding glazed frames running in vertical grooves; imported from Holland into England in the late seventeenth century.

String Courses A continuous projecting horizontal band set in the surface of an exterior wall, usually moulded.

Swag A carved festoon in the form of a draped piece of cloth, flowers or trees.

Terracotta Earth baked or burnt in moulds for use in building construction and decoration; harder in quality than brick, often with a glazed surface.

Tracery The ornamental intersecting work in the upper part of a Gothic window, screen or panel, or used decoratively in blank arches and vaults.

Turret A very small and slender tower.

Tympanum The area between the lintel of a doorway and the arch above it; also the triangular or segmental space enclosed by the mouldings of a pediment.

Voussoir A wedge shaped brick or stone forming one of the units of an arch.

Finial

Gable

Hipped Roof

Ionic Column

Mansard Roof

Tracery

Index

276